A Hot Sailor, A Cold Margarita, and... Trouble

I'm sincerely grateful to the people who champion this book – both friends and strangers that become friends. Here are some of their comments: LZR

"I've read a lot of books this year and this book was one of the most compelling I read. I just could not put it down!"
~ CHLOE GINTHER, *Stay at Home Mom*

"A whimsical and quirky tribute to the pitfalls and joys of sleeping with complicated men. Playful, clever, and poetic."
~ CARMEN OLSEN, *@joycultivation*

"A funny and sexy romp with tons of heart."
~ CAROLYN HAY, *Screenwriter*

"Intelligent beach read. Laughing out loud one minute, goose bumps the next... I was captivated and entertained!"
~ MAUREEN O'BRIEN, *Gardens' Grace Boutique and Coffee Bar*

"On the surface this book is a quick laugh-out loud romp, but underneath there is such thoughtfulness about the meanings of love and life."
~ SANDRA LOGAN, *M.Ed.*

"...thoroughly engaging, entertaining and very revealing."
~ PAULA MACPHERSON, *Actor*

"What I read was amazing! It's always great when someone comes along and breathes new life into a book – creating something completely fresh and original."
~ TIM BALOI, *Customer Experience Manager, Indigospirit*

Also by Lila Z Rose

Sex, Love, and Paradise

(a micro book)

A Hot Sailor A Cold Margarita and... Trouble

My Memoir of Paradise

Lila Z Rose

A Hot Sailor, A Cold Margarita, and... Trouble: My Memoir of Paradise is a memoir of real life events, however, names and likenesses have often been changed out of respect for the privacy of the people depicted. As well, conversations have been condensed for economy and narrative. This work is the author's artistic rendering of these life experiences.

Copyright © 2013 Lila Rose

All Rights Reserved.

www.lilazrose.com
Twitter: @lilazroselove

Cover Art Model: Sara Klinghoffer

Cover Art Photograph: Kurtis Krack

Cover Art Consultants: Andrew Forbes and Patrik Russo

Book Design and Layout © 2013 Andrew Forbes

All Rights Reserved.

www.andrewdforbes.com

ISBN-13: 978-1492972976 (paperback)

A Hot Sailor
A Cold Margarita
and... Trouble

for David A. Richer
Artist. Patron. 'Get it done' inspiration.

And the one person I know won't turn the page –
because the last thing he wants to read about
is his sister's love life.

Forward

As a long time strategy advisor to Wall St. and Fortune 25 organizations, I have spent the majority of my 30-year career trying to understand the underlying motivation for what makes people do what they do. Over the years, I have been constantly reminded that for all of our complexities, we are merely a collection of comedies and tragedies with new actors and plotlines being added on a constant basis. Despite the complexity of the Life story that we write, the version that we share is usually heavily redacted, with our weaknesses and fears carefully edited out lest we reveal the self-perceived mistakes, failures and weaknesses that would prove that we are truly human.

It was in the process of doing what I do that I had an opportunity to meet Lila Z Rose and I knew from the beginning that she was different from the many people that I tend to meet. She asked many questions about Life and she freely mused about her own Life. She was disarmingly passionate and amazingly transparent about her successes and more importantly to me, her difficulties. When she later asked me to read this book with an eye towards writing a forward, I accepted the challenge, assuming that it would be an uneventful read – another candy-coated, inauthentic sharing of only the good stuff in someone's Life.

As I turned the last page, I realized I was wrong. In Lila's journey to discover love, a sense of self and a sense of personal purpose, we see our own story. In her successes, we remember fond memories of our past and when she weeps, we weep in empathy, remembering challenging moments in our own Life. As her journey and ours become interwoven, we realize that this is not just Lila's story. She has in fact invited us to explore our respective journeys together. The collective journey is one of courage and self-discovery, of laughter and pain, of impetuousness and self-doubt, of love and lust and most importantly, of mistakes and victories. It is the journey of the human experience – the need to love, to be loved and to know that when one's end-of-days has arrived, we can proudly say, "I was here and I made a difference".

This book is not merely an expression of Lila's Life journey that she has created. It is an invitation to explore the journey that we are creating together and the richness of our humanity. More importantly, it is an invitation to discover a truth that many of us tend to lose sight of – that when we have an opportunity to see or point out the greatness in others, they in turn invite us to see the greatness within ourselves. It is at that moment that we realize that the heavily redacted Life story that we prefer to share is not the one that inspires others. What inspires others is the Life story that takes as much courage to share as it does to experience.

Stories like Lila's and as you are about to discover, stories like your own.

HARRY TUCKER
Wall Street / Fortune 25 strategy advisor and insatiable student of the human experience

Calgary, Alberta – 2013
@HarryTucker

Panama City – December 2007

I step off the curb into a sultry night darkened by moonless clouds… and ankle-twist on the crumbled pavement.

"Ooof!"

Channeling a vintage Batman cartoon bubble, I SPLAT in a new type of 'urban sprawl': face planted on the broken road – legs splayed – hands outstretched.

VROOM!

I sharp-look up to a careening Vehicular Homicide Taxi. The kind that usually race by me like they're in the Indy 500 and I'm the checkered flag.

Only, this one is racing straight towards me – as if I'm a mere speedbump on his way to somewhere VERY IMPORTANT that he has to get to VERY FAST. That's because cab drivers in Panama City are paid by district – $2 for most downtown locations – $3 or more if you venture further. Hence, speeding from point A to point B is the only way they can make any money.

Double Hence – I'm about to make a career change from 'recently fired writer' to 'chalk outline on asphalt'.

Who knew *SCREEECH!!!*

Would be the sweetest sound in the English language?

Turns out it's the same *SCREEECH!!!*

In Spanish.

I blink up at the blinding headlights of a miraculously stopped-in-time deathcab feeling kid-height short and 'first week in town' tourista stupid.

A rotund male passenger, who looks like an expense account loving exec nearing fifty, hauls his rotundness out of the back seat preceded by the thinner, more agile 'I Brake for Redheads' driver. They yank me to my feet.

"Spanish, Spanish, Spanish?!"

"No speak… sorry," I shock mumble in knee-jerk Canadian politeness.

"Are you okay, Senorita?" Mr. Rotund deftly switches to the

gringette's spoken tongue.

"Uh… yeah… grat-zi…" I murmur some vague form of 'thank you' in pidgin Italian. Raw vanity at being mistaken for a 'senorita' at forty-four flushes out the near-death blush of embarrassment into a pinker shade of pride.

"Are you for sure okay?"

"Um…" I brush what I can only imagine to be terrorist-bacteria laden street dirt from my beige capris. "You wouldn't happen to be going near the Miramar Hotel, would you?"

They stare. Pupils dilating from kind concern to 'loco-foreigner' alarm.

"It has a nice gym," I elaborate as if that explains everything.

Mr. Rotund translates and the driver stares harder.

"Si. Mirarmar. Si," he stammers out, goggle eyed.

"Great, thanks."

I slide into the backseat, touch-testing the top of my head for errant vertical curls that might need a pat-down, whilst Mr. Rotund eases his jiggly roly polyness in beside me. He turns to stare out his window – privileged. As though his I.D. flashes the right address and he never has to explain.

"Well, that's one way to hail a cab in Panama," I murmur and he grunts a mercy chuckle in ride along solidarity.

The driver zooms off like he's auditioning to be an ambulance and gets me to the Miramar in record time.

Naturally, I tip extra.

Returning to Panama two years later, I again fall hard – only this time for a hot Sailor over a cold margarita. Oh, and Trouble too, of course. I can't forget him.

1. TOURIST at LOVE

Panama City – October 2009

Sailor's waiting curbside in a Vehicular Homicide Taxi. I jump in the backseat beside him, only to feel his ripple of sensuality breaking waves on my surface calm ocean.

Don't be ridiculous – I divert. *The thrill is being set free from The Tower – that's all.*

Cut loose from the 32nd story apartment above Via Israel's snarl-tangle traffic – daily tailgaters snaking past the shimmering view like a moat of metal monsters all fighting their way to the downtown core.

Rapunzel is about to be unleashed into the fray. Unleashed into the confusing crisscross of streets stretching out in all directions that have often left me feeling trapped above for the inability to provide an address in Spanish.

"El Marriott por favor," Sailor directs and the driver burns asphalt like he's the getaway car in a high speed chase and the cops are gaining.

"I thought you wanted sushi?"

"It's just easier to tell the driver the closest hotel to where you're goin' and take it from there," Sailor shrugs. "Try looking for an address and you could be goin' around in circles for hours."

Oh, so that's the trick! Panama is a city of landmarks not numbers. Freedom of mobility in a new GPS comes in little bits of information – discoveries made either by accident solo or from someone who's been there/done that.

Little crumbs of intel track Sailor landmarks too. Hidden/illuminated planes of his face as the cab whips around Multi Plaza to Balboa flickering streetlights. Peekaboo – the cheeky 'up for anything' American that has charmed me out of a jealous solitude into this backseat. Peekaboo – the Italian streak of smolder that has me on lockdown, fastening my last clasp of Body Armor:

No pets, no plants, no personal entanglements.

My quipped response to 'why aren't you in a relationship' – a cryptic: "I'm too important to be captured." The line culled from a cartoon femme fatale Russian spy on The Flintstones just before she vanished into a wall.

Only…

Panama is a city best served dark with a slice of moonlight. Like fine chocolate that breaks your diet after a week of being good. Its downtown lights mock my latest six month celibacy streak with the sinful, long gloved wave of a glitter blinged bad influence in six inch heels.

C'mon, gringette – you're past due in the pleasure dept.

Fine, true, but I specialize in "past due".

Past due bills despite workaholic aspirations.

Past due on a novel still hovering on page 100 after 5 years.

Past due in the 'why can't I get over it' department too. A love that lodges in my throat – choking on the three words I've often said with equal parts abandon and tortured-conscience to the man that made me The Other Woman.

Trouble.

So named because he turned to me once as I lay naked, already panging his imminent departure, and said, "I'm trouble for you, aren't I?"

But, Sailor is no trouble. Sailor hints at pleasure without permanence.

'Uh-oh – he's ruggedly, rigorously handsome,' was my thought at first sight as I stepped out of the midday scorchery into Darna's igloo blast aircon to meet this stranger for lunch. A 'friend of your brother' his text had said. A boat captain in and out of port. He sat alone at a table in the middle of the room – one glance and I knew. There's more than one heatwave in this town.

From there, my inner database involuntarily picked up Useless But Important Facts from the surface to the sub-surface:

curly haired like me. Busy like me. Single like me. And in every conceivable way that matters – completely unavailable.

In other words – perfect for me.

"I specialize in 'no fixed address'," was my response to Sailor's 'where's home?'

"I can relate – that's why my home floats." He flashed his wayfarer cred with an easy grin.

"Incoming!"

Yelled intuition – like Radar from M*A*S*H reruns. Hints of which had prickled as early as plane-touching-down in this sultry city. Though, ironically, another city led to the first interlock like the Panama Canal clicking into place allowing the ship to sail ahead…

"I loved L.A." hint of whimsical recall in my voice… regret at having to leave it in my taillights…

"Yah, it's got that creative vibe –"

"You can't walk into a café without tripping over ten writers –"

"A buzz you breathe in along with the smog…"

And there it was. Small talk turned to talk-talk. The kind where one word thread fluidly leads to another…

"But, I wasn't writing then or anything like that," Sailor marked buoys in his past, "I had a company I was trying to get off the ground."

"Oh, so you were a suit," I smiled, trying to picture this casual T-shirted expat donning the constraints of corporate life.

"Yah, not just a suit – the boss. Ten years non-stop 24/7."

"Like TV – it's a runaway train –"

"Buried in emails even on a Sunday."

"All you can do is hang on and pray you don't go over a cliff…"

… until an hour passes as if mere minutes.

"Still up for sushi?"

Had been Sailor's cheery 'back in port' text.

Though why a guy who just spent two weeks surrounded by water would want seafood…

"It's hard to get good sushi in Panama, but this place has a decent menu." Sailor leads the way as we alight from the cab, me tugging the black 'n' white mini skirt down from my upper thigh over black tights, stumbling on kitten heels. An ensemble suitably casual with a touch of 'night out' chic.

Or so I'd hoped – jumping up and down in the matchbox bathroom earlier. Mirror Challenged. Attempting to fit more of myself into the tiny frame above the sink for a last minute Cute Check:

Whirly unruly red spiral curls that Sibling says need their own zip code.

Black button up shirt hinting at ample cleavage 'under the hood' without flashing headlights at high beam.

Mascara swiped lashes fringing eyes of gray... or... er... blue though sometimes green... and in certain lighting—

Focus, Lila!

"I'm thinking we can share the salmon, it's really good here." Sailor is leaning towards me, his menu open to the pictures of exotic rolls and spicy tuna. A typical local restaurant: English/American name, Japanese food, menu in Spanish.

"Then a mix of sushi and sashimi."

Mmmmmmmm...

After making a thousand decisions all day, it's a relief to relinquish the make-things-happen control.

"You choose," I ripple anticipation. "You've been here before."

You choose, platonic – or hedonic?

The evening could go either way. And there's nothing I can do. But wait. A man has to know what he wants and especially who he wants. A charge ahead tempered by civility – a reach not a grab – but the confidence to make 'the first move'.

So, I wait...

Through the sushi dinner, in which he reveals his keystone life traumas, which like many a man, involve a mother and an ex-wife.

A diarist like me, he is open, verbally adept, and adventurous. The Skipper of his own boat – the maker of his own mark.

"Of course, that first year on the boat was crazy..." Sailor pops the last tuna roll in his mouth.

"I bet." I bite into a squishy crab/avocado California roll, only to have it fall apart and sushi-goo my fingers.

"Everything that could go wrong did," he shrugs.

"But, you wouldn't go back to that L.A. life?" I reach for a napkin to de-goo.

"Nah. Now, I just need to figure out a way to spend less time doing tours and more time writing…"

"See, that's the problem. When you're trying to be a writer – all these… distractions…"

Shared conspiratorial smile… a too close for comfort ripple.

Our vanquished plates are whisked away.

And I continue to wait…

Through the post dinner retro '80's MTV video playing rustic patio bar in Bella Vista, where we sit outside in the humid night and lean in just a little closer as his rum 'n' cokes with lime progress while I sip carefully on my half a margarita.

"I'm really more of a Libertarian," he tosses out.

"A libertine?" slightly alarmed, images of S&M rituals flashing by. "You mean like with safety words and… um… leather?"

"No," he laughs. "A Libertarian… It's like old school Republican…"

"Oh right." I vaguely recall hearing the term. "In what way?"

He schools the Canadian in American Politics.

"…a belief in free enterprise – less government – more…"

Freedom.

"Oh so, The American Dream, basically."

"Yeah, you could say that. Essentially free enterprise is more of a socio-cultural faith in the individual's ability to manifest a greater destiny…"

A tiny electric buzz of mental expansion sizzles from my naively eager intellect to my increasingly hungry, pulsating…

Steady now.

Sip.

Wait!

But, it's getting harder as the talk careens from political to personal.

"It can't just be about sex for me," Sailor delivers the ultimate aphrodisiac. "There has to be 'something more'."

"Appliances?" I tease out a laugh.

"That would be a 'no'…" his smile eyes meet mine "… something more than mere lust." He turns thoughtful, "An intellectual point of contact."

I'm forcibly holding back the intellectual impulse to touch his curly hair. Tightly wound statue-of-David curls, classically Italian – capping a crackingly vital American Male buoyantly athletic physique.

Ragged Sigh.

"Natural?" he indicates my own red whirls.

Oh, so I'm not the only one on Curl Watch :) He's recognized veracity in follicle solidarity.

I nod, absently pulling on a spiral, stretching it out only to let it ping back to just below my shoulder.

We compare and contrast – mine to his – his first touch drawing us both in. Strangers at parties pull on my curls. Finally, a chance at payback! Only, I'm not prepared for the silky feel as his chestnut browns corkscrew around my fingers.

Awkward pause.

Tingly Want.

Wait!

But, when he again touches mine, I gently indicate he can position his hand at the back of my neck to the baby coils nestled there and murmur, "The soft part is underneath."

Yeah, I know. Ultra obvious.

Except, he doesn't actually hear me. I have to lean in and say it again, this time louder, "The soft part is underneath!"

The look on his face is, 'Huh? What?'

So, what should be said in a seductive 'channeling Kathleen Turner as Jessica Rabbit' throaty whisper is practically yelled, and I have to grab his hand and literally yank it to the nape of my neck until his fingers make contact with the advertised 'soft curls underneath'.

Real smooth, I know. But if this doesn't...

Lips hit mine!

A stealth kiss airstrike – flash invasion of the space between us as Sailor leans across the table to press first kiss pursed lips to my startled equally pursed mouth!

Smack!

A tease of a kiss. A red glove tossed off a stripper stage... only for the stripper to emerge in a parka.

1.2

WHAT THE...?!

I sit there absorbing the shock as he sits back appearing to do the same.

Meeting eyes in a 'did that really happen' daze of two people who just crossed an invisible border into primitive, unexplored territory. A wild, unmapped landscape fraught with peril – but also the thrill – of the unknown.

Sailor suddenly looks apprehensive as if I'm going to slap him for the insolence and spread the word, "Player Danger!" It's an unexpected bit of concern for propriety.

Endearingly vulnerable.

What I fail to realize is that it's also a 'warning' like when you're speeding through a Malibu canyon and you miss the 'Danger: Falling Rocks' sign. For now, the only thing I notice is that it diverts the ardor, detouring the ram from his charge.

And that won't do.

I lean back to take stock: kiss one – out of the way. So, technically, he's made the first move, hasn't he? I smile at him encouragingly until the initial shock 'n' lack-of-awe passes and we mutually go in for round two.

Better. Softer. Less tight-lipped.

But it's the third kiss – the one I now feel free to initiate – that unlocks the floodgates.

Ardent. Lips parting.

Permission to enter? Granted.

And now, instead of talking American Politics and the difference between a Democrat, a Republican and whatever the hell a Libertarian is, we're tasting each other's cocktails.

Openly. Unabashedly.

And he's taking the lead, probing my salty/syrupy tequila-tongue with his rum 'n' coke sweet/citrusy one as our ardor spills out of mind and into matter.

If E=MC2

Then He Kissing Me = Holy F he's HOT!

He slows his kiss to 'savor' and strays his hand to the back of my neck for an advertised 'soft part underneath' fondle.

We uncork lips long enough to make our way out of the bar. He gentle-touch navigates me through the Minotaur labyrinth bumper-car traffic and scantily clad girls spilling out on Calle Uruguay. Arriving at a nondescript two story building, we climb a flight of stairs to a dark little Karaoke joint swirling with the blue 'n' yellow spotlights of amateur celebrity. A fast song pounds out of the speakers, and he sweeps me into an impromptu salsa.

Uh-oh. He can dance too.

Even slightly intoxicated – this sailor can swing! Taut muscles under his polo shirt tighten to steel under my pleased hands.

When the song ends he puts his arm around me and I nestle in, glue-high on the whiff of newness. He orders a Balboa beer and I wisely stick to 'agua'. We stand around listening to the ear splitting strains of Panamanian karaoke: a Spanish accented off-key attempt to sing English-language hit pop songs – with the odd local singing a Spanish song in a musical middle-finger to American pop culture.

I spot an empty back-corner banquette and we sink into it, making a halfhearted attempt to look at the song list between oxygen depriving French kisses and increasingly bold groping. One more finger-inch south and the vice squad will descend with water cannons.

"At first I was afraid, I was petrified..." shrieks a singer of ambiguous gender.

And then, out of the blue, through a mind-warping version of *I Will Survive* warbling from the speakers, Sailor's touch transcends the sensual and morphs into something more compelling.

Unnerving.

Terrifying even.

Tenderness.

A wave of warmth that emanates as his muscular arms encircle my waist in hardbody strength laced with a heart-centric caring.

A caress-hug.

It's body language Morse code for: this man doesn't just fuck like a sailor – he can love like a poet.

Well, this is unexpected. Not something I'd anticipate in one so former-navy-boy buff. Unexpected, like when the guy who's into stadium Journey concerts turns out to have a secret Barry White collection in vinyl.

Uh-oh…

A stab of fear for the potential Love Hangover as I tumble into the forbidden emotion-grotto I'd be foolish to swim in with a sailor who's in and out of port. A sailor who telegraphs NOT BOYFRIEND MATERIAL no matter how sexy and smart.

Isn't that what I liked about him in the first place?!

But unfortunately, he's not just sexy and smart – he's *lovely*. And that subliminal flood of intel about his underlayer (kinda like peeking into the underwear of the soul) leaves me breathless.

My heart-monitor goes off the scale into the red danger zone: "Intruder Alert! Intruder Alert!"

"What are you thinking?" he chooses this moment to ask.

The answer stalls on the off-ramp from my mind to my mouth. It's too much to explain over the sonic boom next song. So, instead I plaintively wail…

"Could you please tone down your Cuteness Factor?!"

He looks startled, then… knowing. An awareness of his impact grinning cocky.

I glare narrowed eyes and he holds up innocent hands, "Okay, okay – toning it down for ya." This becomes a running joke all night: I glare – he says 'toning it down'. Only he never really does. Not even close.

Instead – Sailor sings.

It's a Spanish ballad, and he's correcting the pitch that the singer on the lit dais at the front of the bar keeps missing. Correcting the pitch in a raspy lead-singer-in-a-rock-band reverb that is the equivalent of Aural Blow.

Oh God, I have the sudden urge to throw my panties at him like a suppressed housewife on a weekend bender in Vegas.

"You like this song?" he asks.

"If it's not disco – it's crap." I divert from the song's impact on my nether regions.

"Please tell me you're not serious!"

I turn to meet his recoiling-in-horror eyes.

"Just kidding!" I smile, but I'm not sure he buys it. Maybe it's too soon to confess my closet mirror ball addiction. Better wait until our wedding when I'm in white platforms and the DJ plays Donna Summer for our first dance. Okay, now I'm really kidding – it would be The Bee Gees. Obviously!

I lean into hardening biceps as he tightens his embrace, my lips caress his ear and steal a nibble. Recognition flame-flickers across his face. Shadowed though it is in the corner we're embraced in.

"You're passionate." He flashes amusement laced with heated discovery, as if he's peeked into my own 'underlayer' and found a black ribboned red lace panty he snips off with scissors of disclosure.

"Um, have you looked in the mirror lately?" I deflect again.

I'm getting smoke inhalation from the rising heat between us and the sudden 'not on a first night' panic has me turning away, only to lock eyes with the disapproving dagger-glares from a clique of baby-faced Barely Legals who've infiltrated the bar.

Look, I was only going for a kiss, okay?

How was I to know his mouth is an accelerant?!

"Yep, passionate." He traces a finger on my cheek now glowing red from the flames of desire licking up the sides of my battlements. And my splash of adolescent humor…

"I know you are but what am I?"

… is singed to steam when he adorably raises his hand to connect with mine.

High five.

And, just when I should be *raising* the drawbridge – I lower it with a crash – going down fast as his lips crush mine in a soulful battering-ram-to-the-castle-gates *astonishingly pleasurable kiss…*

Trailing his lips down my neck, he teases out a shivery breath-moan.

"Let's go somewhere," he murmurs.

Somewhere we can be alone…

1.3

"You're a good kisser," I gasp, my soft voice cracking like thunder in the empty apartment.

"I've been told that," he says modestly, pressing me more firmly into the couch as he orally fixates on my now poofy from overwork lips.

Fabric-yielding couch cushions beneath me – Sailor's embrace above me – I'm floating in a pleasure-ache bubble of slinky languidity. With every touch, every point of contact, ripples of sensuality current through me – as though he's transmitting something far beyond the surface caress.

Mingling molecules...

And I'm torn between wanting him closer – nakedly closer – and keeping every stitch of clothing on lest its removal lead to...

"Look, I'm not sure I'm ready for... I mean it's too soon for..." Vulnerable uncertainty mars my tone, furrows a never-been-Botoxed brow.

"Don't worry. We can stay right here if you like."

I smile up at him, my 'too fast too soon' anxiety attack soothed down a couple notches.

It had taken a few more of Sailor's 'let's go somewhere' urgings before I could bring myself to untangle limbs and leave the 'modesty police' back at the Karaoke bar. Going anywhere near a 3.5 mile radius of a bed felt reckless – but a few more meanglares from the Barely Legals made it clear that remaining anywhere public was... um... irresponsible.

So, I had risen like a sleepwalker in a dream, muttering "Ahem, permiso...' as I'd gingerly passed. Cringingly aware Sailor and I had morphed into poster kids for inappropriate PDA. I pictured us starring in some 1950's Sex Education Film with the gray suited male Narrator finger wagging, "There she goes boys and girls –

Bed Girl Walking!"

Which is partly why I'm not going anywhere near the bedroom now that we are in fact alone. C'mon – everybody knows that's First Night suicide!

I burrow more comfortably into the couch as Sailor leans over for a sip of beer and hands me my 'agua'.

"Again with the water," he comments on the alcohol vs. non-alcohol disparity.

"I have to keep my wits about me when I'm around you."

I take a sip of purity.

"You have to keep your wits about you?" he repeats, amused.

I nod soberly, gray-green-blue-whatever eyes glaring at his hazels to punctuate.

"Or, what?"

"Or, I'll lose what little restraint I have left."

"Oh, well, then here – have some beer," he laughs.

My 'very funny' is muffled as his lips are on mine again.

What begins slowly… ever-so-sweetly… escalates into fierce, fast, urgent. A sensory-overload eruption as we practically tumble off the couch tangled in each other. Well, at least now I don't need to see Pompeii. I know what it's like to be engulfed in a Vesuvius explosion of molten magnitude.

Besides, it's his topography I'm more interested in, the discovery of his landscape. Some people need to scuba dive with sharks to get that thrill some need to hike Everest. You can keep the bends and parka – give me a male-beauty specimen of wit and wantability and I'll explore the ninth wonder of the world myself, thanks (the unofficial eighth wonder being the Panama Canal, apparently). While the rest of the crowd is snapping photos and crying, 'Oh, looky, it's the long lost Dodo! It's not extinct after all! And OMG it's perched on the Island of Atlantis!" I'm a Tourist at Love urgently whispering, "Shut up, Livingston! And hand me the binoculars. I think I just spotted the rare Testosteronerectus-XY!"

Rare, because it's not every day I meet a man with the elusive *je ne sais quoi* to arrest my easily fragmented attention span *and hold it*.

A Hot Sailor, A Cold Margarita, and... Trouble

Trouble had it and he knew it. He didn't just walk into the narrow, fluorescently lit breakfast joint in Toronto's Beaches area that Sunday seven years ago – he swaggered. Swaggered like he knew some secret the rest of us mere mortals didn't. I sat alone at a table filling my notebook with the ink trail of my obscure existence while he rippled through the crowd like a life celebrity.

As he neared my airspace, I made the fatal mistake of looking up.

So, it is with that first sight of Trouble still seared into the back of my mind that I yield in deeper and deeper increments to Sailor's embrace – furtively giving into this fourth 'Escape from Trouble' attempt in the last three years. Uncomfortably contorted on the couch, but determined to stay in the living room as I cling to the purgatory between heavy petting and 'going all the way'.

My clothes are still on, I'm sober.

I can circle this orbit – a lust-hovercraft – all night if I just... *oh God that feels good...!*

"Oh, don't stop that particular..." I gasp.

"I won't," he promise threatens.

Anyway, where was I? Oh yes, orbiting the purgatory between ... "Oooohhh!"

Pressing deeper and deeper into him and arching back as he ravishes my neck with his reign of kisses, to which I must return the favor and nibble on his ear whereupon he melts into me and sighs out a raspy moan that soundwaves from my ear to my...

"STOP! Before you can't stop!!!" Scolds my inner Sex-Ed Film Narrator at his most scandalized.

"He ships out in 48 hours for a whole week," retorts my inner fishnet-stocking, implant-cleavage flashing Music Video Vixen as she buffs her gold tipped nails "It's now or never."

"Tart!" Sniffs Sex-Ed Film Narrator.

"Tightass!" Snaps Video-Vixen, as she fluffs her hair extensions.

And while this virtue vs. vice Fight Club rings to the next round, I cling to the couch as much as I'm clinging to Sailor...

Until...

The aircon spews its last cold death-rattle breath.

Ominous silence.

Sailor opens a window, but the air outside is only minutely cooler than the heatwave inside. He embraces me again, but the trickle of sweat between us intensifies to Olympic runner proportions.

No! Don't. Take. Off. Your. Shirt!!!

And there he is: smooth, tanned chest to my eager, hungry mouth, unbelievably soft skin on his back under my roaming hands. How is it biologically possible that this male member of the species has softer skin than the woman writhing underneath him?

I ask you – is that fair?!

"I like the way you touch me," he murmurs.

Well, I can't exactly stop now, can I? It would be rude. My hands explore further… finding a button… a zipper… a…

"How is it I'm naked and you're still dressed?" He asks moments later.

"Mmm… I like it that way."

"I bet." And he whips off my shirt in one deft motion, only slightly less impressive than his one-handed bra unhooking maneuver that I suspect he learned in the navy.

"You're pushing my boundaries," I complain.

"You like it when I push your boundaries," he says, caressing pink rosebud nipples that have the nerve to harden in agreement. He then presses his chest against mine and murmurs, "Ahhhh… skin to skin." Eyes meeting eyes with a colluding smile… and a blistering inferno of unbearable, sweat-lodge agony.

That's it – we have to move to the bedroom where the aircon actually works.

We catapult on the bed flipping onto our backs. For the first moment we just let the cold air breeze onto our Fahrenheit-abused bodies like lost-at-desert survivors stumbling across a 5-star resort whose 'all inclusive' includes palm-leaf fanning virgins misting us with Evian.

All too soon I become aware of Sailor sprawled on the right side of the same mattress I'm sprawled on. Aware of him lounging naked – fully stretched out horizontal beside me. Exuding the virile aura of a man who's charting his own course. A man who threw his suit overboard in exchange for board shorts, and whatever material comfort he's lost, he's gained back tenfold in a different type of comfort. An ease in his own skin that is breathtakingly sensual.

And it is in this wake that I drown.

My arms reach for him before my mind even registers and I am swept up in his responding embrace as he deftly rips at what remains of my clothes. Only the L.A. tights-under-mini-skirt look involves actual tights. As in super-snug to the body leggings requiring pliers to remove.

"Wow, these are *tight*!" He states the obvious, as he manages to get them half way down before they twist me into a yogic pose I'm woefully undertrained for.

"Well, they're called *tights*!" I explain unhelpfully, now tied up at his side in harsh justice for my fashion crime.

He tugs at them to no avail

"How do you breathe in these things?!"

I attempt to kick them off without causing him bodily harm – a stray knee to somewhere sensitive being all too possible in our close proximity. So close that he sees the black, boy-shorts style American Apparel panties underneath.

"How many layers do you have on?! This is Panama! It's HOT here!"

"Hey, this is my chastity belt, okay? Deal with it!"

"Chastity belt, huh?" He grins and nuzzles my neck again, which only revs up the urgency, until between his pulling and my kicking I finally wriggle out of my constraints.

Free at last!

Equality in this case = clothes falling to the floor in a crumpled heap. Only, where he is relaxed with his nudity, I'm shy and more exposed than I expected to be when the evening began.

"You're soft." He says in an appreciative tone as runs his hand along my waist, to hips to legs now bare, then back up to between them…

Soft.

Only the truth is deeper than surface hand-to-skin contact. My stone castle barriers to other men are mere holograms to Sailor as he lays himself along the length of me and I entwine myself around him in covetous welcome. His face pressed close to mine, I meet his gaze and notice the 'gotcha' teen boy grin peeking through the consenting adult symmetrical smile.

"Hey," he says in a sweet tone, looking into my eyes in a silent nod to the spark begun in conversation – the connectivity-ribbon that has tied us to this bedpost beyond mere lust.

And then he slides his nakedness over mine…

Sigh…

…and wetifies my already glistening silkiness with a caress of his hardness.

"Ohhhh…my… God…!"

"I like the way you respond to me," he murmurs.

"Oh, well – that's the easy part." And I shift underneath the weight of him ever so imperceptibly.

Giving way.

He slams into me like a sensuous hurricane – churning my whirlpool of sentiment with a forceof-nature drive that would be incredible enough – but it's interwoven with affection in a blend so heady-honey-hot that he rockets from *rare* to the endangered species list.

Obliterating every thought in my overburdened mind into a bliss-haze of oblivion.

Rendering me euphoric with each deepening point of pressure – clasping my hand above me like a long-time sweetheart – soulfully kissing me as he's passionately filling me – so that every point of the compass leads to a skyrocketing orbit above whatever planet I used to inhabit.

Thrust.
Kiss.
Thrust.
Caress.

And I'm no longer able to speak. Only…
Gasp!
And moan his name…
And *feel*…
As I'm nakedly… sensually… airlifted to rescue.

1.4

I. Am. Overwhelmed.

Lying beside Sailor in secret paroxysms of post-coital passion-shock, my mind quickly attempts to catch up to what my body already knows.

He's kryptonite.

"Told you to stop when you had the chance!" gloats Sex-Ed Film Narrator.

"Aw, it was worth the risk," shrugs Video Vixen, but she's a little unsteady as she slings a staggering stiletto back on… and… wait… no… are her eyes just a little bit… *misty*?!

It doesn't take an emergency call to an overpaid shrink to get the prognosis: so you slept with a sailor – and you didn't think maybe you'd *like* him?!

Shut up! Who asked you, anyway?

The answer is simple: be cool.

I turn to Sailor with goggly eyes of sparkly love-dust.

Okay, maybe I need to aim for *semi-cool* – you know – not overreach.

Fortunately Sailor is turned in the other direction. He's tangled in the sheet and drifting to whatever dreamland sailors drift to. Tiny-waisted mermaids, perhaps? Sirens harmonizing a sea shanty?? Treasure Island???

I wrap myself in a fresh-laundry scented fitted sheet. It's the only thing I can find in a hurry as the brief, requisite first-time cuddling has now given way to sleep. Pillow talk consisted of arguing over who should have thought to bring a condom – the man or the woman?

"Right, and if I carry a condom in my wallet the woman is like: *uh-huh, expecting something?*"

A sleepy, "Don't hit me with logic past two a.m.," was all I could manage.

We agreed to blame the need for the M.I.A. condom on the aircon malfunction, but then he accused me of sabotaging the aircon in the first place.

"I know this was all part of your master plan to get me naked and take advantage of me," Sailor insisted, yawning and satisfied.

"Me? Get *you* naked?! Who was it that stripped off at the first sign of a little heat?!"

"Yeah, exactly… all part of your master plan."

"No, but then you're the instigator…!"

"That's what you'd like me to believe."

"No, but—"

"It was really you all along."

"Okaaay," I said slowly, as if explaining to the cause-and-effect challenged. "You got hot, which got you naked, which in turn got me hot, which then got me naked. Do. The. Math!"

"See? Your plan worked."

Arrgh!

In addition to blaming the seduced for the seduction, Sailor also appears to be a solo-sleeper. Given that I'm now lying awake in the aftershock of his lovemaking blitzkrieg, I'm happy to stay on My Side of the Bed wrapped in my own 300 thread count with the occasional surreptitious glance his way. I marvel at the ease he emanates casually sleeping in the nude. I sense you can drop Sailor anywhere – a beach, boat, or strange bed and he can sleep like he's back at mamma's house in the bed he grew up with surrounded by the travel posters he probably tacked up beside Farrah Fawcett.

I, on the other hand, had David Cassidy and insomnia. Insomnia I've spent countless hours perfecting since the age of seven. Insomnia that's hard enough to manage when I'm sleeping alone – let alone with someone new. This would be so much easier if I'd already fulfilled my lifelong dream: separate bedrooms. Separate bedrooms with a connecting door like aristocrats.

My own boudoir all pink and soft yellow with that nude painting of me a Vancouver artist once did: a textured dreamscape in which I'm hugging my legs on the shore of an impressionist pond lit by an ancient moon. It would hang by a canopied bed of double-mattress softness floating on a step-up platform in the center of a room scented with French perfume. So feminine that the girly glare from the doorway would cause anyone with a Y-chromosome to back away, trembling from the suddenly uncharacteristic desire for a wax, pedicure, and a Tourettes-like need to voice an opinion on winged vs. unwinged pantyliners.

Instead, the Vancouver artist's gracious work is rolled up in a past-due owing storage locker in Toronto and I'm still lying on my side of a hard temporary mattress for transient ex-pats.

The bed I've longed to sleep in for 7 years? Any bed containing Trouble.

The first four years in Toronto the bed was mine – a $20 hand-me-down queen sized mattress.

Since fleeing Our Situation I've bounced from city to city as a TV story editor while my own secret story remains locked in a Hope Chest monogrammed EFT: Escape from Trouble. But, three EFT attempts in three years have only left me feeling wallside out in the cold.

Emotionally homeless.

Try as I might to tie the bed sheets and toss them out the window – Trouble slips into the room silently behind me – wrapping his impossibly strong arms around my waist and pulling me back from the ledge. Even as he's the one driving me to jump.

A cruel enchantment.

The years on the run have yielded other mattresses on the floor – though with the exception of lovely memories of EFT2 and EFT3, they've been mostly empty ones. They've added to a growing lifetime collection of bed-head memories. From 'Sleepless in Seattle' to restless in Prague to wired in Eilat, the list of hotel/motel beds combined with couches, air mattresses, futons, top and bottom bunk beds and 'spare bedroom' furniture I've tossed and turned on stretch far and wide from tiny towns like Liphook, England – to vast London/New York metropolises.

I've missed sleeping with Trouble the most.

Toronto 2002

"I should go," he says, looking down at me cradled beside him.

I'm startled out of my bliss cocoon. Enwrapped in the arms of this hulking breadth of a man who fills the right side of my bed – for the first time – with so much raw power laced with sweet reverence for what is between us that I had blindingly let myself feel sure…

"It's 3:00 a.m.!"

"Well, if I don't get home before morning there will be problems."

That's when I knew.

Trouble's adamant, "My wife and I are, for all intents and purposes, separated. We live in the same house, but we're living separate lives and we're free to see other people. As soon as the house sells, I can afford to move out."

…was a lie…

"If you have to go home, you're not really separated."

He fixes me with his glowing sincerity, eyes serious. Looking deeply into my suddenly anxious, accusatory stare.

"Do we not go out in public?" he evidences exhibit A. "Do I not hold your hand – openly? Kiss you like this…"

He kisses me softly – full favored lips brushing mine. "Would I do that if I had something to hide?"

My eyes are caught in his – unable to refute Trouble's declarative PDA that has made waiters blush from King West to Yorkville.

"Divorce is imminent," his certainty my sedative – kissing my forehead, smoothing out the lines. "Don't worry."

The number of times in four years Trouble and I woke up on the same mattress: once.

Back to now...

In the wee hours of Panama City, I spare the man now sleeping beside me my current worries – born this night.

I don't tap Sailor on the shoulder to ask, 'you awake?'

I don't whisper, 'Hey, do you have to be that beautiful when you sleep? I mean, it could be considered a public hazard like the uncovered manholes dotting Panama City sidewalks.'

Urban Open Wells.

Concrete abyss steep-drop booby traps that ensnare the unwitting tourist and the chronically clumsy – of which I am both.

Must not fall...

Must not fall...

Must not...

Zzzzzzzzzzzzz...

"I can't believe it's after six!" is Sailor's idea of 'good morning'.

2. THE MORNING AFTER

He bolts out of bed at 6:24 a.m. like he's still in the navy and late for a drill. I lean up on one elbow barely restraining the urge to yell, "Drop and give me twenty, deckswab!"

6:26 a.m. – he hits the shower.

6:57 a.m. – standard Sailor time – a hurried kiss-parting.

"Thanks for the uh… tryst." He smiles almost sheepish.

"Have a great trip," I go in for an awkward hug, now cold-light-of-day prepared to not see him again – steeling myself to shrug a simple 'so long seadog' and chalk it up to that almost-never 'one night stand' indulgence. But, he hesitates in the doorway, surprising me with…

"Let's grab a bite later today," adding casually "if you're free." A grin punctuates, fun and infectious.

Only sophisticated nonchalance pours from my pouty lips, "Um… yeah… sure… that would be… nice."

The eyes that linger on mine are warm.

So much for the 'one night stand' theory.

2.2

The next day...

"You should come on the boat some time," Sailor says offhand, sipping coffee. "We can sail for a couple of days around the islands."

I glance up – jittery from my third cappuccino to Sailor's first 'American style' drip coffee – having coked up on caffeine prior to his arrival: walking towards me wide awake and buoyant in a white T-shirt and beigey cargo shorts – radiating an 'up to something' mischief – pulling me into a quick squeeze with a grinning "Que pasa".

Fluttering me shy.

We're at Saquella. Squeezed into a round, white bistro table spilling out into the Multi-Plaza atrium. Just another tousled 'morning after' duo in the weekend brunch crowd. Only, this is now 28 hours later as our get-together good intentions of yesterday tailspun into mañana. Drill sergeant sticky note 'to dos' at my end…

…and Sailor calling mid-errand – mallcrushed – "Looks like everyone in Panama City woke up today and said, 'I think I'll go to Albrook'."

Albrook, an insider's anti-tourist retail Mecca where the prices plummet for locals who recoil from the Punta Pacifica sticker shock pretentions of Multi-Plaza.

"It's the end of the month and everybody got paid," Sailor had sounded harassed against the sale stampede murmurs in the background. "They're all here spending it on things they don't really need, but think they can't live without."

"And you're in the line of fire." I, on the other hand, was standing in the living room, cell to ear, swaying on my feet in desperate need of a nap.

"Have to be if I want to get everything done before I leave tomorrow."

"Look," I said with what I thought was extreme nobility and sacrifice on my part. "If you don't have time to get together before you leave that's okay."

"Nah, we'll figure something out." I could hear the smile.

But, by late aft the potential for heavy petting unraveled into heavy texting. A He Text/She Text volley of two people spending more time talking about getting together than the time it actually takes to get together.

"What is this texting obsession?!" I finally dialed at 8:00 p.m., interrupting his raspy…

"Hey you…"

… with…

"If I'd stayed in L.A. I would have needed a thumb transplant… and now you too!"

"Welcome to the 21st century," he said then added, "So, you up for doing something later?"

'Later' now meant 'late night' as Sailor had to meet boat clients first. 'Later' sounded like a booty call – a booty call that takes on new meaning when said 'booty call' is in and out of town and I'm already one month into a three month visa. If I don't see him tonight – I don't see him naked for who knows how long.

But, tomorrow's tasklist loomed…

Sunday – the one relatively quiet day I could squeeze in some early morning 'writing time' on that stalled novel. If by 'writing time' one means staring at the blank page. Staring until anxiety escalates to all out panic and I'm forced from said blank page in defeat telling myself 'losing the battle does not mean losing the war'. Doodling with blog scraps in an attempt to finish *something*. Not to mention that my über-buddy, Lewaa, emailed me his latest feature length script and I still haven't read it… Wonderboy Lewaa, who reads my fledgling chapters in Mach 2 writer etiquette – never making me wait… always pointing out the positives before he hits me with the hard stuff…

"I'm halfway to my jammies," I'd sighed.

"Jammies?! Have you noticed it's 80 degrees?"

Pacing the living room, I turned towards the narrow hallway and ambled to the bedroom in socked feet.

"I reserve the right to wear jammies in all weather – though 'jammies' consists of yoga pants and my green, vintage Turtle Wax tee, so don't be getting any 'flannel matching set in floral' ideas."

"Oh well, that's all right then. Though, I looked over at one point last night and thought I saw you wrapped in a fitted sheet," Sailor sounds like he's scratching his head even through the crackly cell.

"Yeah, so? It was the only thing I could find in a hurry."

"Okay, but you could have asked me. I'd have shared the flat sheet."

"You looked comfortable. Besides, flat sheets are so *ordinary*." I was no longer covering nakedness, but awkwardness. "It's so passé. Fitted is the new flat."

"Absolutely, why be normal?" A smile seeped into his voice.

Scrambling to save the situation, I draped on the bed in sight of strewn about pieces of a limited, functional wardrobe and slipped in some 'above my pay scale' flirting.

"Well, I wouldn't mind a French lingerie collection complete with custom corsets."

"Oh. Really?"

"A girl can dream."

"Oh yah? Well a guy can too."

I'd curled up into a rare enchanted sleep, the little teasing jokes of our conversation wisping around my body like a white smoky afterglow of our first night. The Decapolis – with its crack mojito I've sipped only once two years ago and can still taste on the tip of my tongue in sweet mint reverb – dangled for 'next time'. Sailor met clients in Casco – the crumbling 'romantic ruins + contemporary hot spots' old city – while I lay in bed imaging us there someday. A fantasy acute in the scent of fine Cubans and cocktails laced with rum.

Hey, I spent 40 years in a country where a 'hot night' can mean a space heater, a hockey game on TV and the guy burping out 'beer me'.

And now Sailor is upping the ante…

"Ever dived into the Caribbean on a sunny day?" he grins my way across the tiny Saquella table as I shake my head 'no'.

"Ever been to the Caribbean at all?"

"Um… no," my calm sip of cappuccino a camouflage for the rebel leap of heart as I flashback to a Caribbean screensaver I had once to get me through the cold Toronto winters. Staring longingly into that crystal water dotted by a white sailboat and tiny palm treed island with strip of sandy beach.

"Diving into that cool water after lying on the deck in the sun."

OMG that sounds incredible!

And the way he's looking at me as he describes it – the way he leans close…

"Nothing like it…"

Heat waves of island perfection squiggle in front of my eyes, hazing my vision.

"Do you like lobster?"

I nod despite a shudder at how the poor lobster meets its maker.

"Have you ever had lobster caught fresh?"

"Does Peggy's Cove, Nova Scotia count? They had instructions on how to eat it on paper placemats."

"These are Caribbean lobsters," Sailor smugs. Something tells me these lobsters won't come with paper placemats and a plastic bib. "Cooked up fresh – we can eat on deck and watch the sun go down."

Scorching days surrendering to orange pinky sunsets followed by calm, moonlit waters. Brunch on the boat – lobster at night… sharing the Captain's cabin…

"You ever lay on a deck under the stars?" His expression reflects a near celestial glint that ricochets like a stray shooting star landing on my own suddenly glowing smile.

"That sounds amazing," I say muted, trying not to show just how amazing…

Oh Sailor, you can batten down my hatches (whatever the hell that means) any time!

Only, my faux tranquilla outside is not just disguising excitement – it's suppressing the rogue thought…

Wait – are we *dating*?

"You'll love it," he says. "Trust me."

2.3

I used to joke that guys come in five categories:
- One night stand
- Three day weekend
- Six months/discovering you're the one for me... or not
- Relationship
- The Rock! (AKA: Maximum Security)

The leap from one night stand to three day weekend is different for everyone. For me, it signals 'exclusive'. EFT3 agreed with this hypothesis.

Flashback to the road from L.A. to Vegas:

My feet are on the dashboard of my bright yellow Cobalt SS while EFT3 is at the wheel. A businessman with impeccable manners, he's also a planner. Hence, early into our encounter he booked us into a hotel on the strip.

"Look, since you're nice enough to take me away for a weekend, I won't be sleeping with anyone else as long as we're sleeping together." My red painted toes screamed 'wild abandon', but my tone was geekily earnest.

"Me neither. I'm not built that way," he admitted whilst speeding.

We agreed what 'dating' looked like even though we knew it had a shelf life courtesy of my temporary visa. I don't 'break up' — I just leave town.

Simple. Easy. Direct.

The leap from six months to 'relationship' is far more significant. A shared dream. You and me against the world, kid. It's that one-up from 'exclusive' that signals we're not just sailing the same sea for a while — we're going in the same direction.

"I can do commitment," Sailor had said at some point in our topic leaping conversation that began at Darna. "I've done it. Ten years of marriage. When I had the business in L.A. Worked my ass off, but I did it. I got us our dream."

The duo dream that shipwrecked into a solo voyage.

I have that treasure map too. The one with the missing X.

"Maybe once she got that dream she discovered it wasn't really hers," I said, then wondered if I should have.

"Yeah, well, I tried. I did everything I could to support her in what she wanted to do."

There are three dreams in any relationship: His, Hers, and Ours. And if any of those dreams are in conflict…

"I admire you for getting the job done," I had grasped at some form of comfort, "even if it didn't exactly go the way you wanted."

"Yeah, thanks. I'm over it." His shrug hadn't convinced me. But, at least he's got the guts to go back to Ground Zero: the place of parting.

"Of all the places in all the world my friend could have chosen to meet up…" he had glanced my way and I smiled at his nod to Casablanca.

"Well, maybe you'll make new memories this trip – better memories."

"Yah, that's what I figure too. New memories would be good."

The end of a marriage is not just the end of a relationship – it's the end of all the dreams you had for that relationship. That's the hurt that lingers. That you tried and tried – only to choke on betrayal.

And if there is some inherent irony in this moment – it's that Sailor and I are squeezed into a tiny table at Saquella surrounded by chatty couples and the occasional family in a mélange of well heeled locals and T-shirted expats – not just because we had dreams of travel, but because of that other more traditional dream that blew up in our faces. Forcing us off the main road – to a road less travelled.

"You've never seen San Blas." Sailor snap-shuts his menu decisively and lays it on the table. "You gotta come." His smile says I'd be crazy not to.

But, this could make 'goodbye' a lot harder.

And that makes me more nervous than when he first saw me naked. This is the problem with removing your clothes before removing your emotional armor. Smoothing out the hem of the same blue print dress I wore to Vegas, I'm about to turn to Sailor and joke that I don't breed well in captivity – when he casually adds…

"You're brother's been. Said he wants to go again." He catches the waiter's eye and nods him over. "Theo too – he wants to take his girlfriend. You guys could get a group together."

Oh! He's just being a good tour guide!

NOT dating.

Phew.

Wait.

Whaddya mean we're not dating?!

2.4

"You like order? College Kid Waiter arrives, inadvertently getting to the crux of the matter.

Yes. No. I suddenly don't know what I want.

I mean, yes, he's über-hot…

Mmmm… the Caprese looks good – a sensual indulgence.

But, my career is floundering, I have so much work to do and getting any more entangled is a bad idea.

Better stick to eggs. A safe, predictable choice.

Wait, what does he want?

"I'll have the Western omelet," Sailor says and College Kid Waiter scribbles.

"Um…" I look from College Kid Waiter's patient gaze to Sailor's puzzled one at my long hesitation then stare back down at the menu like I'm deciphering ancient Egyptian hieroglyphics.

Sigh.

"Would you please translate?" I turn to Sailor with pleading eyes.

Of the many languages swirling around us from Spanish to Italian to Hebrew to German in this port city Citizens of the World crowd – Sailor's raised eyebrow 'diva alert' at my complicated order is the loudest. He's practically having to secret handshake the College Kid Waiter for my 'Caprese with extra basil and extra olive oil on the side, but no balsamic, and with two fried eggs, but hold the toast'. I catch the kid's 'above my security clearance' shrug as he walks over to the touchscreen to key it in with a female colleague looking over his shoulder and pointing. I sit up a little straighter and lift my chin in my best 'don't everybody?' bat eyes blonde.

"You were saying?"

Sailor smiles and shakes his head. "You need to learn Spanish."

"Hey, I can say: 'Buenos', 'Comme Sta', and 'Cappuccino super-caliente por favor'. What else do I need?"

"A full time translator, obviously."

I laugh and our eyes meet in a flash of warmth that momentarily short circuits the jangly nerves that have been growing by the minute.

"That's Sibling's job," I smile.

"How's he doin'?"

"Great! He's lovin' it."

"Where's he now?"

"Jerusalem." I inward sigh in wistful memory.

"So, you're housesitting for him."

"Yeah, and he flew me out here."

"That's a nice brother."

"He's the best." We share a Sib moment – me the proud older sis waxing poetic like a 'best Bro in the world' Hallmark card – Sailor admitting…

"Y'know, I've never been able to figure out what your brother actually does."

"Well, he's in Finance."

"You don't exactly know do you?"

"Haven't a clue," I cheerfully confess. "I majored in theater."

"Gotcha." Sailor smiles.

"But, he paints and does music too. He's a world travelling Renaissance kinda guy."

"Yah, I've seen some of his paintings – he's good." Sailor takes another sip of coffee then adds out of the blue, "He doesn't read your work, does he?"

I throw a little sideways glance at the worry lines suddenly clouding his usual confidence.

Hmmmm…

Of the markers and buoys that signaled our potential to torch a mattress – exchanging words was a big clue. Not in the 'screw you' and 'your mother' way of 'exchanging words' – but in the reading of each other's fledgling 'birth of a novelist' attempts at prose shortly after we'd met for lunch.

His revealed a 'Jimmy Buffet' affability beneath the sexy-at-first-sight. Mine had the opposite effect.

"Intriguing…" had been his texted surprise. Surprised to discover the 'nice woman' in a long sleeved, button up blue shirt by day – was camouflage for a legs-wrapped-around-him kitten by night.

The sin under the sincere.

The Ann-Margaret under the Margaret Atwood.

The…

"Just goes to show you never know about a person," he had said a tad insultingly.

Sigh.

But, this is a theme I've heard before as summed up by a former lover with a blunt delivery. "Most people with your passion wear that edge somehow," he had mused, "but there's not a trace of it in your face or how you look. You look like a teacher or librarian – but get you in bed…"

I think every teacher and librarian should protest this un-sexy stigma. Bare midriffs are so… *obvious*. I mean, the centerfold is INSIDE the magazine, isn't it?

"First I'm having an intelligent conversation," Sailor had said last night "and next thing I know I'm sitting there thinking, 'I want to kiss this woman'!"

Perhaps he didn't get the memo that teachers and librarians are the new hot.

"You sure your Brother doesn't read your work?" he asks again with a suspicious glance towards the Multi-Plaza atrium, as if my Bro is going to parachute in any moment and punch his lights out. "Maybe he's just not telling you." He sight swings back my way, brow furrowing.

"My Brother took one look at what I was writing and shut down the laptop like it was on fire. I mean, he knows I have a propensity for… um… meeting people when I travel. Or as he jokingly puts it, 'travel booty' –"

Sailor huffs out a 'huh' at that one.

"But, trust me he doesn't want to know the details."

"Details? Just how detailed do you plan to go?"

"Well, all the way I guess at some point."

"He's gonna kill me."

"He doesn't read my work! And besides, he won't care if we're dating," I say off-hand then freeze.

H E Double Hockeysticks! I said the D-word. As in out loud!

"Or, whatever, I don't know that we're actually dating per se… I don't know what we are…" Mercifully the word burp ends – but the tension has just begun – as Sailor takes another sip of coffee in uncharacteristic silence and College Kid Waiter returns to lay down cutlery.

Just like Sex on the First Night being 'too soon' – mentioning the 'D-word' The Morning After is also taboo. He's liable to bolt like a pirate catching sight of shackles.

Haven't I?

Isn't that exactly what I've done if over morning coffee my Night Before lover turned to me with hearts in his irises?

Quick! Think of a safe topic!!!

"Can you believe people in Columbia don't know where San Blas is?" Sailor asks indignantly a few sips and silence later.

Uh-oh.

I try to nod with what I hope is an appropriately appalled expression, whilst inwardly panicking that he might suddenly pop quiz me from *Lonely Planet*.

"I mean, Columbia is just one country over from Panama!"

It is?! Jeez…

"How can Columbians not know the geography of their own next door neighbor?!" Sailor's practically vibrating outrage.

"Mmm-hmmm, " I say in a soothing 'I know what you mean' tone while mentally resolving to Google 'San Blas' the first chance I get. If only Sibling were here! He can recite *Lonely Planet* backwards. I land in a new place like a blank map from explorer days, and fill it in as I go. A guidebook feels like cheating.

Fortunately, Sailor and I are saved from whatever awkward thing either one of us was about to say next by the arrival of brunch.

I fall onto the Caprese's soft buffalo mozzarella atop plump red tomatoes anchored by crispy edged fried eggs 'on the side' like a wild tiger that hasn't eaten in three days.

"How's yours?" he eyes my multiplate buffet crowding our little table.

"Mmmmm…" I mumble mid bite. "How's yours?"

"Really good."

Luckily, the conversation shifts again to an even safer topic – like how the ex-girlfriend he's meeting in San Diego later today wants to have his baby.

"So, um… are we talking natural conception here or turkey baster?" I can't help but ask, glancing towards his fluffy omelet avariciously.

"No, there's gonna be none of that first part…" he says firmly and I'm embarrassed by the little sliver of relief that darts through me.

"She's strictly a friend," he continues. "But, she wants to raise a kid on her own and with all the travel I do, this may be my only chance to be a father."

"Well, I can see why your hotboy gene would be in demand," I tease.

"Ah, not exactly," but the corner of his mouth twitches into a near smile. "It's just this one opportunity – I'm not planning to take out an ad and make a career out of it. I'm not even sure I'll go through with it."

"I guess you'll have a week to discuss it on this trip." I fork a tomato.

"Ten days actually."

"Oh, that's nice." I put down my fork, confused by the stab of missing someone I didn't even know existed two weeks ago.

But, people are not interchangeable – the intelligence behind the eyes – the particular crook to the smile – the tone of laugh.

And this one has given me a crash course in all things Sailor. His truths surfacing like submarines. Ocean depths of murky camouflage giving way to clearwater transparency. As visible as sunlight glinting off a periscope.

And if he's going to be honest about the whole sperm donor thing – if we're at that level of sharing – then maybe I better unfurl my sails too…

"Um… I think there's something you should know."

He sits up a little straighter, laser focusing my way.

"It's interesting you're at the stage in life where you're considering a last chance at fatherhood – when I'm at the stage of possibly having to retire my uterus."

I sigh a little inward sigh, relieved to be able to talk about it, having brushed aside the warning signs heralding the 'bad days' ahead. Impatient to get it all over with – picturing a full on retirement party – bigger than a wedding – more booty pops than a Bar Mitsvah—

I catch the look on his face.

Uh-oh.

"You see…" I squirm, rushing to clarify, "I have a little problem in the female department… it's nothing contagious or anything… but it does affect me."

"Why you are you telling me this?"

I freeze in startled silence.

Maybe I misheard him.

Maybe he means it sincerely – the 'why' being actual curiosity. Maybe he…

"Why are you telling me this?" Sailor harpoons any attempt to soften the blow with, "someone you've known all of five minutes."

Staring back at his discomfort bordering on irritation, I realize I've just proven the basic tenet of Einstein's theory of relativity: it is in fact possible to be 5'5" while simultaneously being smaller than a three inch salt shaker.

And yes, time does move glacially slow when you're *mortified*. Although, *mortified* doesn't quite cover it. Layered on top of the mortification is shock.

Dude, you told me all about your ex, your mother, your baby daddy options, the married women clients who slip you their numbers right under their husbands' noses – okay, so you toss them overboard (the numbers – not the women) – but who died and made you the 'overshare' police?!

Only, I can't point that out – can't throw back the intimate details he offered up that led me to believe we had an open door. Okay, so turns out it's a trap door, but that doesn't give me a one-free cruel card. When someone entrusts you with their life markers it's sacred. At least it is to this writer. So, instead…

"I've slept with you," I blurt out. "That means I know you more intimately than most people I've ever met."

I'm hoping I look smartly Kinseyesque – but I'm getting an internal memo from Cupid, "Um… Lila… could you be a bigger dork?!"

"Well, anyway…" too late to shut up now, "On the off chance we might sleep together again at some point…"

I catch him stiffen – and not in a good way.

"…I feel obliged to be scrupulously honest."

OMG, does embarrassment kill? Because I think I'm having a dork stroke. I sure hope that glowing white light up ahead is just the Louis Vuitton store and not actually heaven.

College Kid Waiter asks if we want more coffee and I glare at him, wondering how fast I can get an antidote for the social-suicide truth serum he must have slipped into my meal in revenge for ordering off menu.

But, hey… it's not like I admitted how much I actually do love vintage disco, okay?! Plus…

You'd think Sailor would be thrilled to learn it's not something requiring shots. I mean, if someone I'd just slept with said "I think there's something you should know," I'd be totally relieved if the sentence that follows has zero to do with:

The HIV or any other nefarious STD

A drug mule day job

That he accidentally 'borrowed' my rose print panties and is now wearing them.

I mean, it's not like I turned to him and purred, "Although you know me as Lila I used to be Luke – but don't worry – I'm still an Aquarius."

Of course, then he'd probably demand to know why I hadn't mentioned it sooner. When is it okay to tell someone what you're going through? If sleeping with someone doesn't give you one-free-reveal what does?

"My ex had something similar…" Sailor struggles to find common ground and proceeds to regale me with the tale of medical insurance and mood swings.

Why are you telling me this.

Maybe because I'm scared.

He seems to get that his knee-jerk reaction could be mistaken for an all out 'jerk' reaction and turns to me with compassion-eyes. "It was night and day after the operation – trust me – you'll feel a lot better."

I smile wanly at the reassurance.

But, my cover is blown and instead of vanishing into a wall with a cartoon spy "goodbye, you stupid good-looking" nonchalance, I've tripped the alarm.

"C'mon, you don't want to get involved with a scallywag like me," Sailor says offhand as we split the bill.

It's possible that no one has used 'scallywag' since Blackbeard bit bullets in 1718, but the throwback term charms even as it chills.

Unfortunately, I appear to be walking the plank.

"Woah! That was one lame kiss," I blurt out after Sailor's peck goodbye leaves me reeling from the lackluster contrast to his usual talents.

"Well, there are people all around," he glances defensively left to right at the chic Saquella crowd, suddenly the shy one.

"So? Does that mean you have to kiss me like your Cousin Tilly, three times removed from Peoria?"

"No one has ever called my kiss lame." Sailor tugs me close, pressing his lips to mine.

Cold – hard – arrogant.

Holding me tight enough for the scent of laundry soap and coffee to dizzify senses. Close enough for his tensing muscles to reach past the flimsy fabric of my dress and imprint the strength of him on my suddenly weak form.

He steps back, satisfied.

"Ah… that's… better." I feign fanning myself as if faint.

"Well, it's gonna have to do ya for now," he says with a brusque contrast to the half tilted smile – giving my waist a tiny squeeze. "I'm late."

And he rushes off to make those 'new memories' whilst I sit back down and throw open my notebook to write…

The Pirate has jumped the rope and swung away to his ship – the H.M.S. Booty. Setting sail full speed ahead – eye to telescope.

I catch a glimpse of his tailcoat flapping in the breeze.

And sigh with relief.

As long as someone's running, all's right with the world. A world in which traditional rules have been thrown out the window – and sex is a High Seas Adventure.

3. MONDAY

I can't believe it's after six.
    6:37 a.m. to be exact.
    I reset the cell phone alarm to 6:45 a.m.
    6:45 a.m. trilly alarm…
    Snooze button!
    Just five more minutes…
    7:25 a.m.
    Sailor would be up by now.
    Mother Teresa – if she were still alive – would be up by now.
    Even the Euro is up by now.
    7:27 a.m.
    Fuck.
    Dragging mutinous 'let me sleeeeep' body out of bed. Gingerly putting one foot down on the floor and then the other – standing shaky and exhausted – taking wobbly step after wobbly step towards the matchbox bathroom with its glass enclosed shower box, repeating a spiritual mantra I learned over ten years of daily disciplined meditation:
    Coffee.
    COFFEE…
    COFFFEE!
    Escaping The Tower twenty minutes later in blue dress, black tights that cut off at the ankle, and flip flops – the boldness of a Panama City sun making me laugh at its 'ta da' show offy glare. Cornflower blue, cloudless sky. So hot it's impossible to believe this isn't high noon. Toting the laptop Sibling bought me a couple of years ago a few blocks by foot to the Sheraton Hotel. Careful to avoid the open urban wells – stepping around potholes – towards a beacon of civility. The S h e r a t o n lit sign on the roof of the hotel a mere blip in the view from Sibling's apartment window –

calling me last night – a sign I'd been staring at for weeks – finally noticed.

I enter the lush green with plants and center fountain 'throwback to Casablanca' lobby and sigh. Relief.

$2.25 for a cappuccino and I can sit for three hours. Except, I only have one. I flip open the laptop and pray the words come…

8:50 a.m.

Shut down.

Dragging mutinous 'let me staaayyy - I just got started' psyche away towards commerce – towards 'earning a living' tasks that demand time-sensitive attention. Bracing myself for the onslaught – for the 'bad days' as pain starts to rumble and I cringe at having revealed myself so… damaged.

A Brief History of Goodbye

Toronto 1970

Dad is pulling me into a hug. He's standing by the door of our one-bedroom, basement 'immigrant family' apartment on a cold, rainy, gray November morning. He's going back to his birth place – Bucharest – for a two-week vacation. I wonder if he's going to see the Brother I've never met. I don't even know his name, I just saw him in a photograph once. A little boy older than me from Dad's first marriage.

This 'previous marriage' concept feels foreboding and strange. I thought marriage was forever.

I wrap my 7-year old arms around his heavy woolish navy coat and smile up at him.

"Bye Daddy! Have a good trip!"

Crazy Uncle Y jingles his car keys, convinced Dad is going to miss his plane.

"Just a moment." Dad says and fiercely hugs me to him, tight.

Too tight.

Tight enough for me to feel a discord of remorse slice through him. Tight enough to feel a longing ache in his embrace that I'm too young to have words for. Tight enough to know…

Something's wrong.

Six weeks later I leap out of bed and walk out of the bedroom I share with grandma 'Omama' into the living room where Mom sleeps.

She's gone. Already left for work – but she's dropped a Strange Man in her bed.

"Hello," I chime in my most gracious 'welcome to our humble abode' smile.

"Go away, kid," he growls in a Montreal Canadiens fanteam accent, irate at the bouncy pogo stick of a girl who's got the nerve to wake him up.

Tabarnac!" he spits out and pulls up the covers – turning away towards the wall.

I stare at this grouchy home invasion.

This is my first clue.

Dad's AWOL.

Toronto 1990

"I want you out! You and your *issues* and your drama!!! If you don't leave, so help me God I'll make you wish you had!!!"

Even buffeted by my husband's rageblast I am grimly amused to note that he's accusing me of drama whilst starring in his own Drama Queen musical.

I love the way you make me laugh… is what I used to say.

But, now I'm lowering my voice to 'appeasing' – making myself as small a target as possible.

And hating him for it.

Totally bewildered by the mood swings – the self-hating eruptions – the couch huddling depression – the erosion of the dimple-smile 'college sweetheart' brainiac I fell in love with.

"You have thirty days to GET OUT!" I won't last 24 hours.

It doesn't matter that deep down I don't believe his fist will ever hit anything other than the wall he punched a hole in. He's rocking the 'married residence' living room with violent fury and I'm standing in his epicenter, extremities so cold they're numb.

"Did you hear me?!"

Nervously twisting my wedding ring, mentally packing.

Prague 1994 – Ryder's Apartment

"… Andre just informed me the party tonight is actually my surprise going away and I might not make it home until the crack of dawn."

I stand at the kitchen table reading the first lines of Ryder's handwritten note and my heart sinks. I pick up the note in my right hand and catch the next line. "I'll try to get back before you leave for the train station in the morning – but if I don't make it – just want to say how great it was meeting you. You have a lot to offer the world."

Oh. Really? What?

On the right margin, Ryder has drawn a little happy face and scrawled the words: "And Oh My God incredible sex!"

Oh. Haha. Well I ain't offerin' that up to the world, Mister – that was just for you.

"Are you always this bold?" the American-in-Prague had asked when our intellectual arguments gave way to a two-night tryst fueled by the fantasies I spun for him, low voiced in the dark.

Are you always this bold?

No, actually.

But you are my first. The first of a Tourist at Love tendency after the parameters of marriage and anything resembling a normal relationship left me feeling caged. On the outside doing my utmost to be loving, giving, positively working towards 'our future' – on the inside guiltily clawing my way out.

Like a hostage with Stockholm Syndrome.

"Keep the chain on at all times," the conductor said sternly at 5:00 a.m. the next morning as I settled into my rudimentary private compartment on the train from Prague to Bucharest. A station I'd only found two days before despite repeated attempts – until finally I burst into a tony crystal shop – mimed a pull-chord and chimed, "Choo-Choo!" Half hour later, I had the ticket – tucked into my passport holder beside the multi-country visas.

"Even when the border guards knock on your door..." the Conductor paused and met my gaze to make sure he had my full attention, "DO NOT OPEN THE DOOR WITHOUT THE CHAIN ON until you make sure it's an actual guard in uniform. Better still, keep the chain on and slip them your passport like this..." he demonstrated slipping a passport through the chained doorway.

He then grabbed a pillow from the 'sleeper' bunk and placed it against the square air filter near the floor.

"That's so the gypsies can't spray you with a paralyzing spray and rob you."

"Well, this is an adventure," I gasped out.

"Adventure?" He looked startled. "This is not an adventure," he shrugged. "This is just routine. Now, bolt the door after me."

I dutifully bolted the door as he returned to his post, and sat on the bottom bunk, unfolding Ryder's letter – re-reading it as the train left the station for the twenty four hours it would take to reach my father in Bucharest.

An hour for every year apart.

4. A MAST FROM THE PAST

Panama – a few days after Sailor departed...

Beeep!
Rat a tat tat!
Whistle!!!
Despite the lofty view from Sibling's 32nd story apartment I'm aurally assaulted by the beeping cars/marching band smackdown on the street below. The school kids doing their weekday formations in the schoolyard. A drumroll escalation of my life hangover. Exhaustion akin to being run over by a Panamanian bus like the one turning left below towards the 'no go' Shanty Town. Converted school bus rejects billowing smoke and near-missing pedestrians. Each vehicle graffiti-tattooed with its own elaborate ink emblazoned on any available side from flower power to an irie rasta to Osama Bin Laden.

Beep! Beep! From the Shanty Town to the left.

Rat a tat tat/Piercing whistle! From the robin's egg-blue uniformed schoolkids to the right in the gentrified heart of San Francisco adjacent to Punta Pacifica.

The gap between rich and poor exemplified in Sibling's protective comment as he handed over the keys, "When you leave this apartment don't go left – go right."

Turning instead into the master bedroom that doubles as an office, I smile at Theo the Greek Surfer as he clicks along online – laptop perched on a small desk against a wall – a photo of his dark-haired self in red surf gear gracing the desktop.

"That's funny – you're surfing on a laptop with a wallpaper photo of yourself surfing."

"That's how I roll," Theo hums a few bars of the Hawaii Five-O theme.

"Is that the biggest wave you've ever caught?"

"One of. But, if I go to Australia with Mali this spring I'm hoping to top it."

My hand shoots out to grip the edge of my own borrowed desk against the opposite wall. Air squeezing out of my lungs in a gasp of pain. The abdomen vice-twist is like the baby space-devil spawn in Alien. Only – instead of Ripley breaking down the door with a badass future-weapon, my only 'kill me now' recourse is to reach for the Advil.

"I'm telling you," Theo says as I shake out a few precious pills like a raver on E, "you need to see a doctor." He attempts a stern 'brother-by-proxy' knit of eyebrows, but Theo is too nice a guy to dish out tough love. A Greco-American expat friend of Sibling's, I've been leaning on him too much in Sib's absence.

"Don't worry," I wave a hand, hoping an airy tone will ease his concern. "It's not like I have cancer or anything." I swivel towards my laptop and pop another Advil. "I'm just waiting to see the specialist back home. Socialized medicine – long wait lines – but it's free."

"Well at least get some rest," he says.

"Haha, you're funny." I hit 'send' on an email.

Theo grabs his half-eaten *espinaca* pastry 'to go' and shuts down his laptop.

"I've got a showing." He stands.

"Good luck." I follow him to the door.

"Thanks, I need it. It's been the usual Panama Chill."

The Panama Chill is not to be confused with the Costa Rican Chill. One is a cold shoulder as the locals can be slow to warm up to foreigners (which in turns results in the Expat Huddle) – the other is a perma-smile *Pura Vida* relaxing type of chill that Sibling first fell in love with when he landed in this part of the world.

"It's a great condo, Theo. You just gotta believe someone will see what you saw in it and make you a decent offer."

"I hope so."

I lock the door after he gets into the elevator and turn back to the white living room. I ache to lie down, but instead I shuffle back to the desk anticipating a skype call.

The days since Sailor left have been a blur of pain and pills. Pushing through to get things done – only to collapse by evening unable to corral scrambled thoughts enough to write.

Couch spud crunching my Bro's off-limit Pringles while watching *Bridget Jones II* last night.

Like I needed to be reminded of my weight gain, phantom cigarette cravings from an amputated addiction, and boy-issues.

By a sequel no less.

Awww… look… they're kissing. I popped another Advil.

"Are you teacher?" the pretty barista girls behind the coffee bar at Deli Gourmet had asked this morning with a knowing smile.

Sigh.

Rat a tat tat!

Beep!

BINGBONG! Skype adds to the cacophony.

The caller name flashing on my laptop is unusual and invokes best friend smile status: Lewaa. Pronounced "Lee-wah". I whip on earphones and answer.

"Buddy! I misss you!"

"Apparently. You threw a parade," he grins from his current crash pad on his latest L.A. whirlwind.

"Haha, cute. That's the marching band from the school yard 32 stories down across the street. Through closed windows. But, nah nah nah I see palm trees too." I say this while recalling snowdrifts as high as semi trucks along Route 99 in Edmonton – Lewaa's hometown and my first Escape from Trouble city. Kinda like the Arctic minus a Santa. Driving to work was taking your life into your own hands. A Canadiana heartland where I discovered people who were conversely as warm as the thermometer was cold.

And one renegade talent – half my age and twice my genius.

It took only ten pages of a screenplay he'd written in college and a poem for me to know he had 'it' – that elusive storyteller quality that can make an unknown a star.

When we hired him as my assistant his first words were, "I'm writing another screenplay – so I can't work after five or on weekends."

I stared up at him from my 16 hour days and said, "As long as you get the work done."

And he did. But, he brought something more to the party than mere talent – he brought heart, loyalty and drive. Plus, he started working out shortly after, so he's buff and easy to look at.

I hold up his latest screenplay, ink scrawled with my comments on the title page.

"So, *The Star Kingdom*," I smile. "Wow."

"Yeah?" His handsome face tenses with its onyx eyes and full lips. His head shaved bald for a badass effect that belies his perfectionism. "I mean, obviously I'm confident, but if you tell me it's not on track I will throw myself into traffic."

"Um… may I remind you – you're in L.A. at the moment. Bumper to bumper? You'd get more damage from a hockey body check."

"I meant vegan Venice cyclists."

"Don't do it, Buddy! It's suicide!"

"Just kidding," he says simultaneously shaking his head, "No, I'm not."

I laugh. "Oh c'mon – you know it's on track."

"I love the way you lie."

"Oh my God," I laugh harder. "I read it twice. And you know I never say it if I don't feel it."

"Yeah, that's true."

"It's not flattery it's observation. You make me feel for people who don't actually exist – at the first freakn' draft. That's how much your characters leap off the page."

"So, what you're saying is: it's shit."

I laugh – again.

"I might be better off if it was, because if I hear 'I love it, now get out of my office or I'll have you arrested for trespassing' one more time I'll lose my shit." He hunches in his chair.

"Well, that's not what they're gonna say when they read this script."

"Ahhh... thanks, gorgeous."

"They're gonna say – 'your script is brillliant'."

"C'mon, Lila, I know there's a 'but' in there somewhere."

I hesitate.

"Hit me. No c'mon, honestly hit me, because if I have to look at this draft one more time I'll—"

"Okay Buddy – here goes." I put on my old 'Development Exec' hat and act out the role, "Your script is brilliant – but it's about cancer."

Lewaa's eyes flash. "It's about using your imagination," he fires back. "It's about fighting for someone you love. It's hope. What's not commercial about that?"

"I hate the cynicism behind that comment – the..." asinine whine... "I love your script – but the kid has cancer."

"Yeah, well, some kid lying in a hospital somewhere deserves to have a story he can relate to."

"But, that's an indie movie – not an epic fantasy adventure."

"I don't see why you can't have an action movie about a dad trying to save his son!"

"It's called money. Big money!" I shudder, "Ugh, Buddy, these words taste like dirt in my mouth!" I scrunch up my face, "Blech."

"Yeah, no doubt," he smiles. "But, I get it – worse case scenario."

The stakes are not small. Lewaa's a lightning fast writer – but a screenplay that blends reality and fantasy on the scope he's planning can take a long time and multiple drafts to really 'sing' – all on spec. It's just him and his laptop at that dimly lit coffee shop on Melrose with a dozen other writers hunched over their laptops all trying to out-type their neighbor. A scene repeated at virtually every other coffee shop in L.A. and even Whyte Ave when he's back up in Edmonton. Once *The Star Kingdom* is ready to go out, he has to pitch it 'in the room' – in multiple rooms in fact – and no matter how much people may say "I love it" – if there's no one willing to 'greenlight' it – that's a lot of time invested for a compliment. And yet…

"No matter what I think – you'll do it anyway," I smile. "You march to your own drum track." I add to the accompanying cymbal crash from the marching band.

He laughs.

"And so many truly great, grand things have been created by those who followed their gut instinct," I find myself adding. "I think I'm paraphrasing here – but George Bernard Shaw said essentially 'people see things and say 'why' – I dream of things that never were and I say, 'why not'?"

"Wasn't that the '90's rapper – the one who got shot coming out of a whorehouse in Vegas?" Lewaa looks pensive, like he's seriously trying to remember.

"Buddy!" I cry out. "He was a famous playwright! He wrote *Pygmalion*, which became *My Fair Lady*, which –"

I catch his smirk.

"Damn it! You get me every time!"

Lewaa laughs, delighted, "It is kinda spectacular how often you fall for that."

I scrunch my face in a pinchy 'grrrrr'.

"So trusting – you just take everyone at face value."

"Ummm… I think you mean 'gullible'. I actually believe a guy when he says 'I'll call ya'," I do the wink and point/gun hand gesture that accompanies that obvious line, "Even when he hasn't asked for my number."

"Haha, I bet you do."

"Then again, I'm usually the one dialing."

Lewaa laughs again, "Ditto."

"And I don't even have the luxury of claiming I'm drunk."

"Yeah, we both need to work on that. Dialing sober is embarrassing."

We detour to current crushes and the ramifications of ex-ting.

… until circling back to his script.

"Okay, so… what's the biggest leap to second draft?" Lewaa

snaps to as the marching band hangs it up for the day.

"I think you need to seed in the mythical realm earlier –" I flip open the screenplay and glance through the first couple of pages at my near illegible scrawled notes.

"It's a family drama first – fantasy second." Lewaa sounds emphatic as he shifts in his chair, leaning forward as if we're in the same room. "The mythical only supports the real."

"Yeah? Well, it's called *The Star Kingdom*."

"Working title." He laughs

"Don't you dare change it!"

And the sparring begins again. Two passionate people passionate about their work. 'Spitballing' to use William Goldman's famous term. Debating – persuading – seeking the magical 'third' way.

"Let's look at act one and see where real life and fantasy intersect – and where faith is lost prior to its resurrection."

"I love it when you flirt," Lewaa teases.

But, two hours later, the exhaustive back and forth is done for the day and he adds, "These notes are totally gonna help me punch it up. I'll send you the next draft as soon as it's done."

"Wicked. Can't wait." Because I'd rather be doing this with him a hundred times over than what I actually get paid to do.

"And when your book is done – I'm there," he promises.

I feel a pang of envy for his artistic output – he's prolific while I'm still floundering. But, all I say is, "I'm holding you to that. Payback, Buddy!"

Hanging up in a 'bye', 'love ya', 'miss ya' drawn out parting – I smile at the welcome artistic respite not only from drudgery and discomfort, but also from daydreams. Senses recalling what the mind is trying to forget.

Sailor – the goodbye kiss tussle.

My hand auto-brushes away the thought like a pesky fly. "I will not think about him," as if saying 'don't think of white sailboats' doesn't automatically make you think of white sailboats. But, I'm determined to let it go – I mean, it's not like he's thinking about me.

"Hey…" pops up a Sailor email from mid-vacation.

A cheery few postcard words that evoke his 'que pasa' wide grin and flashflood a total recall of his hard body pressing against my submissive pliancy. One upping the memory from visual to body heat visceral.

Eliciting a full blown Exorcist head spin from 'forget him' to: *I like him.*

Handwritten with a flourish to fill an entire page of my journal.

I'm surprised I don't start rote-repeating "Mrs. Lila Sailor" complete with hand drawn hearts and Taylor Swift lyrics.

Instead, curious fingers type: www.google.com.

The search bar appears.

I type in: San Blas.

The little circle turns.

"So?!" I defend myself to Sibling's empty office. "Sailor's right, people should know the geography of their region!"

Oh… it's an archipelago. What the hell does that mean?

Hoping to at least expand a few brain cells, I hit 'Images' – and am thrown back against my chair by a memory.

Geo edification now jettisoned for something much more personal as the shimmery blue of a Caribbean scene glows back at me.

A sliver of paradise I recall all too well…

Toronto, November 2002 – my apartment...

"Look outside your window."

My heart slams into my chest at these words, softly spoken, but with a 'gotcha' undertone.

Sharp intake of breath catching in my throat.

I can't see through the blinds covering my living room bay window, but I can guess what's outside.

Trouble.

"You're not."

"I am."

Still holding my phone pressed to my ear, I walk towards the window and it hits me. "Oh, so when the traffic sounds got quiet twenty minutes ago…" He had parked outside my apartment after I'd said…"I can't see you tonight, I'm behind."

"Have you had dinner?"

"Take out – while *working*." Hint, hint.

My ancient desktop computer had long since protested my distracted neglect by switching from my 'based on a true story!' TV script to screensaver mode. The azure blue of sky meeting a turquoise blue Caribbean taunted on this frigid night north of the 49th.

A sliver of paradise I stare at every day – telling myself I'll get there. Some Day. I'll step into that exquisite aqua view – if I just keep pounding out the words.

"Well, how about just a quick coffee?" he sounds all reasonable. "You have to take a break some time."

"I'm in the middle of the contract of my life right now and it's an insane deadline."

I peek through the blinds and spot the sleek, Black Racer gleaming under the lamplight on the residential street – spotless even in late fall's rainsnow slushy messfest. The one impracticality he allows himself.

"I see you looking," he says, almost chuckling.

I pull back inside – and sigh pointedly.

"You know," Trouble's suddenly serious. "We make time in life for the things that are important."

This hits me harder than I care for him to know. It's an echo of Ryder's pointed finger accusations in our recent 'reunion' phone calls – that I've grown cold and solely focused on my career. Ryder – the American in Prague of '94 – he of the 'you look like a librarian…' line. The intervening years hadn't dulled his bluntness.

"You're a passionate woman! You can't just hide in your work!"

"Who says?" I snap.

"You're not connecting with people – not holding open the possibility of relationship."

"So?" I had rebutted. "No one tells a man he's cold and loveless for focusing on his career. It's my life and I'm going for what I want."

"But you're denying a huge part of yourself!" Ryder had hit back from the armchair comfort of his happy marriage in Colorado. He had been single when we met in Prague. Just after the Velvet Revolution – just in time for jazz at Red Hot and Blues – and two nights that had convinced him…

"You need love. You can't be so out of balance."

"Balance!" I sneer the word. "Everyone is so hyped up about balance. Well, let me tell you, balance…" I spit out... "…is highly overrated. There are times in life when to achieve anything of importance you have to go all out. A film – a book – artists know all about a life out of balance."

"Life creates art, Lila… not the other way around."

And now Trouble has walked into mine, confusing the issue.

"We make time in life for the things that are important…"

"Yes, exactly," I'd argued, "And this is the most important contract I've ever had! You have no idea how hard it is for a writer to nail a TV movie contract in this country. It's like I've been asked to join the Olympics and you're telling me to cut my practice time short and go have fun." I say 'fun' like it's an illicit hypodermic drug I fear OD'ing on.

Scared to admit I'm slowly discovering this finish line is not the race I want to be running. That this 'holy grail' contract I've worked so long and hard for – that in fact everything I've worked so long and hard for – is not... enough.

I feel ungrateful to even be thinking it.

But, a relative only a few years older than me is lying in a hospital dying of cancer – and spending the night at her side – hearing her take stock of a life ebbing away with a dream as yet unfulfilled – sharing both her most hurtful and happiest memories is turning a whisper into a shout – 'there is something more...' out there. A blossom-of-roses life I sense – but cannot seem to reach.

And time is running out…

"Oh c'mon, you're capable." Trouble counters with maddening charm, "One coffee isn't going to make or break you. Or, I could just sit outside your window and serenade you."

"With silly '70's songs?" I blurt out, like I'm fourteen again and sneaking into the Floating World disco in denim platforms.

Trouble calls my bluff with… "I'm sittin' by your window…" sung in an eerily '70's style like he's Rod Stewart.

"Haha… very funny…"

"Knockin' on your locked door…"

Goosebumps.

"Wishing you – would give me some time…"

"Very funny. You're killing me softly with your song."

It's not just that his voice is croonmaster smooth with a sexy scratch – it's the sarcasm behind the words…

"C'mon baby, let me blow your mind!"

Damn. He's torching it a cappella!

"Tonight's your night… "

Damn, damn, damn!

"Were you ever in a band?" I gasp.

Five minutes later, I'm in his car.

Trouble shifts into gear and floors it while I sit dutifully in the passenger seat, fulfilling my secret calling as a groupie.

"Just an hour, okay?" I try to reassert some semblance of control.

"Anything you want," he smiles my way. A triumphant little smirk of the Alpha Male.

I squirm, arms folded, sinking deeper into the cradling Black

Racer passenger seat.

"Okay, then," I lamely vie for the last word.

"Okay." He steals it.

A few minutes of halting West Queen West traffic later we're ensconced in the rear of a neighborhood bar called The Rhino. Banquettes run the length of each side of the long, narrow step-up back area and we're the only two people huddled there. Loners in the lovers section while the 'in-crowd' gentrifying suits from downtown mingle with the local artists and near-welfare types on the main floor.

"Why don't you sit here?" Trouble pats the long faux leather bench he's seated on against the wall, as I shift uncomfortably on the hard wooden chair opposite him.

Him: pat, pat, pat.

Me: Hamlet hesitation.

"Look, I'm not really sure about this. I should tell you that I'm not looking for a relationship right now."

"Nice," he responds.

I'm not sure how to react to that – not just to the word itself – but the pleased, happy tone.

"Nice?"

"You don't want a relationship – and yet you're here with me. That must mean your desire to spend time with me is greater than your desire to avoid a relationship."

Stunned silence.

I'm used to reading. I'm not used to being read.

"I just want to get closer to you, that's all," he says softly.

Pat, pat, pat.

I extricate myself from the hard wooden chair.

Despite myself. Surprising myself.

And slide into the bench seat beside him.

The waitress arrives and I order Perrier to his coffee.

"You can have a glass of wine if you like," he says. "I don't mind."

"No, I'm fine, thanks."

"Honestly, it doesn't bother me. I want you to have whatever you want."

"It's okay, really. I don't actually drink that much."

We stick to small talk until the waitress returns with the goods. Trouble stirs cream into his non-alcoholic coffee while I sip the virgin bubbles in mine. I like this mutual sobriety – mine by choice – his by necessity. It's not so much the alcohol he has to worry about – it's the pills it might lead to. This is only our second face to face alone time, but he's already confessed his demons. All his demons. At once.

"I overwhelmed you a little the other night, didn't I?" He finds my eyes in the dimly lit banquette.

"A little," I understate. "You told me your entire life story on the first date." I can't help a little 'it's all about you' resentment creeping into my voice. Hard to tell him where to go now that I know where he's been.

"Well, at least you consider it a date," he bright-sides then jokingly stretches out with a pretend yawn, so that his left arm lands on the top of the bench seat behind me.

"Haha, cute," I laugh up at him.

"You like that?" he says, repeating what I'm quickly learning is his favorite word, "Nice."

And he drapes his left arm over my shoulder, pulling me close.

That's when the impossible occurs. When the 'tingles' I'd only ever read about in a romance novel race into my bloodstream as if ordinary cells have just been transplanted with rosebuds. Rosebuds all bursting open at once – blossoming – in a desert I hadn't even known was previously empty and arid.

I fit into the crook of his left side like Eve to Adam – the marble hard muscles of his arm and torso enclosing me in protective custody – the oak strong legs running the length of mine. A tight jeaned, sinewy temptation.

My life until this point has been words. Written pitches – verbal pitches – screenplays – proposals – cold calls – emails – my first movie contract.

Words, words, words.
Only now I am…
Wordless.

Sensation has just electrocuted reason. Sensation that will prove both my salvation – and condemnation.

And as he pulls me in even closer all I can gasp-whisper is, "Who are you?!"

Back to now…

I'm still sitting in front of my open laptop in Sibling's home office, staring at the same azure blue of sky meeting turquoise blue Caribbean screensaver that I returned home to that night.

Forever changed.

But, the tiny island that blinks back at me from the computer screen hasn't. Still showing off its towering palm trees like sparklers on a birthday cake.

San Blas.

Oh. My. God.

It's San Blas!

I had no idea where the screensaver had come from – I just knew I wanted to go there. Desperately.

The Google search has yielded it like a lost treasure.

A mast from the past.

Sailor's recent words boomerang into my mind, resurrecting a lost dream:

"You should come out on the boat some time. We can sail for a couple of days around the islands."

The Island Nation of San Blas.

It's here!!!

The last shred of a dream from a time in which desires were thwarted and aborted – when falling in love became a fall from grace…

… has slipped back into my fingers.

A white sailboat on the Caribbean.

"You should come out on the boat some time…"

Just outside of Panama City – it's here!!!

A surge of bittersweet joy…

… stilled by dread.

Three seconds can steal inspiration – can replace it with abject fear. Three seconds. That's the time it takes for my hand to reach for the landline to dial in for my Canadian messages.

"Hello Miss Rose. This is Dr. K's office. Please call us back right away to schedule an appointment – the doctor has some test results he needs to go over with you…"

Uh-oh.
Rat a tat tat!
Drumroll!
SIREN!

5. SIDEWIPED

SIREN!

"Oh my God!" My heart slams into my chest as the Town Car swerves to narrowly avoid a side swiping Vehicular Homicide Taxi – only to careen towards a bus.

GASP!

My heart is now in my throat as the Town Car course corrects again to avoid hitting said bus.

BEEEEEP! The Taxi voices its misguided rage.

Wheezeqquaaack!

"Is that our horn?!" I whip turn to Driver Mark, who's pressing his palm on the horn only to elicit a pathetic wheeze.

Wheezequaaack… sputter.

BEEEEEP!

Taxi laughs mid-middle-finger and tears away.

Mark throws me a 'whaddya ya gonna do' shrug.

"Well, I'm glad you're at the wheel and not me," I mumble from the front passenger seat.

A taxi driver himself, Mark also pilots Sibling's Town Car when required. A pleasant, quiet Caribbean-Panamanian, his usual 'speak softly, but carry concealed' introversion isn't doing anything for my spiraling anxiety. Neither is the black cloud diesel that just fumigated the car from the roaring bus.

We're racing to a doctor's office at the height of rush hour and I'm not sure what's going to kill me first:

a) Balboa's lethal traffic

b) The outbreak of Dengue Fever that Sibling called to warn me about

c) The 'unusual cells'

It took serious pleading to extract 'c' from the nurse in Dr. K's office in Calgary.

"I can't tell you over the phone," she kept repeating, exasperated. "You have to make an appointment!"

"Look…" I refrained from adding 'bitch' since that:

a) is impolite – (a felony in Canada)

b) only works in movies

c) only works in movies when said by Queen Latifah

"I'm out of the country and if I need a biopsy I need to know *now* – I can't wait until I get back!"

Reluctantly, Canadian Nurse divulged over the phone, which they're not supposed to do. That's how I knew it wasn't good news – the doc never calls if the test results are okay. Unlike the guy you just slept with – dead silence is a good thing in a doctor. Well, not *dead* silence…

And what's with this 'unusual cells' description, anyway? Who knew that just like in middle school 'unusual' is a bad thing! Couldn't they call them 'individualistic cells' or 'cool maverick cells'?!

Now clutching a sticky note with the name and address of a doctor who speaks English, I ride a rickety deathtrap elevator to the second floor of the strip mall where Mark just deposited me. Ten minutes of waiting room later, I discover 'a doctor who speaks English' means a pleasant labcoated female with a friendly smile and an apologetic, "Talk Espanõl?"

All I can do is point to my abdomen and explain in my most scientific Spanish…

"Ow."

* * *

BANG!

Die Hard rages on screen as Theo and I sit side by side on the couch in Sibling's apartment.

"It'll be okay, you'll see," he attempts reassurance as I grab the remote and turn up the TV volume.

"Yipee Kiyay Motherfucker!"

Bruce Willis is bloodied but unbowed – determined to save his own life and that of his estranged wife. Shooting up the bad guys in English with Spanish subtitles while a monsoon rages outside – darkening the azure blue of early evening sky to near blackness – rattling the windows and forcing us to take cover with 'Hawaiian' ham 'n' pineapple and 'double cheese with pepperoni' delivery pizzas.

Eyes glued to the screen in shared cultural morphine.

A snippy Uniform lips off to Bruce Willis as he's trying to get through to the cops for help.

Bruce lips off back with a couple of choice swear words.

Theo offers me another slice. I hold up my plate. Fuck the carbs.

Soon the chubby cop's car is shot up. Hello! When Bruce Willis says there's a problem – you better send back up or someone's gonna get hurt!

"This won't hurt," the English speaking Dr. V had said earlier today, picking up a lethal looking instrument somewhere between steel pliers and a salad tong.

"Um… I think I'd like to take another Advil," I'd said from the ceiling.

"Bueno. And, try to relax on the table."

Soon, my legs were up in the air and not in a good way.

"Your ovaries look good." Dr. V observed the monitor.

"Well, that's a relief," I sighed. "The true meaning of 'beautiful on the inside'."

He grunted a half chuckle. But his eyes never left the screen.

KERBOOM!

Several *Die Hard* scenes later, Theo says, "The biopsy will come back negative – you have to believe that."

"Yeah, I'm sure you're right." I smile wanly. "Theo?"

"Yeah?"

"You're a very nice man."

KABOOM!

The FBI helicopter is aflame – temporarily distracting from the spider web of fear spinning through me at the possibility of hearing 'you have cancer'.

*　*　*

BANG!

A car backfires on the street below and my eyes fly open.

It's 1:00 a.m. in The City that Always Beeps.

WEEE-OH CAR ALARM! WEEE-OH!!!

I lie in bed, catching breath to still pounding heart. A new appreciation for the teeming life the cacophony represents.

BEEEEP!

Throwing off covers, throwing off claustrophobia, I pad pink-toed bare feet out of the bedroom, switch on the hall light and hit the living room to slide open the Suicide Window.

Shortly after I arrived here I wrote about it – essentially – thirty two stories above Panama City and it opens so wide two lovers outta Shakespeare could jump out holding hands and hurl to their 'cruel world' deaths below.

Leaning out as I often do, I squint for a sliver view of the bay to the right, breathing in the 'real' air outside – trying to breathe in calm.

Wondering about the jump.

Simultaneously amused, scared and surprised to feel that pull – that great leap into the sky. Finally knowing why Da Vinci strapped on wings – that acute desire to fly is the human condition.

Only the plummet to Earth would be hard. That split second when you realize you've made a horrible mistake and it's too late to correct it. What you thought was taking fate into your own hands – was really giving up all power.

Gravity's a bitch.

And Sibling would lose a sister.

It was him and me dancing around the living room while Mum burned dinner after a long day in her 'locker' of an office behind a drug store. A dadless trio – and then there were two. Losing Mum taught us death's cruel permanence.

"Are you sad?" Lewaa had asked. "If this means you can never have kids? You've never mentioned wanting kids, but –"

"But, it's different when the choice is taken away from you?"

"A hundred percent."

"No – y'know – I'm the luckiest person in the world. I got to witness a human being grow into a remarkable adult from just days old."

A quick to laugh little boy with sapphire eyes of infinite compassion – laying his hand on mine at five years of age to my fifteen – telling me, "It'll be okay," when I cried after yet another teen battle with Mum. A little brother who's been trying to teach me the meaning of life since his first smile.

"For someone who never met the right person to raise a child with – I've been extremely lucky. Plus, I'm an 'Auntie' to some amazing young people."

Except that I had to admit the one time I felt that pull to procreate was with Trouble.

Lewaa gets a protective look on his face. He holds it for three beats before saying… "Yeah."

"Hence, you don't see me with a stroller and the Celine Dion lullaby collection on DVD."

"No, I see you more in the penthouse in Manhattan with finger holes in your jacket where I'm hanging onto your coattails," he smiled.

"Ahhh… Buddy… it's me hangin' onto your coattails."

"Which explains why we're goin' around in circles," he quipped and I laughed.

Glancing at the cell – 1:12 a.m. – I turn my gaze to the left – to buildings and glimpses of Punta Pacifica. Still wingless – but thoughts at least able to fly in all directions – to the flipside truth – that I envy Sailor for having every chance at fatherhood whilst I'm waving 'bye bye baby'. No pets, no plants, no progeny.

Realizing I spent my last childbearing years loving Trouble. And while that may seem like a foolish choice – confusingly it too taught me life's meaning.

Doubly confusing is that L.A. was the final clue.

"I'm standing in a spectacular palm-treed city. I can see the Hollywood sign. And y'know what?"

"What, my little darling?" Trouble replies on cell from the gridlocked Gardiner Expressway on a rain soaked Toronto day.

"It's not just the mansions – it's the sweet little houses off Melrose. So much character – not cookie cutter at all. And the sun! It's a clear, glorious day in November, can you believe it? Sunny is 'normal' here – not an aberration!"

"That's wonderful, honey. Where you've always wanted to be."

"And… it's gray," I confess, looking up to a perfectly blue sky.

"What?"

"It's gray without you."

Dialing the number I swore I'd never dial. Again.

But, it's untrue to say 'better to have loved and lost than never to have loved at all'. Post-love embezzles your future – entrenching the belief that no matter how well you do from here on – it no longer matters.

One night in Bella Vista has challenged that hypothesis.

"You're passionate," he'd said.

I didn't think I could ever feel that passionate again.

Sailor's 'rescue' is not of life over death – but of misperception. A misperception that has darkened my life since I reached for Trouble one last embrace. A final glimpse of him getting up from the bed wearing only the clean shaved skin of an Olympic swimmer, taut marble-statue muscles I can still feel under the palm of my hand. I leaned back on the pillows wishing my eyes were infrasoul cameras. Microscopic shutters capturing his one-of-a-kind paradoxes.

That was my last autumn in Toronto. And it's taken a long time for the leaves to turn from brown to gold let alone vibrant red.

Sailor is vibrant red. Siren red.

An EFT airlift that has defibrillated my ardor to an unexpected intensity.

Pulling me out of the rubble of my crumbled faith.

The grayworld running on empty existence without Trouble – the living death of the secretly convinced, 'the best has already come – and gone'. Only slightly less excruciating than the soul blows whilst with him.

Maybe love is not behind me but ahead.

It's this thought that makes me realize just how far I'd spiraled down.

It's not that I think Sailor is the love of my life – it's that he's reminded me I still have life left in me to love.

And, I'm all too aware standing in the dark how ironic it is to plunge into this scare just at the moment of renewal. The 'wait' – the unknown – prickling under my skin eroding bravado minute by minute causing fear to push out pain as my primary state – bringing up a craven desire to avoid the ravages I've seen of that serial killer disease if the test result comes back with bad news. The roller coaster emotions making me wonder if the Suicide Window would suddenly appear a tad too appealing – I mean, what's one more carbon footprint in an overcrowded world?

When…

… Lewaa's words fill me, "It's about fighting for someone you love." And I smile at the night, suddenly getting why *The Star Kingdom* – why a story about a kid facing what I'm so terrified to face – and the dad who wants to save him by resurrecting his lost hope – must be told – not just for him. But, for me too.

It's about fighting for someone you love.

And speaking of love… there's still some off-limit Pringles in the kitchen.

I step back from the Suicide Window and…

Wooosh!

Hot air rushes indoors and…

Kerfuffle!

Sibling's painting in progress is wind gusted off its easel.

I leap in a…

CRASH!

… too late (!!!) bid to save it from the tile floor!

24" by 48" figurative abstract acrylic on canvas and I am lifting it up, anxiously examining the dramatic red and blue brushstrokes for chips by the bright hallway light. Queasy fear slides to whirlpool relief when I realize there's none. Gingerly, I cradle it back onto its easel.

I only hope his six weeks in the Holy Land will make Sib all forgiving and stuff. Or, maybe I just won't tell him his house sitter needs a babysitter.

I'm about to go close the Suicide Window – when I notice Sibling's painting features a white four-petal blooming flower.

Well, this is a first.

Huh.

He must really like his current girlfriend, the willowy, local, part-time model, Giselle. A half black/half Asian beauty with an exterior cool that cracked when we saw a romantic movie the other night and she admitted with a teary little sniffle, "I miss your brother."

I figure she's seen this painting, since it sits in the living room. White flower – dramatic red and blue backdrop. The splash of color in a neutral room.

"An artist has to have a broad horizon," Sibling had said when he flew me to Panama – first in 2007 and then again this trip, "to be exposed to other cultures."

He understands that's my 'baby on board'. The quest to artify.

To leave another type of footprint…

To write the way he paints. To contemplate Sailor and Trouble the way Sibling paints his own life story – interpreting form and shape in color and richer meaning. Like Monet's impression of a sunset or Andrew Wyeth's *Helga*.

A half-finished book is like a partial canvas. A sad, abandoned what might have been. Death = the ultimate deadline.

Screw the test – I ain't going anywhere with my book unfinished. I want to dedicate it to my Bro.

Plus, I owe him money.

I again step back and…

Swish.

What the hell is that???

An accidental foot brushby of an unknown object has me looking down.

A lone brown leaf.

Oh. Must have blown in with the wind.

But, my now alert eyes catch another leaf on the floor in the dim light… and then another… and I follow the trail of leaves to a spindly, terrifyingly decrepit shape looming in the shadowy corner.

Mouth opens in silent scream – eyes recoil in horror!

Nooooo!!! It can't be!!!

Sibling's condo has a PLANT!!!

I run to the kitchen and crank the tap to 'geyser', praying I'm not too late. Scurrying back trailing droplets on the white on white living room, cooing 'nice plant – pretty plant' – willing resurrection of this wilting rebuke with a flood of its earthly home, escapee drops splashing. Imagining it shaking its leaves my way with a mournful, "Self involved, much?"

Guilt bomb detonating.

All Sibling has done for me.

And I repay him by killing his plant.

"Fight plant tree thingy – fight! Come on! Livvvvve!!!"

Oh, man!

All Sibling has done for me – including…

Miraflores.

What made this country what it is today.

The axis that connects the Atlantic to the Pacific.

The Panama Canal.

6. SIBLING'S SUPERTANKER SURPRISE

Panama Roadway – December 2007

"I know of a great dessert place," Sibling had said with a sly smile.

We were bumper to bumper and the usual bad traffic was escalating to 'nightmare'. Yet, Sibling stubbornly insisted on taking us to this legendary 'great dessert place' despite our Canadian friend, the slender, health conscious Dr. Super-D repeatedly stating she didn't need dessert and couldn't' we just get the hell out of the smog?!

I didn't want to admit I thought it was worth what felt like asphyxiation by diesel fumes for a little crème brule. Plus, I had a feeling Sib was up to something and if she just had a little trust…

When we hit Miraflores, Dr. Super-D teared up in tourista joy.

Yeah, good for you Ph.D., but where's my sugar high?

If it was a choice between an important monument to human ingenuity or, say, chocolate mousse I felt it was no contest.

Give me chocolate. Every time!

Fortunately, Sibling led us to the promised 'dessert buffet' in a restaurant with a terrace – handshake close to the canal. Ogling the cheerful array of tortes, tarts, fruit flan and trifle, I nearly missed the huge tanker scraping by.

"They're expanding," Sibling explained. "They didn't anticipate these super tankers when they built it."

'Jeez, everything today is supersized,' I thought, scarfing a five layer chocolate cake.

Bet they didn't have this dessert place here in 1878 when the French began to build the canal.

Instead, they had yellow fever and malaria – so much so that

Panama became known as The Fever Coast.

28,000 lives lost for what is essentially a glorified shortcut.

Taken over in 1902 by the Americans who finished the job – the Panama Canal is the ultimate monument to a man's need to avoid asking for directions.

While some beer swilling Australians at the next table ooohed and ahhhed over the steel gate doors and water rising mechanics…

…I was struck by the lithe worker limberly running across the top of that same lock gate like a gymnast on a balance beam just before the gate opened to some unseen 'password'.

And while Sib and Dr. Super-D debated the economics…

"How much do you think they make in a day?" she asked as the super tanker inched forward through the now open gate.

"Not sure – but I think it's about 450 billion a year. Divided by 365," Sib calculated on his cell, "about 1.2."

"That much? Are you sure?"

"No matter what, D, it's a lot." Sib took a bite of cheesecake. "Cheaper than the two weeks it takes to go around."

"So, the American lease expired in '99, and now all that revenue is localized?"

"Like Balboa beer," Sib grinned. "And potholes."

Big haired Dr. Super-D laughed as they clinked glasses. "And a good tan and…"

"Rain," laughed Sib with another clink.

"And…"

… I stared at the crew.

The same men staring at us.

And wondered about their daily habits and experiences.

One stubbled sailor read a book on a lower deck. It must have been good, because no matter how much we waved and the other sailors waved back he remained engrossed in 'same sea different day' indifference.

His life was steel and grease, bad food and boredom.

Ours was powdered sugar and cheesecake.

His was confinement to a metal can floating in a vast, open

ocean.

Ours was the rolling hills of Miraflores cradling the canal as sunset gave way to starry sky and we returned to the car with the come 'n' go freedom of landlubbers.

I wondered what that sailor would encounter when he got home weeks later. What woman would rush into his arms? Bottle Blonde? Streaked Brunette? Would she be wearing an apron feeding the kids – or a plunging V-neck 'howdy sailor' tight dress? Either way, she'd kiss his stubble, laughing and crying… happy to feel the warmth of his body heat pressed up against her.

Until he next left her in port.

Funny how my peak-moment memory was just another day of ennui in the life of that career shipster.

Even tonight, Panama remains the city the canal built – the teeming screaming loudest metropolis I've ever tried to catch some zzz's in. I snuggle back in bed, sheet wrapped, hugging the pillow and recall its flagship wonder as another man of the sea strays into my mind.

That chestnut curly haired incendiary kisser…

Day 3 to Sailor's return.

Day 2…

Day 1…

But, I'm not counting or anything…

Tossing and turning through a midnight heatwave – glitter streetlights below morphing into moon dusted stars above. Sailor 'n' me on the gleaming white boat sailing by that postcard perfect island. Flaming out all other thoughts as yet another sultry night becomes a fever of another kind – the fantasy of a future encounter fueled by naked memory of the first.

Kiss.

Caress.

Unzip…

I whip off my cotton T, letting air hit skin.

But, it only reminds me of being exposed to him – soft submission under his adept, intuitive hands as tropic days ember into scorching nights.

Holy Heatwave! I've become the girl in port.

And if Sailor doesn't come back and make love to me soon – I will spontaneously combust.

7. THE GIRL IN PORT

"I can't get into my apartment – I'm locked out." Even exasperated, Sailor's Aural Blow rasp is like a shot of smooth, sweet liquor after a ten day prohibition.

"Come here," I blurt out.

"My roommate'll be back with the key, but it could be a couple of hours…"

"Don't worry about it. You can wait here."

"Ya sure?"

"Of course, be nice to see you," I purr in socialite calm.

"Okay, thanks," he sounds relieved. "See you in five."

I stand there for a moment thinking how nice it is that he's back and…

Wait…

FIVE?!

I look down at my lurid green vintage tee from L.A. – the one with Turtle Wax in red letters emblazoned across my chest – which hopefully distracts from the holes fraying by the back collar – and my black yoga pants courtesy of Lululemon in the famed West Edmonton Mall. Which means I got them in Edmonton, which was before L.A., which means they are three years old.

Ack!

I run to the bedroom and rip clothes out of the closet.

Okay, nice dress.

Too obvious.

Okay, nice black pants.

Too office.

Okay…

Nice jeans. That come up to the waist.

Yikes, too antiquated. What am I? A Mennonite mother of five?

HARUMPH.

It's been 3.8 minutes and all I have time for now is a quick jog to the bathroom mirror to brush on mascara.

Smear...

Arrrgh!!!

I frantically dab wadded up toilet paper onto my blackened eyelid trying to remove the smear without causing another one in the process.

Spotting my toothbrush, I glob on toothpaste and brush in record time.

Skidding back to the bedroom – tossing the previously pulled clothes into the closet – shoving the now bulging door shut with a full on hockey style body check.

I'd kill for a pencil skirt right now.

"Vintage green Turtle Wax T and black yoga pants... perfect!" I convince myself.

Yep, good thing I'm not trying too hard or anything.

BUZZZZ!

I leap to the kitchen and intercom him in.

Okay, breathe. He has 32 floors up from the lobby before he hits the door. You have time.

Knock, KNOCK!

Damn that rapido elevator!

Nerves collide with a 'get a grip' eyeroll as I open the door.

Melt in my eyes GORGEOUS.

Tanned to golden butternut brown, white teeth flashing in contrast as he smiles 'hello'.

Unfair tactics!

I mean, aren't people supposed to gain weight on vacation? But, oh no – Sailor has returned only hotter while I stand Casper pale with my breath caught somewhere south of my lungs. If cuteness were a crime I'd be forced to make a citizen's arrest. Or, invent the male burqua – perhaps something in beige burlap with little eye-holes and—

"Hey."

"Hey, welcome back," I snap to – channeling the cool, gracious welcome of a Hollywood hostess, but in place of a French manicure are bitten nails and Mark is standing behind Sailor, the corner of his mouth twitching.

I'd forked over $45 plus tip to get Mark to pick up "Sibling's friend" from the airport. I think he's onto me. The giveaway might have been the David Baldacci paperback I had him place in the back seat with a little 'welcome back' note. I guess "Subtle" is not my middle name.

"Thanks Mark. I guess I'll see you tomorrow."

He smiles a knowing smile.

"Rock it out freestyle, dude." I add as he hits the elevator button with his trademark chuckle.

"Mañana," he waves and disappears into the metal box.

I close the door and turn back towards the living room.

Sailor sits on the couch in his beige cargo shorts and white T betraying no sign of travel weariness.

"I have Heineken."

He makes a face.

"I also have rum and coke with lime."

"Really?" He perks up.

"Yeah, I thought of you today in the liquor aisle."

"Sounds great," he grins.

"'K… coming right up."

I return to the kitchen completely at a loss. Am I supposed to mix the drink for him? Or, do I pour rum into the glass then put the coke can on the side? I scrounge the fridge for the promised lime, muttering curses at Martha Stewart.

"Here you go," I say cheerily pushing open the swinging kitchen door and proffering the Bacardi and coke the way I've seen cocktail waitresses do at fine hotels.

"What're you having?" He takes the first sip.

"Agua."

He grins up at me, "Oh I see, get me drunk while you stay sober. I see your game."

He doesn't realize I'm already drunk on his smile. I sure hope he's not packin' a breathalyzer.

"So, how ya been?"

"Great," I hedge. Now cautious with disclosure I'm not sure if I should open up about my little 'test' and edge-of-my-seat wait for results.

"How was your trip?" I deflect.

"Great!" he enthuses, and proceeds to tell me all about it.

Yet, despite him uttering words strung together in meaningful sentences, all I hear is, "Wahaah, whha." Brain cells jammed somewhere on the 'woah' setting as I absorb his sudden appearance. Like a unicorn bursting into the living room – the real life presence of a fantasy here on the couch – where I've landed beside him.

"It was weird at first, but then... wahhaaa whaaa..."

"Uh huh. Wow! Hmmm... interesting," spills out of my mouth in some vague approximation of coherence.

"And then we... wahhaaa whaaa."

Easy now.

Attempt to impersonate intelligent life.

"So, am I getting you a turkey baster for Christmas?"

"Uh, that would be a 'no'," he smiles. "We talked face to face about the fatherhood thing, and we decided to give it some time. Maybe meet in another six months."

"Reconvene at a later date."

"Exactly. It's a big decision."

"To go ahead – or not to go ahead – both are big decisions in their own way. I'm glad you're taking the time to really think about it."

"Yeah." He takes another sip.

"From your email it sounded as though things were going well – not as traumatic as it could have been."

"Surprisingly," he smiles.

"Sounds like you anchored some great new memories," I smile back.

"Yah. Exactly. It turned out to be the right place at the right time, y'know? Full circle."

Past reshaping future. Between Sailor's return to Ground Zero and my screensaver rediscovery – I begin to wonder why it seems we tend to meet people on parallel journeys.

"Oh, and I sent you an email about that screensaver I had in Toronto – I can't believe it's San Blas."

"Oh is that the Microsoft one?" Sailor sounds skeptical.

"I don't know," I murmur, brushing it aside, sensing the guy who lives in that view is not going to get—

"Anyway," he says, reaching for his drink to take a sip, "it's a whole other thing to experience it." And it's back – that 'you should see my world' grin.

"Yeah," I grin in turn, and shift a little more his way.

"We should plan something soon," he adds.

"That sounds…"

What is my right arm doing?!

It's rising as if of its own volition!

'Come back here Errant Limb!' I silent-scream.

"Curls… soft chestnut whirls of Sailor curliness…" Errant Limb talks back.

Limbs aren't supposed to talk back. Limbs aren't supposed to have a will of their own!

"Um… yeah… something soon…" I blink at Sailor, trying to maintain outward lucidity like a politician caught roadside in a DUI. Only, my right hand wraps a silky Sailor curl around its forefinger – while flipping me the other finger with a defiant, "My turn to touch!"

Before Sailor I managed six months celibate just fine. Now, I can't last ten days without loss of motor skills.

But, his boy atoms are swirling 'round my girl atoms saying "how you doin'?" and the look he throws me as my fingers make curl contact is a sensual awareness followed by a sudden shy smile and quick lookaway then look back.

Searingly cute.

Instinct reacts before brain kicks in and next thing I know –

I'm a human projectile — mid-leap like I've been shot out of a cannon hurling straight for my target — Sailor's lap.

My legs wrapping around him, my lips finding his.

The kiss a slow deep, fitting welcome home.

Only for my brain to skid back into my rebel body with…

WHAT. ARE. YOU. DOING?!

Ardor collides with panic as I stare helplessly at Sailor, completely out of my 'don't make the first move' depth.

"You brushed your teeth," he half whispers, nuzzling in for a minty taste. "How romantic," soft toned, he laces his fingers into my own curls.

Our eyes meet, smiling. Short circuiting nerves into permisso — the electric air now sweetened with mutual consent. His arms encircle me in a decisive embrace, taking command of the situation as his lips once again find my neck and shiver my timbers.

Breath raggeding out — throat making hmmm sounds somewhere between a sigh and a moan — relief at this longed for touch — a heady mix of sensual and tender. Trademark Sailor.

A heartbeat later, he flips me down onto the couch under him and presses more insistent lips to mine, rapaciously taking what I'd clumsily offered.

Sighhhh… mmmmm…

And racing alongside aching desire is a relief that replaces any lingering embarrassment over that 'overshare' fiasco at brunch — because he's kissing a woman who's been honest — who hasn't pretended she's 'perfect'.

And those kisses are increasingly ardent, demanding response, flaming out any shred of restraint with escalating heat — absence having intensified the want — one that evokes the echo of that first night — but in place of discovery — is a furtive grope for a pleasure already known.

Catapulting us towards the bedroom in a vortexual lust tunnel.

All thought of 'letting go' forgotten — unless by 'letting go' I mean letting him lift my vintage T and reaching up to caress my cleavage — hand brushing my black Frederick's of Hollywood push-up out of the way – while his mouth crushes the moan that airrushes up to my lips from somewhere between my –

Well, at least it no longer matters what I'm wearing, because I'm not wearing it anymore. Green/black/rumpled fabrics hit the floor, abandoned in favor of skin to skin.

We tumble onto the bed, a different kind of top and bottom. Ahhhh….

He places lips where his hand just was, once again hardening rosebuds as he simultaneously softens me towards him, my own caress escalating urgent as I gentlescratch nails across his back.

His skin just as soft against my hands as I remember – only darker - even more surfer boy. Contrasting butternut brown against whipped white cream.

His hand reaches for my softness – triggering wildness in what was already a precariously urgent need – releasing moans from memory into audible reality – escalating at his intuitive touch.

Fast – furtive – barreling straight for the finish line as he positions himself on top of me with unmistakable intent.

"Okay, just so you know," I unlock lips and gasp, "it's been ten days and I need you to be gentle. I revirginize quickly."

"Revirginize," he does a little head shake grin. "I like that."

He slows – gentle-izing his approach on my landing strip.

Enter slowly…

"Mmmm… ahhhh…"

I'm sensitized submission under him, nails tracing pleasure lines along his tanned, bare back, bringing him into me deeper and deeper, as if I can't quite get him close enough.

Feeling him stretched out the length of me, kisses on my neck shooting up nerve endings like 'trystal meth'.

Sensationalized both above and below. His molecular charisma distracting my busy mind – while hands caress body into whipping want.

"Ahhh… Mmmmmm… Oh my God!"

Increasingly urgent desire one upped by his thrusts into me – his hard to my wet – only ramping that desire higher, as if I'm an addict who mid-shot is already craving the next hit.

Mainlining him.

Again.

And again.

Until the energy swirls around us…

… mingling molecules…

The initial shivery restraint of 'new' replaced by the trembling of raw, honest need. Carried aloft by a rising tide that rushes what lies beneath to the surface.

And there it is – Sailor's playful, wide grin exuberance looking down at me – eyes alight. Beneath the hardbody American do-it-himself sufficiency – past the sensitive helix of Italian male beauty layering over the hotsprings sea I'm more deeply exploring. Lifting me up in its surf. Pushing me towards the whitecap peak…

Only, just as the wave crests, we crash onto the shore of aftermath before I've even stood up on the surf board. Let alone caught the wave.

That first night, he'd whispered in my ear, "I want to make you (insert crude word for orgasm here)." A whisper that shot hot anticipation through every inch of my writhing body.

Only, it seems we end on his.

And he's left me stranded 'south of the border'.

What do I do?

He carefully detangles and lies beside me, spent. Caressing my hair – sweet and spooning.

Maybe my enthusiastic response to his skillful touch has confused the issue, making me sound like I've hit the jackpot of all…um… completions. I never fake it – that would be an insult to both parties. But, maybe I should tone down the moaning? How, exactly? Is there a speech therapist that specializes?

Maybe I should just say something.

But, that feels about as appealing as wading barefoot into a pack of dieting piranhas that missed lunch. Besides, how would I put it?

"Please sir, may I have some more…?"

Too orphan.

"Go ahead, make my day…"

Too hardass.

"Um… didn't you say you wanted to make me –"

SCREEECH!!!

My thoughts leave skid marks as I stop mid track. If being with Trouble taught me anything it's that men don't like to be reminded of what they said they'd do. So, I employ a time honored female trait – I turn the frustration on myself.

Don't be ridiculous. It's no big deal.

And the grain of truth in that is just how acutely pleasurable it already feels to be this close to him. 'Skin to skin'. I mean, Einstein was God's gift to math – but he didn't even know his own phone number. And Sailor is God's gift to foreplay.

"Here."

I take his forefinger and guide it along the smooth V.

"I removed all evidence of my being a natural redhead."

"I noticed." He keeps his gaze there as his hand traces the smooth above the wet.

"I'm not likely to slave over a hot stove for you, so it's not like you can make appreciative sounds over my pot roast or anything like that," I smile up at him. "So, this is your chance to appreciate something I did with you in mind."

The full on 'Brazilian' torture hit I took until tears sprang from my eyes and the wax specialist had to step away from the table to wipe her brow – guilt-sweat pouring down her face at the gringette's 'low pain threshold'.

"My chance to appreciate…" he rolls the words around, smiling as he continues to touch – each caress taking the sting out of the trauma flashback.

"Okay, I'm appreciating," he says, stroking silky soft.

Mmmmmmm…

Stroke.

MMMMMMMM…

Stroke.

Intense pleasure sigh.

But, he stops short of the 'ultimate' stroke.

Oh man, what do I have to do? Frame it? Offer incentives? Like at Wal-Mart? What if I threw in a free pinup calendar and a supply of motor oil?

But, as his amused gaze meets mine, I warm at his 'silly girl' little head shake and force-remind myself of what's 'ultimately' important.

Connection trumps climax.

Aren't the sensuous, silly moments between us more memorable anyway? Honestly! If having an orgasm every time was the harbinger of happiness, I'd still be married. Besides, if arching back in OMG touchdown ecstasy is that important to me I can always mention it next time, right?

That is, if there's gonna be a next time.

And that is the bigger question as Sailor and I seem to awake as if out of a trance. As if some carnival hypnotist snaps his fingers, and we stumble out of opposite sides of the bed, blinking at each other like we're confused as to how we ended up horizontal.

Again.

He hits the shower first and after a pause for post-coital hygiene we meet back in the living room, still scratching our heads like it's a mystery worthy of CERN scientists pondering that first Big Bang. In fact, we could probably figure out the origins of the universe easier than...

"What are we doing?"

"Yeah... I know." He throws himself back on the couch into the indent he'd previously made that's probably still warm. I sit, legs tucked under, on the floor beside him and look up – too late realizing I've accidentally assumed the 'groupie' position. Or more accurately, Mary Magdalene at the feet of a bad-boy Jesus.

He tosses me a 'what'cha doin' way down there' raised eyebrow.

I'm going for the Most Awkward Moment Award... and I think I just nailed it.

"Come up here." He pats the couch cushion beside him and I

scramble up, again tucking my legs under the too short wraparound dress I had thrown on like a mini robe.

"What is this…?" I hesitate. "Are we like…"

Dating.

Sigh.

"I don't know about that. I just know that when we were sitting here talking earlier I was thinking 'there it is again'." And he points to his temple then to mine like there's a ribbon linking the two, "That intellectual point of contact…"

I'm relieved to hear him say what I'm feeling.

"It can't be just physical for me," he reiterates what he had said that first night. "There has to be something more."

Yeah. Something 'up here' not just 'down there'.

But, there's only one 'dingaling' in this encounter and since it isn't mine, I can't take another caress without 'context'.

You like order?

Yes. Context. Clarity.

A little safety net under the nude acrobatics.

No matter how much I hate having 'the talk'. No matter how much I'd rather strap myself to a target wheel for a knife-throwing magician who's got DT shakes from heroin withdrawal and has just been diagnosed with Parkinsons. No matter how much I'd rather take up with a gang of metalmusic mercenaries and accidentally blow my eardrums in some punkapalooza reverb-amp-turned-up-to-11 mishap. No matter how much I'd rather have Sailor pull me into his arms and murmur, "Whatever this is, let's hit the Decap tonight and make the most of it."

None of those scenarios spare me what follows.

7.2

Sailor runs a hand through his hair, cornered into the white couch beside me downshifting towards Anxietyville. "Your brother's gonna kill me."

"My brother doesn't care who I... um... see," exasperation rising... "...as long as I'm happy."

"And what if we run into each other?" He counters like we're undercover spies in hostile territory – acting it out like we're establishing code. "We'll just be like 'hey/hey' next time we're all out some place and see each other."

'All' being the expat clique.

'Hey/hey' sounding disturbingly like the casual greeting of two acquaintances that have never seen each other naked.

"What do you mean?" I ask, trying to ignore the sickening dropkick feeling.

"Well, obviously we have to be... discreet."

"You mean like a secret?" I squeak.

He doesn't refute.

"I can't do that. I can't hide." I'm unable to soften the appalled tone creeping into my voice. "If I like someone enough to sleep with them then I'm proud of them – I'm proud of the person I'm with. I don't ask them to be a secret. That implies I'm ashamed of being seen with them."

He doesn't refute... or even slightly backpedal.

All of a sudden I don't feel very pretty. Or even halfway to cute.

It's like I'm walking through a high school hallway and the cool jock who kissed me under the bleachers last night is hangin' with his posse who have little use for the sensitive arty girl who sits in the stairwell writing bad poetry. Black clad artsy teen-me glances his way trying to catch a glimpse of the dreamboy who made me feel like I was twirling on starlight last night. He pretends I barely exist, but for an off-hand 'freak sneeze'. His friends snicker. His 'cool' cred preserved.

"Look," I shakeout the image and go for broke, "I like you."

"I like you too."

"No, I mean I LIKE you. More than I expected. You're interesting, plus seriously good looking." And before I can stop myself – the 'checklist' of his attributes whooshes out, "Do you know how hard it is to find someone attractive who also has an agile mind AND is fun to spend time with?! Not to mention you can actually dance. I mean, you've got moves –"

"You flatter me a lot," he says like he's filing a complaint in triplicate. "I don't think I can handle so many compliments."

"Well, man up and deal with it!"

OMG did I just say that?!

"Look," he says.

Uh-oh.

"I'm not looking for a relationship right now. I've just got too much going on."

This is my cue to pipe up my standard "I'm not looking for a relationship" line too.

But, somehow the words die somewhere on the way to my mouth. This would be so much easier if I were only here two weeks and could invoke my usual travel booty credo, but I'm here another two months.

"And besides, it's not like you live here," he counters. "You're leaving Panama in what… December?"

"Not necessarily." I'm vaguely aware how argumentative I sound, but I can't seem to stop the runaway train from heading straight for the cliff. "I might stay. My brother and I are talking about maybe finding a way so I could live here long term."

Silence.

"Well, I also want to spend a year in Spain," he volleys back. "Alone."

"Well, I want to spend a year in Manhattan. Also alone."

"But, between the boat and trying to write and hitting Europe later this year as well…"

"But, those are just excuses."

Ooops, did I just say that too?!

I lean back against the couch into the startled silence that follows – wondering what happened to the girl who specializes in 'temporary' – the girl who loves the come and go freedom of being unencumbered. Or as EFT3 put it, when I joked about us getting an Elvis-impersonating Rabbi in Vegas: "This from the creative Bohemian girl who wants to wander the world."

She's met her match.

The man of the sea sitting beside her can outdistance that girl stride for stride in the hundred yard 'freedom' dash. And who knew she'd like the chase?

Turns out as long as the guy keeps running – she's intrigued. The second he'd stop – turn around 'n' say the 'R' word – she'd be the one running like hell in the other direction. And just when I need all the rationalizations I can get, my mind revs into overdrive with 'what about equality'?!

I mean, when a man chases a stiletto-to-the-heart femme fatale it's because he 'loves a challenge'. But, when a woman still reaches for a fascinating man who eludes her she's 'codependent', 'dysfunctional', or worse, 'desperate'. Every possible negative label for the same conquest a man gets a 'hero' card for. My own stilettos stubbornly dig in for equal rights. Although in this case – it's the 'equal right' to make a fool of myself.

"Okay, well, for me, once I like someone – once we're intimate – I don't like sleeping around. I don't like… cross pollinating DNA."

"You want to be exclusive?" he asks sharply.

"Well, maybe… I guess," I backpedal, cowed by his irritated, incredulous tone on the word 'exclusive'.

Jeez, buddy I'm not asking for a kidney!

Sailor's looking at me now like the handler of a troublesome D-list actress who's just demanded Burberry plaid M&M's® in her dressing room – and they don't make Burberry plaid M&M's®.

"Look, this is why my girlfriend broke up with me," he says in gentle 'don't upset the diva' tones. "I can't say where I'm going to be one month to the next."

He leans back into the couch as if taking an emotional pit stop.

"Well neither can I. But, at the same time, we're already sleeping together – and exclusive doesn't necessarily mean… it just means…"

What, exactly?

Is there a 'semi sort of seeing each other' category? And even if there were, I don't think Sailor's gonna go for the nuanced difference between 'exclusive' and 'relationship'. Each to his own categories.

"I just got out of a relationship," Sailor's tone chimes finality. "I'm not ready to dive into another one."

"Well, whether you realize it or not – we are interrelating – and in a way – you're always in a 'relationship' with someone you're intimate with."

Now at least I know for sure that embarrassment does not kill. Because I'm still breathing.

"In the 'big picture' sense okay, yeah, maybe…" Sailor trails off as he looks away, perhaps exasperated at the formerly 'nice redhead' who suddenly morphed into the wannabe girlfriend from Planet Commitmatron.

Of course, it doesn't occur to me at this moment that the intensity of my emotions is possibly a tad mitigated by the intensity of Sailor's hot-sex brand of lovemaking – leaving me as high strung as a Stradivarius. And, that maybe, the conversation might have gone in an entirely different direction if *both* people sitting on the couch had crested the wave to the big-O…

ALTERNATE UNIVERSE IN WHICH LILA HAS BEEN SEXUALLY SATISFIED:

Sailor: I don't want a relationship.

Lila: Mmmm… sounds good. What I want is a nap. Would you mind letting yourself out?

She stretches and yawns.

But, in THIS universe...

Sailor and I are still sitting side by side on the couch, the 'magnet to steel' attraction having morphed into two magnets repelling each other.

"Okay," I say softly, white flag waving. "Obviously I'm more impacted by this than you are."

"That's not true," he says in a 'falsely accused' tone.

"No?"

"No. And it's not fair." I meet his sincere eyes with surprise dilating mine.

"But, this is complicated. Your brother's my friend and I'm still... my ex and I are still..."

"Oh, you're still seeing each other?" I say it calmly – but it's shock-cover. Our mutual single status was openly declared between lunch and dinner, so if he's otherwise –

"No, we're friends."

Okay, phew.

"But... it's complicated," he trails off, reaching for the rum 'n' coke glass still sitting on a delicate wooden side table. He takes a swig – radiating 'Man down in hostile territory!'

Sigh.

"When did you break up?" I try to put myself in his flip flops.

"Two months ago."

H E Double Hockeysticks! I thought it was a lot longer.

"I see. Tell me about her – what drew you to her?"

"Well, first of all she was smokin' hot!"

He shifts on the couch, bouncing up a little as he makes himself more comfortable to talk about what now appears to be his favorite subject.

"It was kinda Romeo and Juliet when we met. She was standing on the deck of a 60-footer and I was on the dock below. I looked up and there she was – just beautiful."

Julisa. The girlfriend of the last year plus – now ex-ed.

"I'd been in town for months and had met some beautiful

women – but she was smokin' hot…"

Uh… yeah, Sailor, you said that… I have a clear image of a 'smokin' hot' local. A slender brunette with long legs – and I'm clubbing myself with her beauty just fine thanks. Good thing I'm smart.

"But she was smart too."

Sigh.

"I asked her out – and she said essentially 'in your dreams.' I had to chase her until I finally wore her down." He relives it with an 'act out': "'C'mon just one drink – we'll have fun – what can happen in one drink?'"

I'm wondering where I can get a pair of welding goggles – blinded as I am by the sparks shooting out of Sailor's eyes.

"And when I brought her on the boat she was amazing – a lot of women couldn't handle it – but she was so capable!"

Hmmmm… this being a 'good listener' thing is highly overrated.

"I couldn't believe how much she waahh wahhh… and we could waah wahh."

Sailor's face is now entirely transformed with that look. That sheen of aliveness – that totally engaged enthralledness.

This isn't a man who wanted to break up any time soon.

"But, of course she's Catholic. Of course, right? She couldn't tell her family…"

"But, you're Catholic." I'm confused.

"I'm about as irreligious as they come. Plus, the whole marriage thing – once was enough down the aisle for me. Nah… they definitely wouldn't approve."

"So, she wanted you to be her secret?"

"Had to be."

Oh I get it. Funny how the untenable becomes acceptable for the one we love.

"Okay," I say softly. "But you know that's terribly unfair. No one should ever be put in that position."

He's quiet.

I'm quiet.

"Scooch over," Ghost Julisa says as she squishes between me and Sailor, draping a proprietary arm over his shoulder.

"Not so fast," Ghost Ex-Wife wedges in between them, not-so-accidentally elbowing Ghost Julisa in the process.

"Ow, stop it you cow!"

Ghost Ex-Wife merely smiles a 'gotcha' smile.

The couch is now crowded as the past jockeys for position, making itself comfortable hogging two couch pillows – well, three actually. Sailor's ex-wife that made him swear off marriage, the ex-girlfriend who left him because he had sworn off marriage – and Trouble who's still married.

"Hello my little darling." Trouble caresses the back of my neck as he squeezes himself between me and Sailor's entourage.

Sailor and I sit with our broken places between us. Two hearts with 'Reserved' signs.

"I'm sorry."

"Nothing to be sorry about," he says. "It's not your fault."

"I know, but it's a Canadian thing to say sorry at the drop of a hat. Or, more accurately, toque. And, what I mean is… I feel for you."

"That's life. Besides, I don't believe in that one big love."

"You don't?" Surprise.

"I think love is like one of those cool concept CDs."

"What… like The Alan Parsons Project?"

"Yah – though sometimes more like Supertramp's *Crime of the Century*."

I laugh. "That's good. But you're kidding, right?"

"No seriously – think about it. Each one is special – memorable. You play it over and over when you first get it – but as time goes on the meaning somehow changes. Many of my exes are now friends."

"I can relate to that." I flash to the sweet Euro romantic intellectual nature of EFT2 – a photographer from Italy – then to the ultra courteous worldly intelligent vibe of EFT3. Friends now in different cities.

Sailor continues, "In some cases my exes have been friends longer than when we were together." I again relate until he adds, "Relationships aren't forever."

To that I'm silent. It's one thing not to find lasting love – it's another thing not to hold open its possibility. It's as if the paramedic who defibrillated my heart has himself a weak ticker.

"Well, look... let's just continue as we are..." Sailor untangles himself from the couch and stretches upright. "Just take it one day at a time."

'Secret 'n' Stringless' is what he means.

"Okay," I pretend to agree.

I stand up to walk him to the door, imagining his thoughts now as one simple word repeated, 'Extract! Extract!'

"You must be jetlagged," I say. "Sorry to bring all this up now – I didn't mean to keep you." I'm oblivious to the deeper allusion.

Open door.

Kiss.

Close Door.

Lock the door.

Stand, staring at it for a moment.

Super. Swell. He wants to be my Unboyfriend.

I rouse myself to turn off the aircon and throw open the Suicide Window. I catch a glimpse of Sailor walking home on the street below.

Let's just continue as we are.

This isn't dating.

This isn't even friends with benefits.

It's more like 'pretend strangers with benefits'.

PSWB.

And now I know what THIS is. This is a recipe for Low Self Esteem.

Take one secret.

Add a dash of naked flailing.

Separate sex from status.

Remove from heat, rub in salt.

Low Self Esteem Soufflé. Serves one.

I understand not expecting too much too soon, but Sailor's expectation that I have zero expectations is an impossible expectation.

"Darling?" Trouble says, still holographed into the living room. "Do you honestly think he'll ever reach you –"

"Don't say it."

"In all the places –"

"Please don't!" I tell the empty room, but it's too late.

Doorways fly open that I had kept closed – padlocked and painted over – giving way as if unhinged.

The layers of interconnected points-of-contact that *he* reached in me are multidimensional entry points as if Cupid's arrow splintered when it found the bullseye and shot my heart full of Trouble... which in turn sent him all through my bloodstream...

"You and I both know you can be with anyone you want," he says softly. "But you'll always be thinking of me."

'Wishing it were me' – is what we're both not saying.

"That's what you want to condemn me to, isn't it?!" My voice rises. "That's it, isn't it?! I can't have you – but you don't want me to be with anyone else! You want to condemn me to a lonely wandering – an endless longing. Well congratulations! Mission Accomplished!"

I'm no longer holographing him – I'm face to face with Trouble for the first time in three years – reunited via skype video.

Blooming in an all out blush as he holds me in the crosshairs of his brooding gaze.

No longer just a sexy phone vox long distance. Trouble is filling the screen in front of me like my own, personal movie star anti-hero.

And he looks goooooood.

8. TROUBLE IN PARADISE

"No, that's not what I want for you. What I want…"

He shrugs.

Trouble has toughened. His former sales executive suit is now a bustheads navy blue-collar designed to intimidate. As if he wasn't already intimidating enough. Sandy blonde crew cut, 6'1" muscular frame, coiled force crouched to spring from a rockwall core.

Power.

Intensity.

Sad eyes.

Green with hazeling flecks of brown. An endless pool of swirling emotion.

But it's not just how he looks – it's how he looks at me.

"The way I feel seeing you… even after all this time…" voice catching on emotion with a hint of surprise. "Maybe I'll get on a plane and surprise you in Panama."

"Please don't…"

I'm grateful he can't feel the tremor he sends through me.

Trouble is my San Andreas faultline.

It's midnight his time and he's sitting behind a large mahogany desk in the office of the company he now owns. Dark circles testimony to the crushing hours he's working. As usual.

I'm in a red dress in Sibling's office. It's the only red dress I own and I figured it met the 'scarlet woman' criteria. Skype is both the vehicle of our reunion – and the wall I still need to keep myself from melting into his arms.

Did I say he's my San Andreas faultline?

Well, he's also my Everest and Empire State. If life is made up of moments we look back on with a flash of wonder – the sharp "I was here" color pics in an otherwise 'dull routine' existence – then Trouble is a walking peak-monument.

"I can't be in the same room… alone with you… until you're legally separated. I just can't." Because my heart would explode with undbridled joy at the first touch.

Time.

Distance.

Hasn't changed a thing.

"That's all right," he says in that tone that always implies 'it's not'. "But sooner or later…"

The words hang between us – as they always do. And I silently curse myself, because deep down… I still believe him. Or worse – want to believe him.

"Where are you?" he asks.

"In my brother's home office."

"Nice."

"How about you?"

Trouble pans the camera around his office to show me his entrepreneurial homegrown office – the thing he's most wanted – worked for.

"I'm closer than I've ever been…" he says meaningfully.

And feeling further than I've ever been, I snap, "And what am I supposed to do in the meantime? I can't be your Lady in Waiting forever."

"Understood," he ducks.

"You do realize it's been seven years since we met?"

"And you look the same honey," says Trouble the master of deflection. "Look at that cleavage – your creamy white skin. You never age. You're just as you were."

"No, I'm not." I lash out. "I'm a shadow of what I was when you met me. Constantly exhausted courtesy of my Angry Uterus and terrified. Not sure where my next income source is going to come from and still trying to finish a novel after all these years. The last thing I feel right now is attractive."

What I should feel is embarrassment at the sudden pity party, but instead I feel a surge of relief to outpour to the one man man enough to take my most hyper sensitive…

"Honey," he softens. "I know this is hitting you where it hurts the most – your feminine identity."

Bullseye.

"But trust me." He leans and turns slightly towards the camera at his end into a direct-gaze close up.

"You're. Still. Beautiful."

Each word emphasized. Injected with sincerity.

Coating my hurt in candied kindness even as it guilts me to partake of it. Even as I think of the person unknowingly betrayed.

Conflict love is like conflict diamonds. Doesn't make it any less real or shiny – but someone is getting hurt.

I simultaneously embrace and curse it – bubbling up as it always does – the ripple of that first moment he put his arm around me. A cozy quilt enveloping me in his caring – contraband – gaze.

And it doesn't escape my notice that the reassurance I unconsciously wanted to hear from the man I'm currently sleeping with has arrived courtesy of the man I've been trying to escape. And worse, the recognition that the 'those are just excuses' I hurled Sailor's way were really meant for him.

Trouble.

Who always knows the right thing to say.

Trouble.

Who stares back at me as if he sees through me to a nakedness beyond nudity.

Trouble.

Who burrowed into my deepest corners and took up permanent residence.

Toronto – November 2002

"I want to be your *boyfriend*."

Trouble leans over his steering wheel as he says these words – gripping it with both hands as if for support. I'm watching him, tight long sleeved T atop jeans that leave little to the imagination, from my close-up post in the passenger seat as we park outside my apartment. It's not the quaint 'boyfriend' from a fortysomething swaggering magnet for every eye in every restaurant we walk into that touches me – it's the tone with which he says it. The achingly vulnerable boytone that contrasts the outer manstrength.

It's now our third 'date' – though later I will deny myself that term.

"I don't want this to be casual," he says quietly, only half looking at me as he stares mostly ahead out the windshield into the past midnight street. The glow of street lamps illuminate only a few blocks ahead – the street disappearing in the distance – a curve ahead leaving no hint of what's beyond our little lit hub.

"I want to be your boyfriend and you to be my girlfriend." It's just like Trouble to spell out exactly what he wants.

"What do those terms mean to you?" I ask gently. Afraid. Thrilled. Confused. "Boyfriend and girlfriend?"

"I don't want us to see other people. I want us to be exclusive."

Soft-voiced vulnerability continues to compete with steely determination. An irresistible cocktail of entreaty/command.

And, a glimpse of 'us possible'.

Earlier we'd driven past pawnshops on Church and Queen talking of 'The Future'.

"If I can stay on this TV movie – presuming I don't get fired like the other writers – and it actually gets financed and made I'll get a production bonus, which would be amazing."

"I'd love that for you – I'd love to go to your premiere—"

"Well, we don't actually have premieres in TV – more like screening parties when it first airs. But, we could go to the film festival galas."

"Either way, I'll be the guy in the tux who's saying 'I knew her when'."

"Just remember the phrase: first day of principal photography. That's payday."

"Nice. I like that you're ambitious. I'm not a man who needs a woman to play small, so he can feed his ego."

I glance over at him in the driver's seat and smile to myself at his incredible Hulkishness minus the green.

"Hate to tell ya, but it would take a whole lotta woman to make you feel small."

He smiles, "What I know about you already, honey, is that you're not the type of woman to try. You're too sweet for that."

I blush-squirm under the look he sends my way before turning his eyes back to the road and making a left on Richmond. "Besides, I'm going to be the CEO of a major firm in five years," he predicts. "That, and a nice mansion or two will feed my ego just fine."

I laugh, delighted to encounter a fellow dreamer in an oft 'conservative' town that specializes in conformity.

"Hmmmm…"

"What?" he asks, amused.

"You're a 'blue sky' thinker. You just project what you want without the self inflicted censorship that stops so many people in their tracks."

Yet, as much as that inspires me – in the back of my mind is a little warning clang – a ping of concern that his optimism could also lead to over-extending himself – to miscalculating what it really takes to get what he wants.

"The average man wastes a lot of time convincing himself the possible is impossible." He wipes trepidation from my mind like a windshield wiping off yesterday's rain.

I glance up at him as he drives, speeding ahead only to have to stop suddenly… a speed-up-stop… speed-up-stop jarring driving style of a man in a hurry.

Impatient with the traffic signals of life.

I can relate.

"I just want to put something good out into the world and actually make a living doing what I love," I muse, as yet unsure how. "TV can be exciting – the camaraderie – and the fact that millions of people can see what you do – or in Canadian terms – your relatives and that agoraphobic shut-in across the street."

Trouble laughs at that, "You make your living by your wits. I respect that."

"Thanks. No one has ever put it that way, but I suppose I have to – because if I had to make my living by my cooking skills I'd starve."

"Don't tell me – dinner is dialing take out."

"Pretty much," I confess. "I've been known to burn water."

"Don't worry, I can handle my way around a kitchen." The way he says 'handle' and 'kitchen' he's talking about a different kind of heat. "Stick with me, kid, you'll never starve."

I laugh and then smile up at him – at the contradiction between 'modern man' who can handle an independent woman – yet also prides himself on being a good provider.

But, the laugh has an extra shot of delight afterglow – because it's dawning on me that no matter what we're doing – sushi on West Queen West – walking hand in hand to a convenience store to pick up cream for his coffee – cozy in his car – I'm... happy.

How strange. And new.

"I've never relied on a man, but, I've always believed in the idea of partnership. Building something together. Even if that's just encouraging each other's individual pursuits."

"The salesman and the scribe," he smiles. "Nice."

"I love that you want your own business," I beam up at him, "I meet so few men in this town who think beyond the paycheck. And sure you can make a living – but can you create a life worth living?"

"A lot of people are afraid to live large. I'm not. And I'm not afraid to work for what I want. Whatever it takes."

"Me neither."

He drops his hand on my knee between shifting gears. I put my hand on top of his and he interlaces fingers.

Two people from humble beginnings entwining dreams.

Just how similar those 'humble beginnings' were became apparent when we passed a luxury condo.

"I used to work there," I say in passing, "as a teenager."

"No you didn't – I did."

"What?" I sharp turn glance his way.

"When I was eighteen."

I do the math and realize we'd overlapped.

"No, but I worked at the drug store at street level beside the cafe," I clarify.

"So did I."

"You're kidding!"

"As a stock boy."

"I was the cosmetics girl on Sundays."

Trouble proceeds to rattle off the names of the pharmacist and the store manager. Names I haven't heard since...

"Do you remember my mother?"

"Your mother?"

"She was the bookkeeper."

"Your mother was the bookkeeper?!"

"How do you think I got the job? Nepotism."

"That's funny, you work in the entertainment industry, but nepotism only got you a job at a drug store."

"Hey, it meant I could afford jeans and cigarettes."

"Don't tell me you smoke?!" Trouble sounds horrified.

"Used to. But, I don't think vice was what my mother had in mind when she got me the job. She raised two kids on a bookkeeper's salary. I don't know how she did it."

"I remember her. Nice lady."

"Do you remember her name?"

He shrugs apologetically, "That was a long time ago."

"Lea. Her name was Lea," I say softly. Missing her. I'm guessing he's just being polite – saying he remembers her.

"She asked if I was Jewish."

"Oh my God!" I cry out, a bolt of memory lightning through me.

"What?!" he swivels toward me in alarm.

"She introduced us." Goosebumps shiver down my arms.

He shakes his head, drawing a blank.

"At the store," I prompt.

"I don't..." he hesitates.

"You were tall and um... not so buff as you are now."

"Yeah, I was skinny back then."

"I had to look up to you. I was... uh... in my uniform which was too tight especially um... on top." I redden at how this sounds. I'm being factually descriptive, but I sound like a Hooters applicant bragging about my credentials.

"I would have remembered that," he says with a jokey leer.

"Yeah, well... trust me. My mother introduced us."

The memory sharpens.

"We were standing near the street entrance of the store towards the pharmacy. You had your back to the window. It was... awkward."

"I bet you were cute in that uniform."

"Well, not cute enough obviously, because it's taken you over 20 years to ask me out."

"And I plan to make up for lost time." He throws me a self-assured grin at his romancing prowess.

We hit Bathurst and turned left then right onto King Street West, a gentrifying area of old Victorians dwarfed by new, overpriced box-like condos and lofts.

Trouble muses, "The stockboy and the cosmetics girl. Nice."

I return the smile, even though I'm probably the only one who remembers that cringingly awkward 'hey/hi' first meeting.

The aftermath was a full on teen tantrum, "I don't need you to find me a boyfriend, Mum!"

But now, she has an accomplice.

"Don't you see what this is?" Trouble later idles his Black Racer in front of my apartment like it's straining against restraints – eager to hit the track – eager to win.

He traces a finger across my cheek.

"This isn't casual, this kind of... meeting of minds," he says softly. "It's rare. You may say you don't want a relationship – but here you are. In a way – you're already in one. Why are you afraid to call it what it is?"

His voice is low, but his message is like a sonic boom – breaking through my 'single career girl' sound barrier.

"But, can you be my boyfriend? I mean... I know you said you and your wife live separate lives and divorce is imminent, but is that really a promise you can make?"

"I wouldn't be making it if I couldn't."

He pulls me towards him then, pillow lips finding mine with a gentle caress-kiss, his hand lingering on my face, tracing the angles from my hairline down my cheekbone to my jaw then turning my head so he can nuzzle into my neck.

The sigh-moan that escapes out of me is easily decoded.

"You're so afraid of the thing you want most," he murmurs.

And as his cherishing gaze meets my skittish one – that long denied desire for romantic happiness ignites. Ignites in interweaving ribbons of pink promises and moonlight. Being held by the boy I met long ago – now a man for whom my romantic feelings vie with an entirely unexpected sensation...

Home.

Warming me on a cold night – winding around my heart.

Squeezing tight.

Soon after, I let myself into my 'character' apartment with the scratched hardwood floors and shabby kitchen cabinets.

Reeling.

As I fire up the computer, kidding myself that I'm actually going to get any work done, the Caribbean beckons again.

An Eden alternate universe.

The 'us possible' Trouble glitter glued onto my bedazzled eyes.

Falling in love with a man's potential is for amateurs – I fall in love with a man's potential to love.

9. HOSTAGE TO SECRETS

"Why don't you get back together with Julisa?" Sibling is unwittingly kicking goals into his own team's net, scoring for the opposition. Lounging on the white couch kitty corner to the loveseat I'm sitting on – talking to Sailor on cell. "You guys were great together."

My SIM chip local number has reverted to Sibling's cell and he answered Sailor's call to a flurry of "What is goin' on, Bro?!" guy talk. Unfortunately, instead of the usual topics guys are supposed to talk about like who caught the bigger wave and "how 'bout them (insert sports team here)" – they're talking about women.

Sailor's women to be exact.

"Julisa's beautiful." Sibling continues to score for the opposing team while I silently scream, 'No! PASS THE BALL TO ME!'

"You love her."

He shoots! He scores!

"She's about as perfect a woman as you're ever gonna get, Bro."

The opposing crowd does the wave as cheerleaders take to the field with 'Julisa' on their spankies!

On my side of the stadium it rains and the guy selling hot dogs just overturned his cart in pique at all the empty seats.

The more Sibling innocently counsels a friend – a friend he's unaware I've slept with twice – the more invisible steam shoots out of my ears. Does Angelina Jolie's brother sport a 'Team Aniston' football jersey? Nuh uh! And worse, Sib's unaware of his faux pas, because his own sister didn't bring him into the loop.

There are things Sibling does NOT need to know:

a) The Pringles are sneaky replacements – I ate his original stash due to Addict's Amnesia. I kept forgetting the carb count every time I thought of their yummilicious crunchy goodness (damn, I could use a tube right now)!

b) His painting-in-progress was blown off its easel repeatedly until I got the hang of opening the Suicide Window gradually, so the outside air wouldn't whoosh in like an art critic typhoon.

c) Details.

The thing maybe Sibling DOES need to know is that the friend he's giving love advice to is his sister's latest round of 'travel booty'. He doesn't need to know the nitty gritty, but deceiving him with silence to respect Sailor's rabid need for privacy is in turn disrespecting my Bro. If he found out some other way, he'd wonder why his own sister withheld the intel. Plus, if he had all the facts, he could at least root for the home team now that he is in fact home.

"Where are you?!" Sib had urgent celled as I was racing to the airport to pick him up.

Late.

Late like that time I kept him waiting 45 minutes at LAX because I forgot to factor in L.A. rush hour traffic. Only this time, I'm on a dark, unfamiliar road a language away from understanding directions even if I could find someone to ask. Well, technically, Spanish would be good in L.A. too. But, I don't think my ability to order a cappuccino in half-Spanish is gonna cut it out here.

"I missed the turn off!" I wailed. "I'm lost in Panama!"

The happy 'welcome home' detoured in favor of panic and a Sis stress bomb. I could feel him rolling his eyes at the other end. The calm brother to the anxious 'Seester' – what else is new?

"How could you miss the turn off? There's a big sign."

"I couldn't see it until it was too late! There was this big truck, and –"

"You were following too close again, weren't you?"

"I wasn't!"

Ever since Sibling saw me tailgating on the 101 he's been on this 'you drive too close to other cars' kick. He doesn't get that in L.A. the sheer volume of cars means you're always driving too close unless you're on the sidewalk. Come to think of it – I got us lost in L.A. too and it was Sibling who bought the map.

"Well, find a spot to turn around," he said, adopting the

reasonable tone of adult to tantrummy toddler.

"I'm trying!"

I panic-pictured myself lost for hours on a pitch black outskirt divided highway with no means of turning back in the opposite direction.

And right there in front of me was a gas station at a 4-way break in the road. I blinked at it like a mirage, then sharp turned Sibling's town car into a hard right that barreled me through the brightly lit gas stop/convenience store.

Okay, well… that was easy.

I zoomed past a rickety ancient truck, startling the field workers in the open back, and turned left onto the side road perpendicular to the highway. I took a deep breath and raced across a break in oncoming traffic, hard left back onto the highway taking care to watch for the airport off ramp. Screech-stopping curbside when I spotted him at the terminal.

"Sorry, sorry, sorry!"

Sibling stored his suitcase in the trunk and folded his lean, 6'1" frame into the passenger seat. He'd turned his brilliant Bro blues my way, offset by a deep tan and jet dark hair with flecks of silver cropped short.

"Looking good Sib."

"Thank you. How's my Seester?" He flashed his Sibling smile and my face broke into a reflective grin. The only time we bear any resemblance to each other is when mouths tilt upward, and our faces align in familial angles.

"She's happy to see you," I beam.

"I'm happy to see you too," he says in warm tones.

Yay – a Sib induced Happy Spike!

If I'm orangey exuberance with purple polka dots – Sibling is muted shades of blue. An elegant Clooney to my clumsy Lucy.

"Don't you want to take the wheel?" I ask.

"You're driving back."

"Uh… you sure that's a good idea? Or do you enjoy getting lost in a foreign country at night?"

"It's the only way you'll figure out the route. Go ahead, I'll direct you."

Somewhere along the way little brother, who didn't even hit the scene until after my tenth birthday, morphed into 'Big Bro'. The capable, mature one. The good advice giver.

Too good.

"If you really want to be a father…" he sits cozy on the couch, advising Sailor on his complications. Only for Sib, it's simple, "Be with someone you love."

He's right, of course – but oh, man.

I leap up off the loveseat and head for the office like an outlaw in search of a hideout.

Just get me out of earshot!

But, for some reason, Sib picks that very moment to grab something from said office and trails me in.

"Get back together and then have a kid with her. Your kids would be cute… I mean, not because of your DNA, bro… haha… but *she* is smokin' hot."

Damn cell phones and all cordless appliances!

Whatever happened to the good old days when phones were nailed to the wall – tethered to a short leash coily cord?! Who the hell decided phone mobility was a good thing?!

"Honestly, buddy, if you want to be a dad…"

I flee to the kitchen.

Sibling strolls into the kitchen on my heels to pour himself a Balboa beer.

"…be a full time dad. Not this part time thing."

I bolt through the springy kitchen swing-door back out to the living room, and stand like deer caught in headlights. Again. Unsure what direction to go in – until Sib follows me out.

"C'mon man, Julisa is everything you could possibly want in a woman."

Arrrggggh! Make it stop!!!

I bolt down the white-walled hallway in a silent impersonation of a scream queen running from some dagger-hands psycho in a horror movie. Barricading in the office, closing the door and putting my hands over my ears, but Sib's voice wafts in deep and resonant…

"Life's too short to… muffle… muffle… happiness."

Okay, that's it!

No more secrets from my DNA match!

9.2

"I like him."

Sibling looks up mid-bite from the fish I attempted to cook after a loco Monday following him entourage style around Punta Pacifica. From bill paying – to lunch with Theo – to the 'wealthy area' well stocked supermarket at Multi Plaza – where Sib waited for me while I snuck in a $6 chair massage.

"Where were you, I thought you were starting us off?" Sibling asked when I finally showed up pushing an empty shopping cart.

"Just had a quick errand," I said – my face sporting red lines from where the massage chair facepad had imprinted.

He looked at me for a beat – then headed for the liquor aisle.

By seven p.m. I had dished up a dinner of sautéed fish, rice and steamed broccoli – secretly hoping the red wine he uncorked would make him all mellow and stuff whilst simultaneously dulling his taste buds.

"How long did you cook this fish?" His face scrunched as if biting into a lemon. In the desert.

"Um… until it looked done."

"Next time, maybe cook it a little less. It's kinda dry."

"Really?" I said, taking a bite and trying to swallow the arid lump, "Seems fine to me," I reach for the bottle, "but, here, have some more wine." I hastily overfilled his glass.

The clinking of forks on plates provided a little symphonic accompaniment to the Sibling talk of relatives seen on his trip and a brief update on how the Med looks since I last saw it. As soon as we segued to boats and Sailor I confessed…

"I like him."

Sib looks up from his plate, startled. "I don't think he feels the same way." Around his eyes is a slight hint of 'my poor deluded sister.'

Ouch.

"Well, indications are otherwise based on that night we spent in Bella Vista."

"I just had a two hour conversation about relationships with him. He didn't mention you once."

Double Ouch.

"Okay, well… but –"

"Did he say something… or… do something…" Sib hesitates, wary… "…to make you think there's something there?"

"Well, yeah in fact he did. He sort of… um…" OMG, how do I sanitize this to make it Bro appropriate??? "He sort of *kissed* me that night in Bella Vista." I sit back, pleased with my G-rated version.

"Huh," Sib nevertheless raises an alarmed 'too much information' eyebrow.

"Never mind, I'll spare you the details," I spear some broccoli with my fork and focus on my plate as if it's a five star gourmet meal.

I expect him to drop it at this point. Dismiss it with a wave and his standard, 'Well, Sis, as long as you're having fun – just play safe.'

Instead, he roadblocks with, "But, he's my friend."

Whaaahat?

"Okay, but… sorry… what does that have to do with anything?"

"Well, it's… weird."

This is a first. For our entire adult lives the age difference has forestalled this awkward moment. Sibling's only dating rule is: no one older than my sister. My dating rule in turn is: no one younger than my brother.

Okay, so I've broken that rule – the Italian photographer took me to a cliff overlooking the Pacific on our first date. I challenge any woman to resist, particularly since we forgot to factor in dinner and I was weak from both hunger and the spectacular view. The Pacific was nice too.

But, with Sailor being my contemporary, this long averted weirdness collision has just careened into the Sis/Bro meridian.

"But, you don't mind do you?" I ask, incredulous.

"Well, actually yeah, I do."

Whaahaat?!

Sailor was right! How could he predict Sibling's reaction more accurately than the sister who's known him since he first hit the scene all cute and babyish?!

"I can't believe it!" I gasp, irate.

"What?" he takes a sip of wine.

"You're the chill one – the one who's always saying I need to work less and socialize more!"

"Okay, but that doesn't mean I want you to 'socialize' with my close friend."

"I thought you were more acquaintance friends. I didn't realize you were *close* friends."

"Well, we're getting to be. And, there are rules about that sort of thing back where we grew up."

"What rules?! It was Willowdale!"

Willowdale – a whitebread suburb of Toronto – not the Bronx! Willowdale, where every weekday morning commuters lined up single file in well spaced apart 'after you' courtesy to get on the bus. Even in a snow storm. It wasn't some switchblade Jets vs. Sharks rumble! But, all of a sudden Sibling thinks he's in West Side Story and he doesn't even like musicals.

"A guy's supposed to go up to his friend and say, 'I like your sister, is it okay if I ask her out'. Otherwise, I'm supposed to punch his lights out or something."

I stare at my über-sophisticated brother who taught himself Spanish as he sits opposite me in a white cotton shirt with a white stitch design atop a pair of jeans that would be at home among Young Hollywood at the Chateau Marmont. His idea of 'throwing a punch' would be spiking juice with rum and inviting ten people over.

Sigh.

It's not bad enough I quagmired into a marital triangle – now I've tripwired into a Bromance triangle!

"Oh, and I think Jorge is dead," Sib adds out of the blue.

I follow his gaze towards his sole beloved plant in its coveted corner. It's now brittle and brown-leaved all over.

"He's not dead, he's just sleeping."

Sibling raises a jury verdict eyebrow.

He's dead and I killed him. First by not watering him – then by watering him too much.

"Jorge has gone to plant heaven," Sibling says wistfully as Jorge looks down at me from his afterlife, shaking a j'accuse brittle leaf my way…

"Her! That planticidal red head! She done me in!"

9.3

The next day, typical of family argu-discussions, the 'Sis likes Sailor' conversation is picked up again – weaving in and out of our day like a loud, obnoxious in-law cousin at holiday dinners. It even follows us to the Amador Causeway, where Sibling takes me for lunch perhaps in self preservation after sampling my cooking skillz.

"Mmm, mmm, mmm…" he digs into the spinach and feta pizza at Alberto's while I pick at my slice with a knife and fork, too aware of the pins and needles of discomfort poking holes in my already perforated ego.

The Causeway is gracious living atop a dirt pile. Literally. Dirt and rock from Panama Canal excavations were deployed to create the combination roadway/walking path with its picturesque waterway views and eatery patios.

Only, I'm heatstroking in the blinding midday sun.

Sibling adjusts the umbrella to shade his fair sister, who's sprouting new freckles by the second, but he can't save me from myself.

"Look, Sib," I squint greeny gray blues towards his unflinching cobalt gaze. "At least he's a fellow writer I can actually talk to."

Except, we haven't actually talked since 'the talk' – and the contrast between our original easy banter and the strained avoidance is acute enough to irritate – like sand particles scraping against each other – sparking that longing to get back to 'the pearl'; the ease and flow of one thing leading to another. The before this after.

"Okay, but his life's a bit of a mess right now." Sib plates his slice with more than a hint of impatience. "He just broke up, he's all over the place –"

"Well, nobody plans these things. It's not like I scheduled into my calendar, 'like a Sailor on Saturday'."

"You might want to schedule, 'like a guy who's at least halfway available on Sunday.' I mean, I wouldn't want you to sprain something by liking someone totally available until at least next Thursday."

"One muscle group at a time?"

"Something like that."

"Cute." My tone implies 'not cute at all.'

Bite.

Munch.

Hmmmm... this pizza is yummilicious, even if it lacks serious protein, since Sibling hasn't eaten meat since he was sixteen. A decision that prompted cabbage rolls 'n' stew specialty Mum to call me in a panic, "Oy vey, vat do I cook now?!"

"There's a reason I... um... don't get involved... for long stretches of time: I wait for that 'magic click'. And I don't feel it often." I continue to wade into murky water, while dabbing at a bit of spinach that lands on my skirt. "It's different for you – you're always in a relationship –"

"But, it's not a relationship. He's –"

"Yeah, I know. He's like that Eagle's song, 'Take it Easy'. I get it."

"Don't get me wrong – he's a good friend." Sibling picks up another slice. "And he's a great writer, you should read his work – you could learn something."

My eyes narrow to flinty slits, but since the sun's already making me squint, Sib fails to notice.

"Though, he did crash my car five minutes after borrowing it," he munches thoughtfully. "And bottom line, I just don't think he'll make a good boyfriend for you."

"I never said he was boyfriend material –"

"Well then?"

"He crashed your car?" I deflect.

Mark joins us at the table, and we Siblings clam up. The rest of the lunch is a strained pause in the deliberations interspersed with

Sibling and Mark discussing the week ahead with its 'to dos' in a mix of English and Spanish.

I look out to the royal blue and white superyacht that's docked in front of Alberto's as the uniformed crew loads supplies. I wonder what it would be like to live on a floating boutique hotel. The yacht's name is *Just the Two of Us*, but it looks like it sleeps ten in five star luxury with crew deck below. Sibling follows my gaze to the stately craft and smiles. He sees a floating jam session with his musician friends on the high seas, girlfriend dancing top deck in a bikini.

I see the iceberg.

9.4

"But, no one is good enough for your sister, no?" Giselle turns to Sibling as they sit side by side on the couch later that night, adding in her honey toned Spanish accent, "She's your sister."

"That's not true," Sib insists, "I liked one."

"One," I hold up my index finger. "One guy in a thirty year dating span."

"Why this one?" Giselle asks, now intrigued.

"Well, he's a great guy," Sib says, fiddling with the video game controls as he inadvertently reveals his brother-in-law criteria. "He has his shit together. He's intelligent, successful and a good person. He cares about the world – he's not just in it for himself. Plus, he's been good to my sister."

"So, why are you not with him?" Giselle turns to me as my brother puts down the controls and puts his arm around her.

"I have two words for you. New. Zealand."

"Oh, he lives in New Zealand?" I nod as her face gets that 'lightbulb' look.

"That's my Sis," Sibling smiles, "she never dates a guy within her own city limits."

"We met in Vancouver," I elaborate, "when he was in town on a business trip. I had a feeling I was going to meet someone on the beach that day – so I went down to the seawall. He was sitting on a log writing in a notebook and he approached me as I was walking back towards English Bay. He had me at 'pardon me' with that Kiwi accent. He calls every year from Wellington."

"Is he still single?" Giselle asks, astute.

"No." I smile. Glad that one of the best men I've ever met is happy.

"That's the kind of guy you need, Sis," Sib says, as though I've let the prize fish get away. "A guy who's got it together."

He hands Giselle her Wii joystick, picks up his own, and coaches her through the new game. They're soon kicking each other's virtual butts, yelling, "Baby! You got me!" and "Baby, you nearly got me!" and "Baby! I'm gonna get you!!!"

I wash the dishes and retreat to the inflatable mattress in the office – lying there reading Charles Pelligrino's *Return to Sodom and Gomorra*, until my tired brain screams for Nora Roberts. But, it's better than thinking about Sailor – or Trouble for that matter. I guilt-shift uncomfortably to one side – only to shift restlessly to the other side as I simultaneously avoid texting Sailor.

One guy driving me crazy was bad enough. Two is too many. Trouble talks enduring love – but I can't endure the wait. Sailor is straight up, 'I don't want x,y,z' – but his touch transcends to 'something more' that makes it impossible to dismiss so easily.

Confusion is not a good color on me.

And worse, just like the intuition I was going to meet someone on the beach that day, my inconvenient Inner Voice is nagging like some wannabe Oracle at Delphi – warning – *it ain't over.*

"Baby, you shot me!" Sibling yells and laughs as Giselle cries out delighted, "Baby, did I win?!"

It ain't over.

I put the pillow over my head.

9.5

The next day, Sibling and Mark burst through the apartment door after a mysterious errand. They haul a queen sized mattress and boxspring across the threshold.

"Surprise, Seester!" Sib has a huge grin on his face.

"Is that... did you?" I ask, wide eyed.

"It's your new bed!"

"Awww... Sibling! You didn't have to!"

But, this is brotherly love in action as Sib determinedly tears down his own bedroom with Mark's help, turning it into my 'guest room' and moving his bed into his office – completely rearranging his life for my comfort.

"Here, you can use this," he and Mark lift a functional light wood desk through the bedroom door and push it against the opposite wall. "And, I'm giving you November."

"November?"

"Yeah, it's perfect. You have a place to stay in a beautiful country, I'll buy the food –"

"And I can cook!" I jump in, eager. "I mean if you're buying – I should be helping."

"Uh... yeah..." Sib looks off in the distance as if wanting to say something, but thinking better of it. "Anyway, I'll even give you some money, so you can go to a café if you want. You're finishing your contract aren't you? And, you need to write – the time is now."

"I haven't had a month just to write in... I think never." It's always been a juggling act with work – or searching frantically for work. Writing shoved in a corner like the wilting Jorge. But, Sibling brings up a new plant from the car.

"This is Jorge II," he says, installing the tree thingy in a corner of the living room – all shiny green and flourishing. "Don't water him, okay?" he adds quickly. "I'll take care of it."

"November," I repeat, tingling with both fear and excitement though it's still a couple of weeks away. November – when dad left. November – when Trouble first reached for my hand. This is my chance to reclaim November.

An accidental celebration follows later that evening when Sibling brings home some teachers from Canada he found at the tennis court and a little party ensues on the rooftop patio complete with a stash of bubbly and a toast to 'new friends'. The city nightlights twinkle around us – like we're on top of the world.

"Are you having fun, Seester?" he puts a familial arm around me and grins down at my upturned smile. Ever rooting for my happiness.

9.6

Chef Sibling takes over dinner the next night, when the obnoxious cousin attempts to crash our party one last time.

We take our loaded plates out of the kitchen, and Sib sits down opposite me at the four-seat square dining room table. He takes his first sip of a trio blend of Cab/Merlot/Syrah with the thoughtful elegance of a sommelier, then takes a bite of his veggie lover's burrito filled with rice, beans, lettuce, cheese, accented by slivers of red and yellow peppers all glued together by salsa and guacamole like he's eating five star cuisine.

I take one bite and the contents of my burrito CSI splatter into a fine mess. Thankfully, my T-shirt is black and absorbs the salsa/guac hit to the chest like a special ops veteran.

"It's the latest in Mexican Foodwear," I cover while dabbing out the stain.

"It suits you," Sib cracks.

That's also what he said when he deposited my new bed – cornered so that the wall acts as a 'headboard' in the now official 'Sis guest room'.

"A mattress on the floor. It suits you."

"Ha ha – very funny." I wasn't laughing.

"It goes with the whole 'bohemian writer' thing."

Still not laughing.

Sibling continues his fine dining while I get up to grab napkins. One for him…

"Thank you."

And three for me.

As I sit back down, my eyes alight on the painting still 'in progress' and I feel a stab for what else I'm not telling him. I pray he doesn't find a chip thanks to its windblown tumbles during his absence. I too know what it feels like to be chipped away at. I have no defense for my less than stellar boy-choices.

But, it still doesn't explain why Sibling's been acting like the shotgun wielding dad of an errant teen.

"I just don't want you to get hurt," he admits quietly.

"Oh!" It hits me with a 'duh', "I get what this is."

"What?" His eyes are alert.

"Peanut butter in the boots."

Sibling bursts out his signature exuberant 'gafaw' – face crinkling into delighted boyhood recall. Remnants of his six year old self. The six year old that snuck peanut butter into the Kodiak boots of a guy his sixteen year old sister had brought home after school, because he thought the guy wasn't nice enough to share his sister's airspace.

"You forgot the crackers," Sib smirks.

"Right, of course. A nice touch."

"How else was I gonna get the peanut butter all the way into the toe part?"

"Good strategic planning."

Bro's eyes sparkle with memory. A shining moment of delinquent glory in an otherwise 'good kid' childhood. A Peanut Butter Protest that proved prophetic to the Sis teen angst that would follow.

"What I don't get is how you managed to get it in there at all when we were sitting in the living room the whole time and his boots were in plain view by the door." Our two-bedroom condo didn't offer much ground cover.

"I'll never tell." Sib assumes an exaggerated 'covert ops' blankness.

I laugh, delighted.

It occurs to me, not for the first time, that Sib and I have taken turns being 'the dad'. When he was a baby, I'd toss him in the air and catch him as he gurgled baby-laughs – figuring that's what dads did. When he was a kid, I'd take him out on 'Grown Up Nights' – my purse bulging with change for his favorite video arcade downtown on Yonge Street and the promise of popcorn at the blockbuster Hollywood movie. I figured that's what dads did too; expand a kid's horizon – at least fun dads.

"Look," the obnoxious cousin takes a last shot. "It's like that time we stopped the car in the middle of the road in Costa Rica. Remember?"

Sibling glances up from his last few bites with a quizzical 'where is this going' look on his face.

"We were driving around Lake Arenal and all of a sudden there was an endangered species thingy on the shoulder and you stopped."

"What? The Tapir? Or, maybe it was a coati, though I don't think they're endangered. I can't remember."

"Yeah, like I said, the whatchamacallit.

"Okaayyy."

"Well, when you see a cute fuzzy whatchamacallit on the side of the road – a road you may never travel again and you know you're probably never gonna catch sight of one of those again – you don't just keep driving by. You stop to check it out."

Sib raises an eyebrow at the somewhat ridiculous comparison. But, I've long since stopped talking about Sailor. I'm instead attempting to explain my romantic raison d'etre to the long suffering brother who was the ring bearer at my wedding. Not for permission – but understanding. "And in this world, connection is an endangered species."

"Okay," Sib shrugs in weary acquiescence, "whatever makes you happy." He then softens with, "Just be careful, okay? And, know you're in weird territory." He gets up to clear.

The second he gives, the wind goes out of my argu sails.

He's right. One Hundred Percent. And worse, I've allowed myself to get sidetracked. Jeez, the only thing I'm fighting for is a diversion that's just going to knock me off goal. It's like I'm a sugar addict body slamming the guy in front of me for that last donut in a closing out bakery sale. Like I need the carbs.

But, it ain't over. Inner Voice intrudes yet again.

All evidence is to the contrary, I cross arm skeptic.

I'm telling you — it ain't over.
La la la – I can't hear you.

When the dishes are washed and stacked, Sib retreats to the office, which is now doubling as his bedroom, and picks up his guitar. While his Bowie style vocals and homegrown alternative music strains into the apartment through the closed door, I retreat to my own room and think…

Forget Sailor. Forget Trouble. Forget everything except resurrecting my shelved novel in time for November.

Grrrr… no pets, no plants, no personal entanglements.

Sitting up in the new bed – pillow against the wall as a makeshift 'headboard', laptop propped open – I scan the hundred plus pages stored on the back burner of good intentions. Words of romance and myth – an urban fantasy of L.A. glam weddings – and amore's fantastical origin.

Like Scarlett O'Hara covered in earth-dirt clutching that turnip vowing, "As God is my witness – I will never go hungry again." I make my own declaration in reverse – to go on a love diet. A repudiation of all frivolity until 'The End' is the only thing left to write.

Clutching a Bic pen I vow, "As God is my witness – I will never go out again!"

But Panama, with its 'come hither' nightly hot spots giving way to twisty, tangled outskirt roads through a lush green veil, has another type of twist ahead.

10. JUMP!

I'm shakin' it Sheba-chic. Swinging my Haifa-born hips to a Mid East beat beside an ankle-bell-braceletted belly dancer that pulls me in beside her like a harem sister.

Swivel, jingle, shake!

This is Beirut on a Friday night. Well, Beirut the restaurant across the street from The Marriott in the heart of Panama City. Sibling's favorite source of hookah and hummus and the site of yet another 'expat' gathering. One that includes Theo, his girlfriend Mali, a bunch of guys I've only just met… and Sailor.

It's also the scene of my hip-swingy debut behind an imaginary 'seven veils'.

"You've got moves," Sailor says with an insulting streak of surprise as I sit back down beside him.

"Native hips, honey. Native moves." I toss my Mediterranean curls and take another bite of seasoned lamb.

Put that in your hookah pipe and smoke it.

But, my Body Armor is riddled with mortifying dents at Sailor's 'I barely know the red head' body language. Body language I'm doing my best to mimic opposite to the seductive sways of the sequined-bra belly dancer who's now got Sibling in a lock on the makeshift dance floor by our ten-person table.

Sailor induced body language like we're playing charades with gestures that scream: "We did NOT sleep together! See how we avoid touching in any remote way?! Notice how Lila scrapes her chair over to the edge of the table AWAY from Sailor while he leans away from her to talk to his American tourist friend, T-Rick. Does THIS look like two people who even like each other let alone ever lusted for each other?!"

Nuh-uh!

Meanwhile, Theo and Mali sit opposite us canoodling like

two starlets vying for Hollywood red carpet "YES! WE ARE DATING!" tabloid fodder. I steal an envious glance as Theo's hand lands on Mali's thigh while she nestles into the crook of his arm, ensconced in his 'YOU ARE MY HOT SURFER CHICK GIRLFRIEND' pride.

On our side of the table, I accidentally finger brush Sailor's hand as I reach for the Baba Ghanoush and blush furiously like I've broken some anti-co-ed Taliban bylaw.

Sibling sits back down opposite me, taking in the Sis-Sailor interplay with a wary, watchful gaze. I'm worried at any moment he's going to put peanut butter in Sailor's flip flops, but I suppose as long as Sailor keeps them on he's safe from squishy peanut-toes.

Though, Sib is eyeing the hummus like a biological weapon.

I smile at him, but inwardly I'm pleading, 'Please don't say anything!'

Inwardly, I'm also celebrating Dr. V's "Your biopsy is normal" call. The dizzy rush of relief – the marveling that he'd call me directly just to tell me that. It's like having the best boyfriend in the world – only he's feeling up every other hoo hoo in Punta Pacifica.

I'm also semi-celebrating the end of a crazy time with my TV gigs in Canada winding down and while that's scary financially, I'm excited to be gearing up for Sibling's offer of November. Plus, I've just entered my 'good days', so I am hoping for at least ten pain-free sunrise/sunsets.

Woohoo!

Of course, my idea of celebrating was a cozy night fulfilling my Art Nun vow: in bed obscenely early to be up at 6 a.m. to write.

"You can't stay home!" Theo had bristled over the phone as if I was making some diplomatic faux pas on the scale of Iran going nuclear.

"I'm tired." My weariness was a handy disguise for unspoken wariness.

"You're in Panama, you can sleep when you get home!"

"I am home. Home is where I hang my Turtle Wax T."

"Well put it on and get down to Beirut. It's Friday night! We're all going."

'All' included Sailor. This I knew. This I was trying to avoid… until Theo put his secret weapon on the line…

"Please don't make me be the only girl!" Mali wailed.

Arm-twisted by The Girl Code!

Next thing I knew I was trailing Sibling out the door, sporting a black, low cut V-neck/V-back 'social emergency' dress I'd found on Melrose.

And, instead of cozily nestling under the covers with yet another read of *The Da Vinci Code* alternating with Greek Myths courtesy of Robert Graves, and thereby avoiding both reality AND all discomfort except the Gods' revenge on those who try to sneak by fate, I'm supremely uncomfortable sitting beside Sailor, who seems most comfortable pretending there's nothing between us, but air.

"Hey."

"Hey."

Had been our coded greeting – just as Sailor had wanted. Just as I'd dreaded.

A funny thing happens when you try to avoid your destiny, as The Greeks forewarned. It creeps up from behind and smacks you upside the head.

"Why don't you come out on the boat with us tomorrow?" T-Rick is leaning over Sailor towards me flashing a 'bright idea' grin.

"Sorry, what?" I startle-mumble.

Did he just invite…?

"Well, you said you haven't been," T-Rick reasons. "And there's only three clients, so plenty of room."

What a minute… what?!

I goggle down at the lamb as if I'm seeing it for the first time, my brain short circuited by excitement slam dancing into trepidation. The table glows a soft yellowish gold as the requisite tzatziki and famed M.E. dips are passed around to be scooped up with freshly baked pita. It's a Sib style gathering: Canadians, Americans, and three new guys who are either friends of Sailor's or Theo's – I can't quite figure it out – from Brussels and France. Or is it Belgium and France? Or... wait... isn't Brussels *in* Belgium?! Regardless, they're saying 'pass the kebabs' in French. And rounding out the group is Sailor's best friend from air guitar and mall job days, T-Rick. He's leaning past Sailor to flash me a 'c'mon don't be a wimp' grin.

"Uh... how many does the boat sleep?" Looking for an excuse not to go – not to rock Sailor's boat... while desperately wanting to...

"Eight!" T-Rick's grin stays firmly planted on his Towhead surfer meets guy next door face.

"But, how many actual beds?" I ask Sailor, red flag unfurling.

"Four."

"Don't worry," T-Rick gestures a grand 'no problemo' hand in the air, "We'll make sure it's 'ladies first'."

Okay, let me get this straight: I was staying in, my course set for 'snooze sailing', but instead I've lighthoused towards a stranger who's dangling the fulfillment of a seven year dream?

A white sailboat on the Caribbean...

"Well, how do you feel about that?" I gingerly ask Sailor, since it's his boat after all.

"I was just sitting here thinking, 'why didn't I think of that'?" he smiles my way.

But, his pearly whites look a tad forced.

And it sounds more like, "I was just sitting here thinking 'that's a stupider idea than nail flip flops – or worse: lite beer'. I wish T-Rick had kept his mouth shut."

"Look, I'd love to go," I direct-gaze Sailor – trying to guess at his thoughts – only my sotto voiced, "But, I don't want to make you uncomfortable..."

Is met with his, "It's not that complicated," complete with eyeroll tone as he turns back towards T-Rick.

Excuse me?

Mr. 'It's complicated' is tossing out an 'It's not that complicated'?!

Well, let me tell you how complicated it is for me – is what I don't say.

All too soon I'll be mile high flying north of the 49th. And we will never be here again.

Two years after my tumble in front of that Vehicular Homicide Panama City taxi and legendary first Decap mojito in 2007 – all the expat faces have changed. And, while it's true that they all talk about the same thing – not kids, houses, or the mythical 'work/life balance' but the 'just been to x now going to y' itineraries of people who travel to live and live to travel – the people having those conversations revolves. Friendships are forged in the immediacy of 'THIS is the best place in THIS town' shared adventures – while childhood friends 'back home' catch enviable photos on Facebook.

Until, like T-Rick, they succumb and drop by the ex-pat's life. But, it remains just that – a seven day drop by. The hometown crowd is a 'fixed address' familiarity while last year's ex-pats have all scattered to the wind like leaves in a Panama monsoon.

And, I'm next.

All too soon I'll be back in the frozen tundra and a city blanketed in gray like it's auditioning for "Zombiezone V: Undead on Ice". And worse, every other toqued guy with a hockey hard-on will haul out that standard Canuck pick up line, 'cold enough for ya, eh?!'

"C'mon! It's the Caribbean!" T-Rick sounds like he's telling a virgin bungee coward to 'jump'!!!

Standing bridge-edge, a new personal motto shoots up from the subsurface, made no less exciting by its cliché:

GOOD DAYS ARE THE ONES WE MAKE THE MOST OF!

I turn to Sibling out of respect for the fact that he flew me out here.

"Hey brother!" T-Rick zeroes in – playful, "Can sister come out with us tomorrow?"

"Go ahead," Sib shrugs – half smile at having his own Pura Vida 'tude thrown back in his face – half 'I'll have the peanut butter standing by' eyebrow raise.

11. BOUNCING TO EDEN

On the road – the next morning…

"Spanish! Stop! Spanish!!!"

Sailor jumps out of the beater 'San Blas Express' SUV as it screeches over to the shoulder in a daring highway rescue. Wind-whipped by cars rushing by, he dashes around to the back passenger side and tussles with an errant rolled up mattress that's flapping free – one unraveled rope length away from flying out into highway traffic. It would have blown off altogether if the chubster guy from Switzerland hadn't shot his hands out the window and held on like it was the first 'ten' who ever gave him her phone number.

"Okay, Wilhelm, I've got it!" Sailor wrestles the windblown mattress like it's a snapping Alligator and secures it back onto the roof of the SUV, allowing chubster to let go.

Wilhelm, Wilhelm – guy who slightly resembles a cute grown up baby is Wilhelm – pronounced 'Vil-helm'!

"I hope he secures it properly this time." The wiry, white haired Australian with pale blue eyes grumbles. "That's dangerous."

I shoot a glance T-Rick's way in an 'Uncle Disgruntled' alert. T-Rick grins back just short of a wink.

"So, um…" I had blanked on Uncle Disgruntled's moniker as we had departed Panama City post grocery shop pit stop.

"William," he prompted.

"William, sorry. I'm bad with names. Anyway, William," I emphasized his name to cement it in my name-challenged noggin. "How do you know Wilhelm?"

And please be gay! And better still – married homosexuals with matching rings who like to sleep spooning. Is what I don't say.

Please be spooning gays, because from the second I got into the SUV at 8:00 a.m. I knew we were mattress challenged in more ways than one. It was obvious from the rows:

Back row bench seat = Wilhelm squished in beside William who's got his arms pulled into his sides perhaps attempting not to crowd T-Rick on his other side.

Middle row bench seat = pretty, angular, bottle-blond Parisian chick who looks like a human accordion folded into the window seat beside me...

"So, Mimi – how tall are you if you don't mind my asking?"

"1.8 metehrr." To my blank look, she translates, "Seex feet."

Whoa.

"I take it you model?" I say stealing a glance at her Vogueish designer khaki pants, matching safari vest over black T, stylish black army cap with visor and high end Nikon cradled in her lap

"Oui. Mais, only... ow you say... pahrrt time," she demurs in her noticeably French accent. "Also, I do not do rrrunway wohrrk vehrry much – mostly catalogue – steels – dat sohrrt of ting."

Front seats = Driver Ronaldo and a curvaceous late-thirties brunette Brit, who every time she opens her mouth...

"Am I right in assuming it will be a while before we can say, 'are we there yet'?"

... Gives me a hit of Queen Elizabeth II addressing her nation. Whereupon I sit up straighter in my seat and try to ignore the craving for baked scones with Devonshire cream served by a white-gloved butler proffering High Tea.

I'm also trying to ignore the math since it's not three clients – it's four. I'm not the only last minute adventurer on this road trip.

With Alligator Mattress now re-tied into submission on the roof, Sailor scrambles in beside me. I squeeze closer to Mimi only to slide back towards Sailor when I bump her.

"Sorry."

"It eees nutting," Mimi replies offhand, shifting away from me and closer to the window.

Unfortunately, Mimi the Model is not a lesbian. She and Bex are female carbon copies of William and Wilhelm: 'friends who met while travelling'. In typical fashion, the non-locals recognized each other across a crowded tourist trap and huddled in solidarity. Nobody really knows anybody except Sailor and T-Rick who were beach boys when The Beach Boys were singing 'Kokomo'.

"Okay Ronaldo – Spanish." Sailor 'supervises' as Ronaldo drives us off the shoulder and merges back into highway traffic.

"All right!" Clapping and cheers all around for the averted highway pile up.

"Way to go," I turn to Sailor.

"Well, if Wilhelm hadn't caught it in time," he deflects.

"Yeah, nice work, Wilhelm," T-Rick tosses him a kudo.

"I vas joost lucky – I looked out zeh vindow ven it came loose and I…" he mimes his hands shooting out.

"Quick thinking," Sailor nods.

"Yeah, good reflexes," I add.

"Yay, Wilhelm – Woohoo!"

Alligator Mattress is the first moment this posse of interlocked strangers stumbles across something in common – a shared memory.

"And the crowd does the wave," I mock wave and Wilhelm reddens in a shy smile that only enhances his resemblance to an adorable baby food ad.

"Hey, Sailor," Brit Girl asks a few miles later, "there's one crew member, right?"

Oh man. Eight! Eight 'boat people' – zero gays – four beds.

"Yah, Diego's great. He's a Kuna so he's lived in that region all his life. He knows San Blas like the back of his hand."

"And how far now?"

"About a couple of hours, but don't get too comfortable, Bex. You're riding shotgun this one time. No one usually gets to sit there but the Captain."

"Oh well, aye, aye sir," she retorts with just the right sprinkle of sarcasm. "But, I'm here now." She does a mock stretch-out that would be cute – but it combines with her accent to emanate a 'carry on, wankers' Ascot middle finger to us commoners in the cheap seats.

I mentally smile and repeat 'Bex the Brit' a few times to cement her name, sealed with 'Bex the Brit with Wit'.

We're twenty minutes out of Panama City in a beater SUV that looks like it's held together by spare parts and duct tape. And, despite T-Rick's assurance it'll be 'ladies' first', I'm confident it will actually be 'clients first', which leaves even my math challenged brain tapping me on the shoulder with a 'pssssst' sum-up smirk:

You're gonna be Bedless in San Blas.

Nah-uh. There's always Alligator Mattress. More than likely that's gonna be my 'room' for three days. I mean, if Sailor's that possessive of the front passenger seat, I figure the Captain's Cabin is off limits. I'm wondering how to call 'shotgun' on a mattress, when we pass a white billboard with the word: *Disponibles* and a phone number. It's the third one we've passed in the last ten minutes.

"What does Disponibles mean?" I pronounce it 'dis-pon-ibills'.

Sailor bursts out laughing. "Hey, Ronaldo, did you hear what she said?"

"What's so funny?" I ask, but he ignores me to explain in Spanish to the driver how I asked what 'dis-pon-ibills' means.

Ronaldo joins Sailor in the chucklefest.

"What?!"

Sailor turns back to me, "It's pronounced 'disponeeblay'."

"Disponeeblay," I repeat. "Okay, but what does it mean?"

"Available."

"What?"

"It means AVAILABLE."

Oh, I get it – these are billboards waiting for ads.

And, I've just asked the second least available man I know what the word 'available' means. And worse, judging from the 'so your brother lives here?' questions it's become obvious Sailor has alluded to my being some 'sister of a buddy' who decided to tag along at the last minute.

Practically a stowaway.

Double Worse, he's looking endearingly tousled this morning after what was probably only three hours sleep. The hot wind whipped 'road trip' a rural contrast to the urban crawl of last night's migration from Beirut to (finally) The Decapolis!

Only, my tête–à–tête fantasy of a date-with-Sailor was a tad crowded with about a hundred of the most beautiful women within a three country radius. A pageant of Latina twenty-something gorgeousity in teeny dresses and tanned legs – the most stunning of whom seemed to know Sibling.

"Hola!" they greeted him with sparkle smiles and hug/kiss/kiss, while the rest of us stood around like the entourage of a Hollywood actor, whose breakout film just hit a hundred million in domestic box office. I even came face to face with a notorious ex – a year too late to say, "Nice to meet you."

"You're brother's cool," T-Rick grinned, watching Sib chat with a gliteratti trio, who looked like they could be a pop star girlband even if they were tone deaf – just on hottie cred alone.

"Yeah, always has been. Even when he was four." I smiled at the ring of admiration in T-Rick's tone.

He's secure enough in himself to pay another guy a compliment.

"Sib's not a player, though. He has a girlfriend. She's in New York for a few days."

"Be my spy," Giselle had recruited over the phone.
"You don't need a spy, Giselle. My brother is faithful."

And, sure enough, Sibling made his way back to our clique – solo.

"What, you don't introduce us?" Sailor said in a half jokey tone.

"Oh, sorry," Sib did a palms up mea culpa with a sheepish smile.

"C'mon! There was three of them – and three of us!" Sailor indicated the male trio of Sib, T-Rick… and himself.

Dude! I'm standing right here! Is what I didn't say. I mean, I know I told him to tone down his Cuteness Factor, but no need to go overboard!

Sailor might have seen the steam shooting out of my ears, because he mused, "You know, Julisa used to literally turn my head…"

he put hand to chin and turned his head my way to demonstrate, "…and say, 'I'm right here'."

Standing right in front of you.

As Sailor got that Julisa-glazed reminiscey look on his face again, I gave a silent grudging nod of acknowledgment to the hardass girl I've never met who keeps her man's eyes on her.

I, on the other hand, was gaping at Sailor gaping at the local glam contingent. Young women so inherently sexy they could rival Hollywood nighttime soap stars lounging poolside at the Roosevelt Hotel. I was beginning to feel like 'the ugly stepsomething' surrounded by fairy dusted Cinderellas.

But, just as I was standing around the Decap looking for a glass slipper to smash…

"Would you like a drink?"

I turned to find T-Rick solicitous. He's taller than Sailor and quicker to smile friendly.

"I'd love a mojito, thanks."

A few minutes later, I was gratefully clutching that long awaited 'first mojito in two years' and as the syrupy minty liquid-silver hit my tongue…

Why is this guy being so nice?

… floated across my mind.

But, as T-Rick looked my way, I was head swinging to Sailor, who was turned in the other direction staring towards a barely legal blonde Shakira hip swinging to the DJ beat.

"Enjoyed that did you, old man?" shot out of my mouth when we were back outside waiting for the valets to bring The Sib Mobile.

Instantly, I regretted it. Instant remorse. Not because Sailor's eyes widened slightly at the barb – but because I had just diminished myself – not him.

Even worse, I'd broken the cardinal Canadian rule. Second only to maple syrup on pancakes – a national anthem even Thumper from Bambi knows: if you can't say anything nice – don't say anything at all.

Now I'm going to have to sing three O Canada's and genuflect to a Justin Bieber action figure.

A fitting penance.

So caught up in comparing myself to the young 'n' beautiful crowd, I forgot who I really am…

A broke fortysomething gringette whose relationship IQ hovers around 13 – circa puberty.

Damn.

Okay. Fine. But, if envying the young and beautiful – if envying Julisa – makes me spiteful – it's too steep a price.

"Actually," I found Sailor's eyes and geeked out on what I really thought. "You're the most youthful forty-five year old I've ever met."

"Oh yah?"

"Absolutely, it's one of the things I like about you."

I smiled and he returned sincerity in kind…

"Thanks. That's nice."

Making me feel truly Princess Gracious. Though, um… without the walking through minefields part… well, maybe social ones…

"Hahaha… dis-pon-ibills,' Sailor again chuckles whilst I fold my hands into my lap in my best Grace Kelly on the day she married that prince. Only, it's kinda hard to channel Princess-G in a dusty, filled-to-capacity beater SUV squished into the middle row. Not quite the Just the Two of Us yacht fantasy. Particularly when we bouncity bounce off-highway – past the passport check point – past the Kuna territory entry fee border shack – and gear grind up a twisty mountain two-lane strip of road through the overgrown green where my short-skirted bare leg brushes Sailor's boardshorted naked calf.

Shock ripple of want.

Uh-oh… three days of being 'so close and yet so far' is going to be a legs-crossed-in-self-defense… challenge.

11.2

"I take it there's no bridge?" Bex pipes up from the front seat as the SUV pulls up to a river that's suddenly appeared in front of us where the road's supposed to be.

"What – we're swinging across like on a tire swing, or something?" I ask picturing us taking turns in a Tarzan tree-to-tree relay.

"Not exactly," Sailor answers as the SUV lurches forward off the bank.

Oh, you've got to be kidding.

SPLASH!

Yikes! Not kidding!

"Um… the water's rising," I try to downplay the panic, but the strangle-hitch in my voice is a bit of a giveaway.

"Oh, this is nothing," Sailor shrugs. "The water's low today."

But, it's not 'nothing'. It's rushing, rising water – as in the murky kind that drowns all except fish. I'm wedged in the middle of the middle row and there's no way out if we…

"Whoa…!" A wobble too wobbly flickers tension through the crowded vehicle.

"C'mon Ronaldo," Sailor back seat drives.

Ronaldo puts pedal to the metal as mid-river we get mired and slow to 'stuck'…

Vrroooomm… creak… metal grind… VROOOM!!!

"Um… maybe we should open the window wider," I say quietly to Mimi the Model, mentally planning my 'swim out' escape route if we tip – though if we tip over onto Mimi's side…

VRROOOMMM!!!

GRINDING GEARS!!!

REVVVVVV…

My heart is slamming into my chest and I can't help the sharp intake of breath until…

VROOOOMMM… and the SUV gains traction.

It lurches forward in a rumbly trundly muddy race to the opposite bank and rolls up it like an aging wrestler raising fist in triumph.

"Yay! Way to go!" The 'boat people' erupt in applause while I attempt an 'I wasn't scared' shrug. But, I am fighting the clawing claustrophobic desperate urge to clamber out over Mimi the Model, jump out through the window and kiss the ground with a joyful howl of "LAND!"

"And you've done this drive how often?" I ask Sailor as we trundle along, back on some semblance of road through a jungly green as if we're the parade and leafy tree giants line each side of the road to watch the procession.

"Oh about a hundred," he says offhand.

A hundred bounces to Eden – a hundred river crossings. No wonder he's all ruggedly 'whatever' while my hands are now un-Gracefully trembling.

We arrive on the muddy embankment of another river where we scramble out of the SUV and transfer Alligator Mattress, personal effects and all human cargo into a long wooden boat that looks like a wedding feast for termites. Sailor has to help me step into the leaky bottom, my short skirt presenting an exposure issue as I attempt to get into the longboat without flashing my American Apparel boyshort undies.

"You came to the Caribbean dressed like you're going to lunch in L.A.," he grumbles.

Nuh-uh – I'm wearing underwear aren't I?

"Well, I've never been to the Caribbean," I spring to my own defense, "I didn't know there was a dress code."

"I hope you brought a bathing suit at least," he adds as we push off from the muddy embankment.

Hmmmm… why do I have the sinking feeling I'm about to dive into the blue with a guy who'd rather swim naked with a shifty-eyed shark coming off a 'shark rights' hunger strike than have this girl, who already knows where his tan lines are, tagalong on this tour?

"Just tell him not to hit a reef like he did when I was on the boat," was Sibling's parting shot when I left this morning. "I want my sister back in one piece."

11.3

Termite Wedding Longboat slices through the greeny blue – a wave making interloper to silence. We are no longer sardine-squished into the hard top SUV – but decanned into the wild – a micro-ark of two by two tourists. Cutting a wake through a narrow strip waterway verdant with foliaged banks on either side, our invasion of the Beauty Snatchers foray into this isolated region is a cocoon-hush birth canal.

"Vy do I haf zeh feelink I'm in an Indiana Jones movie?" Wilhelm muses, attuned to the eerie similarity.

"Yeah, it does look like the opening to *Raiders of the Lost Ark* when he swims out to the sea plane to escape the natives and their blow darts." I agree.

Jokes ensue about whether or not the Kuna have an affinity for poison arrows, but I feel a shiver of trepidation. We're on their turf – foreign guests – and there's no protocol map.

"Vas it filmed here?" Wilhelm draws us back to Indy swimming for his life – miraculously dodging death blows.

"Might have been Columbia," Sailor says.

"You can check on IMDB," I point out.

"IMDB?"

"Internet Movie Database dot com. It lists all kinds of facts on movies and TV shows – though mostly American ones – but it's really useful for trivia like that."

Even as I'm explaining, I feel my voice fading – as if the mere mention of that world where I work in the entertainment industry and am listed on www.imdb.com with only a handful of my credits and one mistaken nod to my having been an assistant on a horror film I've never even seen let alone worked on – feels like a 'past life' – even a 'faux life'. A pretense put on for money that has zero whatsoever to do with 'real life' and its purpose.

Real Life is this moment – this moving through stillness under a cornflower blue sky – letting my fingers trace wakes in the water – touching warmth where I expected coolness.

I don't recognize it – but this is late October. Late October north of the 49th is bracing – both in terms of cold – and in terms of bracing oneself for the next ice age. October in San Blas is a religious conversion. A rare air stripping out of the 'too humid' heaviness of Panama City into a clean breath in with just the right hint of breeze tingling skin to make heaven feel reachable.

If this is fall in the Caribbean then I just fell.

Again.

And yet again, when the vista opens wide onto the first glimpsed Islands of San Blas – teeming with village huts of Kuna life – and there... glinting white off sunlight... anchored to rise up from the water like a proud sea explorer – showing off her port side curve as if to say 'what'cha ya waitin' for?!' beckons the Oceana Blu.

The sleek symbol of Sailor's wanderlust. His 50 foot open ocean dream machine.

"T-Rick, Diego and I are just gonna load the supplies and get her ready while you guys tour the village," he says. "We'll pick you up in about forty five minutes."

I look up to the hut crowded Island in surprise.

Despite being clustered with Bex, Mimi, William and Wilhelm, I feel jarringly 'castaway' as I'm hauled onto the dock, legs dangling. Sailor and T-Rick are the only two people I know from the city, and without them I feel socially orphaned. As feet touch ground on this remote Island Nation, I insta-morph into a lost explorer from another time – each step leading me deeper down a path to the unknown. A Kuna village path well trodden by locals into a flattened sand-packed golden groove that winds ahead – corners around which I can't yet see.

Are we invited guests? Or Island Crashers?

An intimidating intimacy.

Islands have edges – one step too far and you topple into the drink – hence we're geo-organically herded 'inland' towards the populated center. A straggling group of Euros and one Israeli-Canuck so fair I'm practically incandescent.

Conspicuous.

It's not like landing at Tocumen airport and being encased in the bubble of anonymity – disappearing into the teeming P.C. party. Or, Manhattan where I once spent a week mostly solo until some locals kidnapped me from the Russian Tea Room at 2:00 a.m. and took me down to Avenue A to show me the 'real' New York.

But downtown Kuna town isn't some afterhours string of bars littered with college kids and hardcore urbanites pulling an all nighter. This is being unceremoniously dropped into the hub of an ancient civilization with its own 'Kuna Congreso' tribal government in a too short skirt.

And not knowing what to say. Or worse: how to say it.

"Anyone know if the Kuna speak Spanish? Is it 'hola' here for 'hello' too?"

Shrugs all round.

Profound is the lack of language, as I've discovered in my travels – the 'contraction of personality' – as so much of our intelligence and the impression we make is wrapped up in the words tripping off a familiar tongue. Every word-in-common cut is a punchline missed – an insight unspoken – a compliment withheld. Who am I? Is reduced to a shy smile and shrug of 'no comprenday.'

Only, the wide grin staring up at me from a few feet off the ground is hardly shy. It's eager and excited.

11.4

A little boy, toddler height, about three or four in red shorts – no shirt/no shoes – is goggling up at us as if we're his own personal exotic fish bowl.

He turns and runs out of view, and in just a few steps we reach the curve that takes us smack into the kid-hub he's launched himself into with a turn back towards us and a blindly endearing grin flash of pride as if to say, "I saw them first! They're with me!"

And my heart melts at this pint-size master of ceremonies, who despite being younger and smaller than many of his Island cousins vibrates stage savvy charm.

We share a mutual 'fishbowl' moment as his kid stare matches my adult beam. Recalling my own childhood enthusiasm for making new friends.

The escalating chatter of the kids is a soundwave that draws out a few local women sporting iconic multi-hued leg string tapestries dominated by rich red against russet skin. Upon spotting 'the visitors', they display their famous Kuna Squares. Shots of intense color and cheerful images of parrots and patterns that telegraph 'the tropics'.

They hold up language hands as Bex and Mimi rifle through the squares talking about 'pillow coverings' and 'quilts'.

One hand held up = five. Five American dollars.

Two hands = Ten.

Wait, I recognize this! It's SHOPPING!!!

Yay!

A familiar calming retail haze paints me mellow.

"What do you think of this green one?" Bex holds up a two tone dark green on lighter green design for Mimi's informed fashion punditry.

"C'est belle."

A Hot Sailor, A Cold Margarita, and... Trouble

"I'm thinking Mum would like it. It goes with her new sofa."

Bex and Mimi rifle through square after square intently, comparing options and talking themselves into the practical application of the frivolous.

"I can pehrraaps use dees one as a patch on a jackett," muses Mimi the Model, holding up a more sedate mostly brown pattern: the neutral sophistication a contrasting eye catcher to the explosion of color boasted by most of the other squares.

"Wow, that one's brilliant," enthuses Bex.

Being too broke to do more than 'thatched window shop' I utilize the retail diversion as cover for a quick peek into the nearest hut.

Cool, dark, sparse interior.

Dirt floor.

Two wooden chairs, slung low to the floor to allow feet to stretch out – no ottoman required.

A wooden stand upon which sits…

A TV.

I turn away only to snap my head back in a classic Three Stooges double-take.

A TV?!

Out here in isolationville?

But there it is – the familiar box that was my electronic babysitter growing up. An older model complete with antenna.

I wonder if they get Gilligan's Island.

"Oh, look, this one's lovely!" Bex's 'happy voice' wafts over as she brandishes a dusky dark blue on lighter blue double square.

Two hands shoot up – the local artisan who made it basks in the glow of obvious praise.

I stealth creep down the path and peek into the next hut.

Cool, dark, sparse interior.

Dirt floor.

Two wooden chairs slung low.

TV.

Wow.

And then the next…

Dirt floor, wooden chairs. TV.

Huh.

I stumble onto a picnic table area positioned on the Island's tip, where water laps up and I'm struck by having hit the natural ocean border so quickly. The huts are tightly backed together in a combined 'communal life' meets nuclear family no different than a densely populated urban neighborhood where all the kids spill of out their homes to meet and play in a centralized courtyard. The difference is – these kids can't just hop on a bus to go 'downtown' and be kicked out of the mall for shoplifting.

The lone picnic table sports a twenty-something dread-locked hippie tourist who looks like he's been sitting here frozen in time since the late '60's, strumming a guitar while his pierced, tattooed girlfriend tries to get WiFi on her laptop.

Unique. Remote. An Island Nation unto itself.

"Ten Dollars!"

I turn to the sound of a man yelling. He's holding up plastic laundry bins – the kind you get at Walmart – and he's yelling, "Ten dollars!"

Wow. Who needs Walmart greeters when you can get your plastic laundry bins in downtown Kuna town?

Wilhelm catches up with me and we take refuge from the now blazing midday sun by ducking into a rectangular hut with a counter that doubles as a 'last chance to stock up before open ocean' general store. I gape at the array of drug store essentials on display including bottled water. No need to share a dusty canteen. As I proffer a lone American dollar to the man behind the counter in exchange for some 'all natural spring water' I engage in that time honored ritual of customer to merchant that requires no other language.

"They've discovered money," Sailor had said to explain the transition the locals have made from a coconut based economy to cold hard cash. "I'm not sure that's such a good thing."

But the Kuna nation is straddling a razor thin line between

ancient color string/artisan traditions passed down through generations and a complex new world in which commerce, culture, and electronics unites us all.

And they're smart enough to charge for it.

Though, little do I know that spending that one American dollar will come back to haunt me. Blithely, I unscrew the cap and sip gratefully as we wind our way back up the path the way we came and converge at the dock. Forty five minutes have long since passed and still no sign of Sailor.

"I'm famished," Bex speaks for our collectively empty tummies.

"I think we're having lunch on the boat," I assure as if I'm auditioning for 'perky cruise director'. I stare out at the Oceana Blu's gleaming white deck so tantalizingly close – yet still out of reach.

"Well, I can't wait to get on board and change into a bikini. It's far too hot to be standing around." Bex again speaks for all of us as William paces, looking disgruntled again and Wilhelm shrugs his 'Ja' agreeable 'watchya gonna do' shrug while I officially melt and Mimi stands hand on hip as if she's hit a snag on the catwalk.

"Can you imagine what it would be like to grow up here?" Bex asks no one in particular.

Yep, I can... endless sunny days of palm tree predictable perfection. Swimming, feasting on fresh catch, clowning around whilst surrounded by extended family – never needing to feel alone – always part of a community... it would be so...

"Boring!" Bex pierces my thought bubble.

"What?" I sharp turn her way.

"Imagine being a teenager stuck on this island – how bored you'd be."

Firecrackers go off in my cerebral cortex as I flash to Little Red Shorts MC with his joie de vivre vibrancy and mentally speed up time to see him growing up on this 'it takes a village to raise a child' idyllic hub – only to slam into puberty with a 'get me the F out of here' teen spirit.

Waking up to hard edged 'city limits' made of endless waves.

Will he become the village leader – the class clown? Or, will he be consumed with what lays beyond the horizon? Ships passing hints of what TV confirms – that there is a world of wonder beyond this shore.

The Serpent in Paradise turns out to be boredom.

No wonder Eve was ripe for temptation, "All day long it's coconuts this – coconuts that! Gimme a bite of that Forbidden Fruit already!!!"

Bright girl.

She could envision a couch spud, channel surfing ennui Adam on her hands for the rest of eternity and figured she had to do something drastic or she'd be making coconut pies forever.

The fall of mankind = a more interesting life.

She made the ultimate sacrifice for the entire human race. As our brains expanded to a brave new world – one in which we could think for ourselves – read – write – artify – our skulls also expanded to accommodate ingenuity.

And Eve took the hit.

A painful, death defying childbirth process – the price of human consciousness. You'd think she'd be lauded for it – laurels thrown at her feet – rose petals lining her path...

It's Original Blessing – not Original Sin.

And though 'may you live in interesting times' is an ancient Chinese curse – isn't the striving for better what shapes us? And while Island Village life may be more complex than 'same sea different day', human potential strains against complacency regardless of GPS. Perhaps wanderlust is universal whether you're heading for paradise or hailing from it.

"Bo-oh-ring," Bex mumbles looking out.

"Well," I proffer... "They have TV."

11.5

Termite Wedding Longboat finally pulls up to the dock and as we scramble on board – sunstroked, starving and grumbling towards mutiny – I look back to the Island I've just spent nearly ninety minutes on – the Island some people spend their entire lives on. And until Bex's comment it never occurred to me that the sanctuary I so desperately wished to escape to – would be the exact kind of place someone like me would wish to escape from.

I turn towards the Oceana Blu – rising out of the water like a sleek, white temple to a restless heart. And now, more than ever, setting sail isn't just some quaint adventure – it's a vital salt air, sea breeze, 'give me freedom' deliverance.

PETAL SHOWERS:

Rain drops fall like rose petals on bare skin.

Each petal a soft caress with an afterthorn cold bite – a little nip of shiver-cool followed by the next fallen rose petal. Escalating from caress to stroke to tingly, playful slaps.

I am standing alone on deck – dawn attempting to butt in through the water drop cloud army lining the sky.

Perfect.

In solitude.

On a sailboat surrounded by water above and water below – dotted with tiny Islands of palm tree sparklers.

Paradise.

Glistening wet teeming life.

Pura Vida come to life.

Only, if I thought the bed arrangements were… interesting… last night. The first night.

Night Two on the boat is going to be…

"Bloody hell – I'm drenched!"

"Be cahrrful! Eeets sleepeherry!"

Bex and Mimi the Model race by, chattery cold and giggling at their plight as they scramble below to the cramped galley. Chased away from their sky gazing, top deck 'bedroom' by the SPLASH alarm of SLICK uncompromising rain.

Uh-oh. I stare at the canopy where it starts to drip. Problem.

12. FLASHBACK TO THE DAY BEFORE: SAILOR'S FLOATING FRAT HOUSE

"Help! Lila! LILA!!!"

I stand under the canopy on the bridge deck and turn to the stern, towards Bex's panicked voice. She and Mimi have swum out from the anchored sailboat and I can see them bobbing in the distance. Nestled in a cul-de-sac Island cluster that Sailor has sailed us to – we're now officially not just on the Caribbean – but in it.

See, that's the trouble with water – you can shower in it – surf on it – but you can also…

SPLASH… flail… SPLASH!!!

Drown in it.

"LILA!"

Bex is caught in the current – for every swim stroke she's getting… nowhere. It doesn't help that I could hear this coming. Could hear Bex say to Mimi…

"I'm swimming and swimming, but I'm no closer to the boat!"

To which I responded with a vague sense of foreboding.

But, I was straining against the current myself, stroke after stroke only to remain stationary – even though I was embarrassingly only a few feet from the boat. Finally hauling myself out of the drink, I stood there dripping. Half in this world – half in my own water logged rubbery muscles fog where everything moved in slow motion.

"LILA!!!" Mimi yells out, "GET SAILLOHRRR!!!"

As if some invisible force presses 'fast forward' on my belly-button, reflexes ignite.

"Sailor!"

My wet bare feet slap on the boat deck as I race to the opening and peer out of the sunshine into the dark 'below deck' galley.

"Sailor!!!"

"Yah?" he answers from his 'command center' chair wedged into a corner of the galley – where a computer churns out songs from the playlist he's fiddling with.

Well, at least Bex can sink to a soundtrack.

"What's up?"

"Bex can't swim back to the boat!"

To his 'say what?' face now peering up at me I add, "The current's too strong!"

Already shirtless and boardshorted, Sailor scrambles up the wooden stair-ladder to the bridge deck, smoothly dives off the anchored boat, swims to the dingy, and after scrambling in, he one-paddle rows out to Bex.

"Grab the rope!" He tosses it to her.

Bex clings to the rope, legs kicking as Sailor tows her in almost at home in the water as his Kuna friends. I can't help but flash to Mr. Incredible when he rescues that kitty from the tree.

Soon, it becomes apparent that Sailor in the City is a completely different person than Skipper Sailor.

City Sailor is a charming, easy talker – open about his life. As transparent as clear shallow water revealing a coral reef.

Skipper Sailor is always in motion – a 'rough it and like it' hardass.

"Okay, here's the deal – everybody has to pitch in," he'd said in what I gathered was his customary 'Welcome Aboard The Oceana Blu' – Rules and Regs speech. It was essentially, 'I hereby dub thee crew – now stow your shoes – and if ya wanna eat start cookin'.'

Lunch was made by Bex and yours truly in the cramped galley complete with aghast girly looks at (gasp) the ingredients.

"I don't think I've seen white bread since 1979," I held up a slice like it was an archeological find.

"Too bad I forgot to pack my mood ring," Bex abstained. "Are you sure there isn't a slice of multigrain hiding out?"

I shake my head, 'no'.

Pulling out the cheese and luncheon meat for sandwiches…

"That's not actually bologna, is it?!" Bex shuddered. "Anything to nosh on at least?"

Rifling through the boxed cookies/ assorted refined foods, the light bulb went off:

"Oh, I get it. Frat Boy Food."

"Hmmm." Bex's face – already pinched into a 'white glove test' at the sight of an unwelcome buggy little passenger in 'steerage' (i.e. the galley cupboard) – pinched even pinchier.

"Can I make you something else? An omelet maybe?"

"I don't eat eggs," she sighed like a girl facing three days of accidental dieting.

If Sailor's radar isn't blipping by now – he'd better check his scopes.

Bex's disapproval feels momentous, somehow. As if she outranks even William, despite the fact that he's a) the white-haired wiry oldest and b) most likely to voice complaint – be it about an untied mattress – or the doofus coaches of Manchester United – or the uselessly expensive G8 summit. In a champion vs. challenger to Sailor's 'Captain' cred, Bex feels like The Client – the one that notices everything in the environment – including the fact that Sailor of all people knows this terrain – and didn't warn her about the current.

"I can't believe how strong it was! I was swimming and swimming and getting no closer to the boat... if I'd known, I wouldn't have swum out that far."

"It's not the first time that's happened." Sailor probably thinks he's reassuring Bex that her lack of dolphin skills ain't so uncommon and she shouldn't feel stupid – but it only serves to confirm he should have warned her.

Unlike me, she's not bat-lash swooning at the shirtless hero who rescued her – she's knitting her brows together in an 'it was your fault in the first place' scowl.

Any minute now there's gonna be a low carb mutiny.

Only, unbeknown to any of us, it's Sailor who's gonna jump ship first.

Mimi the Model, with her stretchy arms and mermaid long legs, makes it back to the boat in her own wake. Her nautically themed blue 'n' white striped bikinied shutterbug nonchalance contrasts my borrowed one piece, bedless anxiety.

"We need to figure out the sleeping arrangements." Sailor had convened the bridge deck meeting when we first got on board.

"Mimi and I can share," Bex piped up. "Besides, I'll probably sleep on the top deck."

"Oui, moi aussi," Mimi concurs, "I want to see de stahrrs."

"I suppose Wilhelm and I can alternate," William shrugged to Wilhelm's nod of agreement.

"Okay then, William and Wilhelm front right cabin, that's 'starboard', Bex and Mimi back starboard cabin, T-Rick back port cabin…"

Oh, phew – T-Rick's being assigned his own cabin – so here's the part where he's going to say 'Oh no, ladies first', right?

Silence…

Okay, no problem, he's probably just got something caught in his throat. I quick-glance over to make sure he's not like choking and turning blue, you know, just in case he can't get the words out due to a lethally blocked esophagus.

But nope – skin color normal. Breathing – normal.

So, I turn back towards Sailor, waiting for the words that will any second come out of T-Rick's mouth.

Double Silence.

Okay, in just another 1.5 seconds he's gonna turn to me with white knight aplomb and say what he said last night about it being ladies…

Eerie Silence.

Like tumbleweed on the plain.

12.2

In true actor-missing-cue blankness, T-Rick says zip.

I can practically see him whistling into the wind like a cartoon character intent on 'who me?' diversion. Outwardly I'm calmly looking at Sailor. Inwardly I'm staring daggers at T-Rick in 'et tu?' betrayal.

"And you…" Sailor turns to me "… can share the Captain's Cabin."

"Now that's the offer I've been waiting for all day," I attempt sarcasm, but a reckless hope tilts my voice.

Betrayed again – this time by my own vocal cords.

Wait, did he mean that?

Captain's Cabin queen size bed coziness dances before my eyes complete with the tangled limbs of sea nymph nudity.

Reality to Lila – over – come in, Lila. Do you Roger?

Oh, yeah. Right. 'Secret', remember? I'm incognito as the Platonic Pal – the Mata Hari of dating – a spy in the house of lust. Besides, the only 'morning after walk of shame' I could take on this rig would be to walk the plank overboard.

Keep head above water at all times!

So, I try to make the most of being bedless by acting like I'll be more than comfortable with the wooden slatted bench under the yellow canopied 'bridge deck'. Yep, me and Alligator Mattress. We'll be fine. In fact I prefer it.

Prefer to ignore the drop-kick contrast to my original, screensaver fantasy.

Dreams sometimes come true in unexpected ways – sometimes 'even better than imagined' – sometimes in compromised ways that leave hand still outstretched 'exceeding grasp' – reaching for something as yet unfelt – untasted.

Just be grateful you're even here in this beautiful place.

After stowing my packed clothes, notebook, and latest script to analyze on a strip of floor under the galley table – I climb back up the wooden stairladder.

I mean seriously, platonic is way better – safer – smarter.

I arrive top deck, squinting into the sun.

Three days/two nights/casual pals – piece-a-cake!

OMG! Everybody's naked!

Okay, not exactly 'naked', but to a True North girl used to down coats atop woolen 'layers', seeing shirtless boardshorted men – particularly Sailor – in such close proximity is like the glare of a second sun. Male testosterone eye candy – contrasted by a female fashion show of chic bikinis unlike anything I own (or would be caught dead in without a personal trainer on call 24/7).

"Don't you have a swimsuit?" Bex asked, shock-voiced. "You can't come to the Caribbean without a swimsuit – you'll boil."

Why is everyone so concerned with what I'm wearing!? We're in the middle of nowhere – who cares?!

"This trip was last minute and I didn't get the FAQ," I repeat the oft-repeated phrase I've been repeating since I got into the SUV and discovered the $65 I brought for the agreed upon 'food and gas' didn't factor in the 'to and from' expenses. I had offered to compensate Sailor for the last minute passenger, but the 'buddy's sister I slept with discount' makes me reluctant to coin toss for a cabin of my own – and has to be added to a host of other expenses including the $25 each way for the driver and the toll into Kuna territory courtesy of three local guys standing in a shack by the road at an invisible borderline.

Wedding Termite Longboat isn't free either. Like paying the ferryman at the river Styx, a fare does change hands if I want to get to the other side. And if, like the river Styx, there's an equal return fare then I might not have enough to get further than mid-river – and have to swim the rest of the way.

Or worse. Have to borrow a buck or two from Sailor.

This is my first clue that maybe spending that one American dollar on spring water was a bad idea. It's not the first time I've been mistaken for a rich tourista while pilfering laundry change for lunch money.

Meanwhile, Bex's 'boil' prophecy starts to blister on my skin as I stand on the sundrenched deck with even my normally heatless body thirsty for a cooler outfit – in more ways than one.

"I'll lend you my one-piece," Bex says.

I stare at her. What stranger offers to lend another stranger an article of clothing so intimate as to be only 'sister' material?

"That's really nice of you, but what if you need it later? I can't take –"

"Honestly, I won't. I'll just stay in my bikini. You'll like it – it's brand new and I think the chocolate brown will go well with your red hair and skin tone."

What stranger offers to lend a stranger her BRAND NEW bathing suit?!

I stare at white-glove-test Bex the Brit with new eyes.

"But, the thing is Bex, you've only got what you've got on board, and if you end up needing your spare –"

"I won't. It'll be fine. Oh, and have you got a wrap?"

Dutifully, I follow Bex down below, where she rummages through her things and hands me a powder blue cotton sarong – easily tie-able at the waist and a match to the blue trim on the chocolate brown swimsuit she's handing me.

"I haven't worn a swimsuit in quite a while," I confess.

"Why not?"

"Well, I gained some weight and…" I trail off at Bex's size 14 stuffed into a teeny bikini.

"I wouldn't let that bother me if I were you."

And the thing is – she doesn't. While Mimi models her striped two-piece in catalogue hottie leanness – Bex is working her curves like an earth goddess of worship-worthy proportions in a skinny-girl world.

Plus, impressive taste in swimwear.

I slip on the borrowed suit in the bigger of two bathrooms that both emit an 'onboard outhouse' odor. I'm secretly hoping it won't be wearable and I'll be spared having to parade out there, my own skin showing, but for once in my life – the suit fits. A bit big in the caboose, but Bex's well endowed ampleness is enough of a match to my own that the fabric conforms to my curves. One last look in yet another tiny mirror and I emerge with a slit of cleavage that distracts the eye from the cute-wannabe lesser areas.

Tying the wrap at my waist, I again climb the stairladder to join the others, slightly less panicked than I would be if I were say… facing a firing squad.

Breathe.

Focus on this incredible place – not your Cinderella-challenged insecurities.

But, if this were a movie genre it would be: fish out of water.

And, it doesn't help that Sailor is tanned bare chested, bicep flexing comfort-in-his-own-skin as he steers the big wheel, taking us to an unknown sweet spot. An anchor point deep within the Archipelago de San Blas where the water is so crystal you can see right through translucent turquoise to the sandy/reefy/rock bottom, dipping into it like silk slipping on skin.

There is nothing like a man in his element. And Sailor's 'element' is a searingly beautiful remote region he's a welcome guest in – a welcome he's able to extend to the rest of us, because he emanates a 'what you see is what you get' straight dealing that inspires trust in the locals. A microcosm of this visible in his interaction with Diego – call outs to his scrambling, rope-pulling helper with a familiarity akin more to squabbling relatives than Captain-Underling hierarchy.

No uniformed crew formality here. Rather, Sailor's 'white sailboat on the Caribbean' is a haphazard floating frat house with Bob Marley's 'Three Little Birds' the one regionally fitting track in a mosh pit mix of indie bands and classic pop-rock icons.

I Feel Good! Courtesy of James Brown.

A (loud) white sailboat on the Caribbean.

Yet even this long awaited 'screen-savior' vista fades out in favor of his view as my eyes lock on him like glue sticks.

"It's not polite to stare," Sibling's six-year-old voice wafts back through time. I'd look down to the little swat on my arm he'd laid on to catch my attention and find his alarmed, blue eyes looking up at me. We'd be riding the subway and I'd be doing it again – staring at the people. Wondering about their lives. I'd been doing it since before the age of five – bus, train, bomb shelter in Haifa – staring. Sometimes wondering – sometimes worrying for them when I sensed sorrow – or fear.

Sailor can't know that, of course. My affixed gaze must seem like an intrusion – but I don't fear wonder. And I've never understood people who only notice it in nature – or 'cool' technology – and fail to see it in a human being.

At the helm of his own ship, Sailor is 'commander casual' – a flash of dominant control contrasting an unaffected raw natural aliveness. And for this very 'on duty' reason I can't have him – he's the most wantable I've ever seen him.

Four hours later – he's also AWOL.

12.3

It began with the forgotten garlic and onions.

Somehow Sailor had remembered the Fig Newtons – rationed out to us increasingly hungry buccaneers as the afternoon whiled away and the seven p.m. dinner time Sailor had established drew near. But, the garlic and onions necessary for his fabled 'Fresh Lobster Surprise' had somehow been left in the produce aisle of the grocery store in his pit stop hurry. This was a culinary crisis Sailor could not tolerate.

So, he jumped ship.

Paddling out to another sailboat anchored nearby – a more luxurious longer vessel housing a nicely weathered seafaring couple. Boat Buddy neighbors with a well stocked pantry.

"I can't just go over there and borrow ingredients without saying hello – it's been a while since I've seen them."

And that was the last we saw of his curly head as he rowed 'next door'.

"Okay, O-Blu crew, it's nearly seven," I say what feels like hours later. "Our Captain has mutinied and if we don't start dinner soon it's gonna be nine or ten before we eat. I vote we start cooking and avoid scurvy."

This arouses barely a chuckle as a lethargic bunch of boat layabouts gaze back at me. Except, of course, for Bex.

"I can make a salad," she offers.

We're all crowded onto the bridge deck – sitting three and three on opposite benches. I turn to William who'd previously mentioned some kitchen skills (no doubt vastly superior to my own). "What about you – I thought you had experience cooking."

"Yeah, for four maybe like a normal dinner – not like cooking for a restaurant. I can help out with a meal or two – but I'm not going to be the onboard cook or anything like that."

"Fair enough."

I can't blame the guy for not wanting to be banished down below with a skillet when he's paying for the privilege, but the serrated edge tone suggests I've stepped on his toes for even suggesting it. The 'Uncle Disgruntled' alarm goes off again and I tell myself…

Steer clear.

I turn towards Diego, who's perched near the sails on the top deck just slightly above us, but a) he speaks only 'shrug English', a fact confirmed when he smilingly shooed me away from the post-lunch dirty dishes, mercifully relieving me of KP duty and b) the small two-fish haul he'd caught earlier won't feed the lot of us.

"Well, let's at least have the salad and condiments and whatever else we're making ready so we're good to go when our fearless leader returns."

"Ow about ah pasta – ow you say – side deesh?" Mimi poses.

Wow, the model eats carbs! Is what I don't say.

"Good idea…" I smile instead, and refrain from adding 'Engage' like Captain Jean Luc Picard. I fear, similar to the scurvy reference, all I'll get back is blank stares and maybe one 'nerd alert' chuckle. It's bad enough my TV production background has me trying to organizing everything in a 'supervisor' capacity – because I don't trust myself to actually turn on an element.

"If you want to save your own life," said a male friend watching me in action with a frying pan, "I suggest you marry a fireman." The flash of flame shooting up from the gas stove concurred.

Fortunately, Bex and Mimi take charge of the galley. They chop and stir and whatever else people who know what they're doing with wooden spoons and boiling water do.

"Wow," I say twenty minutes later when I survey Bex's 'salad' – a bowl of ripped up lettuce surrounded by smaller bowls of color-bright vegetables. There's a chopped up tomato bowl, a carrot bowl, even a green pepper bowl.

"Everyone always wants something different – one person likes carrots, the next person prefers peppers."

"Oh I get it, Salad Buffet. Smart."

"This way everyone can have the lettuce base then add whatever other veg they want. It's better than mixing it all together only to have people picking out what they don't want. I've also made an olive oil vinaigrette."

"I can't have vinegar." My face squinches in wrinkly nose recoil.

"See what I mean?" Bex deadpans.

"I can have olive oil and lemon."

"Tell you what, I'll put the dressing…

… and she says the magic words

"… on the side."

I go back up and stand watch on deck like some salty seaman in the crow's nest on the lookout for the nefarious and legendary.

And sure enough what rows back raggedly an hour past the originally appointed 'dinner time' is not the Sailor that left, but…

"They plied me with rum and cokes, and before I knew it, I'd had four!"

He triumphantly holds up the mythical garlic and onions – as though getting drunk was the price of this rare treasure akin to calming an angry mob of anti-prohibitionists guarding a produce stand.

"Um… it's nearly eight and we're kinda hungry," I say as gently as possible – hating playing messenger.

"Well, I had to get the…"

Hell, if I'd known a few hours of Sailor's undivided attention could be bought with a clove of Vampire Repellant and a tear-duct triggering root vegetable – I'd be packin' same.

Sailor enlists Diego as *sous-chef* and the calmly methodical girl-power galley team of Bex and Mimi is replaced with a macho hurricane of sauté chaos. This is set to a soundtrack of rapido Spanish as Sailor barks a few chef-like orders to his nimble one-man crew. The aroma of fresh fish and lobster being pan seared with the hard won garlic and onions nestled in melting butter chimes a dazzling 'taste sensation ahead' that only ratchets up the 'hurry, we're waiting' urgency.

Sailor's cell rings as he stands stove-side guarding his creation like a 'secret recipe' bodyguard.

"Yah, you guys got me drunk right before I had to cook!" He crooks cell to ear as he stirs. "I'm having to sober up here in record time!"

My glue-stick eyes unstick into an extreme eyeroll – so far back in my head I swear I see synapses firing.

Dinner is served in the dark on the now crammed bridge deck as table leaves are opened and we arrange ourselves on opposing bench seats. Bex's colorful veggie mélange of bowls attract Sailor's eye like a laser.

"Let's just put all these vegetables in and toss this thing." Sailor reaches for the peppers, oblivious to his chef-to-chef faux pas.

"No!" Bex steps in like a border guard protecting her turf from some culinary anarchist. "It's Salad Buffet!"

"It's taking up the whole table."

"But this way everyone gets to choose."

"We can all just pick out what we don't want."

"That defeats the whole purpose! This way anyone who doesn't want tomato doesn't have to bother with tomato." She pronounces it Brit-style 'tomah-toe'.

"You say tomay-toe – she says tomah-toe." I mumble, catching the flash of antagonism that often passes for a spark in most romantic comedies.

"Adding is easier than taking away," 'Iron Chef' Bex stands firm. "This way, everybody gets what they want."

"All right, we'll leave it." But, while Sailor's shoulder shrug says 'whatever' his expression says 'sheesh – women and their high maintenance schemes'.

Oh… My… God… Mmmmmmmmmmmmmmmmmmmmm.

Sigh.

It's just one bite. One innocent, unsuspecting bite into a tiny Caribbean Sailor-style lobster… but it melts onto my starving taste buds like holy wine.

I reach for the next bite, hesitating. Teasing myself with anticipation… trying not to shovel it into my mouth surrounded as I am by other intently munching O-Blu crew ravenous as galley slaves… trying to savor… but…

Bite. Bite.

Mmmmmmmmmmmmmmmmm…

Too late.

Too good.

To wait.

Each layer of buttery smooth, garlicy tang, oniony piquancy clamoring for dominance, but blended into one-ness submission, gently coating the cooked to perfection lobster center.

I could have six – I allow myself two. Conscious that as with the Fig Newtons there is a limited supply.

I load up on Bex's 'Salad Buffet', reeling in the greedy, clamoring taste buds in a mouth that's now on a pilgrimage to the next bite of…

Mmmmmmmmmmmmmmmmmmmmm…

He would have to be a great cook. The bastard.

12.4

A half naked Sailor drapes himself along my startled fully clothed yoga pants, Turtle Wax T 'n' hoodie body.

Impish grin.

Eyes finding mine in the last flicker of candlelight – our first moment of privacy – the last thing I expected. He holds my gaze in an unguarded lover-look reunion as if no time has passed – no conflicting agendas – since that first night.

Charmbomb detonating.

Stranger Skipper-Sailor brushed away like a scary chalk algebra equation wiped off a blackboard – replaced with a sonnet. What smiles down at me is the man who first kissed me that night in Bella Vista.

Seeing *him* again steals my breath and comets it towards the star encrusted sky.

"Come visit me," he sweet tones.

And, trailing those three little words Sailor takes his cute boardshorted caboose below, leaving me biting my lip in the cool, damp semi-darkness. Stunned to freeze frame, echo-sensing the imprint of him as I lay stretched out on Alligator Mattress, propped as it is on the slatted bench seat.

Sailor's face now gone, my view is of the bridge deck canopy, but with one peek out from under it, a pure Caribbean midnight draws me to its celestial dance – no city smog hiding the twinkling galactic canopy. As nature intended.

"Come visit me," arcs across my mind like a shooting star.

What do I do now?

Bex and Mimi have retired to their skyview bow deck 'beds', T-Rick and William are cozy in their cabins, Wilhelm and Diego are sandman twins, laid out opposite each other on royal blue cushioned benches separated by the galley 'dining table'.

And Sailor surprisingly keeps a side of the queen sized bed ready and waiting in the Captain's Cabin.

Come visit me…

… sparks an instant moral dilemma akin to shoulder perching 'good angel' vs. 'bad angel'.

Or in my case, Sex Ed Narrator vs. Video Vixen, who pop onto the bridge – 'holodeck' debaters on opposing sides.

"He's ignored you all day," sniffs Sex Ed Narrator, tightening his tie.

"He's been shirtless all day," duh-tones Video Vixen.

"No dating status – no sex. That's the bylaw."

"Yeah, in Dullsville circa 1959."

"Oh very clever, the year before The Pill."

"What's the point of a sexual revolution if you can't actually revolt?"

"Oh well, if you want revolting his breath alone will probably give you alcohol poisoning!"

"He's had plenty of time to sober up." Her eyes glint. "Trust me – he's fully functional."

"But…" sputters Sex Ed Narrator, "there are people all around!"

"Yeah, in Zzzzland!"

"Have you no discipline?!"

"If it's discipline you want – I'll get my paddle."

"Promiscuous wench!"

"Prig Puritan pain in the ass!"

She right hooks Sex Ed Narrator, but he blocks and grabs her arm mid-swing.

They stare.

One angry beat.

Then smoosh together liplocked and flailing as Sex Ed Narrator grabs her extensions and Video Vixen wraps a leg around him, tumbling them both backwards.

SPLASH! Splash!

Leaving me alone with my conflicted emotions.

So casually it's practically in tennis whites, a thought strolls across my mind perfectly reasonable and rational:

What if I were a man?

What if I were a man and an attractive woman had paraded her attributes in a bikini all day in the close confines of a sundrenched schooner parked in paradise – and said bikini-babe draped herself over me as soon as everyone else was asleep and invited me to her cabin what would I...

My feet are halfway down the stairladder before I even finish the thought.

Landing softly in the darkened galley, I pray I don't wake anyone, steeling myself to be extra quiet as I step –

CREAK!

STUMBLE/CRASH!

FREEZE!

Inhaling on ragged breath, I exhale slow to calm hummingbird heartbeat.

Ever so gingerly, I take one more step, then another.

Tiny knock-knock...

Sailor opens up.

Taking my hand, he draws me inward to his lair.

And locks the door.

12.5

He reaches for me.

For the suddenly shy woman standing in front of him unsteady on her feet – unsteady in his gaze.

Floor rocking on lullaby waves.

Swirls of sensuality weaving around us like firefly atoms – whisking away aloofness – evaporating distance in the closeness of the Captain's Cabin – so tight there is but a narrow strip of floor beside the queen size bed. A bed that expands the length and breadth of the room – dominating nearly every square inch – telegraphing 'lay here'.

Beside me.

Under me.

I look up at him, security blanketed in my clothes – the final body armor shred of the already surrendered.

He scrambles upright on the bed – bare feet indenting the mattress as he steps to a square window – a portal in the ceiling that opens to the bow deck above.

He reaches up and pulls it shut – sealing in our sounds.

Wow, he really is battening down the hatches!

My giggle is swallowed by his now legend-in-my-mind kiss – pressing my mouth open to his ardency – inviting me to quench withdrawal-parched lips on the hard liquor taste of him.

Vague slits of light filter in from the Milky Way above the windowed hatch, flickers of moonillumination blotted out by his face hovering over mine. A darkness that heightens touch – kinesthetic taking over where sight fades out. Blurring our edges.

His hand traces my waist to hip curve and slides to inner thigh.

Breath sharps out, stifling the moan.

Enforced silence now an added accomplice to the tensely amplified touch sense – intensifying every caress – even the soft cotton slide of Turtle Wax T being discarded – yoga pants slinking off bare legs until… at last… I am once again naked under the suddenly 'disponeeblay' Sailor, whose own discarded barriers thrill me at every skin-to-skin point of contact.

I missed this… is what I don't say.

But, every cell sparks to sensuous life. Arcing me closer into him as he bends towards a nipple and teases it hard in the soft wetness of his mouth.

Mmmmmm… stifle-moan whispers out.

Languidly our bodies shift to interlock closer, and my hands find his bare back again. Tracing fingers, I 'see' by feel as if his tan has texture – melting me in remnant sun rays. Radiating heat to singe my fingers as they travel down the length of him to what was previously covered up – a taut, tensing white-by-contrast tanline border-crossing to what's been forbidden all day.

Kissing caresses entangle our lips – our limbs – wrapping us around each other like Rodin's The Kiss come to life – what was stone now made soft yielding flesh. Melting into him – blending our breaths – touch tasting closer and closer to…

Snap!

Spotlight!

I can't believe it. Sailor has reached over and turned on the bedside light – revealing us to each other like a too-close couple caught in a spotlight dance – his cocky grin staring down at my 'ixnay on the lightay' shock.

That split second sears in my mind – catching a never before seen full frontal view of Sailor's underlayer rising to break the whitecap surface – breaching the coolfront levees to a pure, rash, unshielded honesty – like an overexposed candid photo of the boy under the man.

And two things flash into my mind…

Oh my God, his boyspirit is sooo beautiful…

…and…

He's drunk.

How else can I explain his lack of concern that his cute caboose is now completely visible to anyone on the bow deck who might have noticed a snapped on light and think to look down through the window hatch to see why?

Sailor's taut back view and the soft thighed white legs squirming under him would tattletale the who/what/where of our tryst like a soap opera gossipy neighbor.

"Turn it off!" I shriek-whisper.

Snap!

Darkness wraps its cloak of secrecy around us again – soothing anxiety – but also curtaining that stripped peek of him – shielding it from my thwarted eyes. Except for one last-second glimpse of his 'lighten up' grin.

This time – I reach for him. Pulling him back into the deep. Resuming trajectory so fluidly it's breathtaking.

Almost instantly we arrive at the moment before.

That moment before when he reaches for his hardness – to enter my wetness.

Whisper-gasp at the pleasure tinged with sharpness.

Wince.

"Am I hurting you?" he whispers in alarm, pulling back.

"Just remember – pretend you're with a virgin."

He chuckles and then slows... ultra gentle... until we're finally sliding into rhythm – rocking our own boat – self induced waves...

...Equator Erotica.

And all at once what is within swirls outward – inner light now glowing to fill the room – circles rippling beyond the walls to envelop...

A white sailboat on the Caribbean.

The Islands of San Blas invisible in the cabin, yet ringing us like ancient harvest Moondance rite swaying pagans.

Enveloped by beauty – emanating beauty.

Transcending the physical to slam into the spiritual – as if Tatania is looking up at Oberon. An Oberon so instinctual in his caress – so intuitive in his sway – he draws me into him in 'onement' so encompassing I am borne aloft to a sense fueled height – catapulted until cheek brushes starlight – even as legs wrap around his penetration – sourcing out sensitive pleasure points so deep I feel like the luckiest girl in the world.

Raising… Rising… ROCKETING!!!

OH My God I'm finally going to…!!!

"I'm going to…" he gasps.

"Yes, I want you to." Only wait…

CRASH!

His wave crests my submissive shore – landing on softness like powdery white sand.

12.6

I lay there still under him, gripped by a tumultuous mix of acute pleasure, vague disappointment, and most inconveniently – fear.

Fear of asking for what I need.

So exposed – passionate strength now delicate vulnerability – my hidden, inner self surfaced in all its raw sensuality. Crumpled clothes strewn about the bed a hint of the tangled emotions playing behind my eyes – masked only by the fading blush of delight still coursing through tingly nerve endings – heatwave now cooling.

He's going to leave me stranded south of the border. Again.

He's not going to ask. And I can't tell.

Too out of my element.

Too defenseless to risk him saying 'no' – or appearing even slightly irritated by the request – or worse – teasing me for it.

Sailor's underlying tenderness is not enough to trust him with my own 'bruise easy' tenderest feelings – not when it competes with a daylight brusqueness.

So, I withdraw the treasure – bury it like a dirty secret. Encase myself slowly, bit by bit, drawing veils around my starkness, mentally pulling away from him even as his legs entangle mine – arms going 'round arms in a post-coital cuddle.

Half sharing his bed – half already out of it.

"You're an incredible lover," I whisper into his ear as I leave The Captain in his cabin. It comes out on a breath of tingling recall – every nerve ending still sparking with the Sailor induced rapture he so deftly evokes in me. Not the 'sweet dreams' I meant to say – instead a celebratory punctuation whoosh of uncensored words. A truth mostly – like focusing on the glass half full... ignoring the empty.

12.7

Gratefully, I sink onto the single bunk bed feel of Alligator Mattress laid atop the wooden bench. The bridge canopy doubles for the grandeur of a canopy bed – the sea breeze drafting in from the open side a natural aircon.

Taking refuge in solitude.

Relieved even as I miss the cozy warmth of the Captain's Cabin – the heavenly expanse of queen sized comfort no match for the peace of…

Separate Bedrooms!

Yay!!!

Relaxing into myself. No longer needing to be 'on' or pretend there isn't something else I want. Languidly reliving the heightened moments – the intoxicating rhythm. If it takes alcohol to make him that choreographically instinctive – then hand me the bottle I'll pour it myself.

I smile in the darkness.

A few moments before restless sleep to Just Be.

At ease… private.

13. ATTACK OF THE CREEPY GHOST SHIP

Bump.
 Rock.
 BUMP.
 SWAY!
 BUMMMP!
 I shoot awake as if out of a cannon.
 CRASH!!!
 O-Blu lurches from the impact, swaying sickeningly.
 Murmured female voices from the bow as Bex and Mimi wake to the jolt.
 Turning towards the direction of the offending hit – my eyes widen at a ghostly elongated sailboat. Silhouetted in the now overcast night – emerging from the mist – lapping waves in its 60 foot ghostly wake – sails drawn in – drifting into attack position to…
 Pirates!
 Is my immediate 'this must be a nightmare because it's 3:00 a.m.' thought.
 BUMP!
 I throw off the inadequate blanket – now hot and shivering at the same time – gripped with fear and instantly conflicted between primal instinct – and 'that's not rational' rationale.
 What would pirates be doing in a cluster of anchored boats? They would have to be the dumbest wannabe Pirates of the Caribbean ever! Real pirates are out at sea where a boat is isolated and easily taken down not in some nautical cul-de-sac. Not here, where neighboring boats could produce an angry mob ready to defend the women and beer.
 But, Ghost Ship didn't get the memo as it plays boat bumper

cars – adrift from its anchor.

I'm about to run and get Sailor when Diego shoots up from below and lightning quick reaches the bow deck to push Ghost Ship away from its impact point.

Only, Diego is slight. It's like watching a windup toy soldier take on a battleship.

A lone ghost on Ghost Ship emerges from his own below deck and tries to help Diego – pushing off the Oceana Blu to gain some distance – but the tide doesn't cooperate and he's towed back towards us.

BUMP!

Two ships that don't pass in the night.

I rush down the stairladder and pad bare feet across the dark galley to Sailor's door.

It's braced open with a bungee chord – revealing the captain sprawled on his back – still bare chested and boardshorted – one leg bent – eyes closed in snooze oblivion.

Hmmmm… it must get stuffy in the cabin, so he sleeps with the door open. Double So, nocturnal loitering of any 'guest' is pretty much impossible.

I shake myself back on mission.

"Sailor!" I whisper, pssst quiet.

Nothing.

"Sailor – wake up!" I ratchet up the volume.

Zip. Not even a toe twitch.

Oh man, this is gonna take physical intervention.

I step into the room, bend over him, administer the shoulder shake.

"SAILOR!"

His eyes fly open.

"There's a boat bumping your boat!"

He scrambles up. Navy training 'this is not a drill' speedy. He's up the ladder before I've even stepped a foot from the doorway.

I follow him above in time to see him waving his arms at Ghost Ship.

"Hey! Spanish, Spanish, Spanish!"

Ghost Guy Spanishes back – replying to Sailor's waved 'road rage' arms with his own palms up 'sorry amigo' arms.

"I know that guy," Sailor shakes his head as Ghost Ship finally clears enough distance to re-anchor safely beyond the Oceana Blu.

"Thanks for waking me," he adds before retreating below – back to bed.

I reclaim my lookout post on Alligator Mattress, shivering both from the damp and fading adrenaline. Not quite the nefarious knaves 'n' thieves attack I feared. Technically, we're unarmed and no match for the truly malevolent. But we are packin' white bread and cookies – so marauding diabetics better watch out.

Shutting my eyes, I attempt sleep as the boat resettles into its rocky wave cradle, but it's no use. I'm wide awake – mist-ified and burrowed under cover to stay warm. Long after all sound has been muted to softly lapping waves, I finally drift off to Zzzzland only to wake early to…

…drip.

14. DAY TWO: CLUELESS IN THE CARIBBEAN

"You look like you're on narcotics," Sailor pronounces me ready for rehab without the excuse of celebrity. Sleep deprived, droopy eyelids glare back at him.

Hey, the only thing that needs 'drying out' around here is Alligator Mattress, which – courtesy of this morning's petal showers – is now soggily uninhabitable – laid out in the hope of catching some rays before nightfall like a Hollywood starlet with a fading tan.

Still, I can't complain. That's the trouble with Paradise – you look truculent if you find fault with it.

San Blas has yielded 24 hours of unparalleled beauty – the blazing day – ethereal moody night – drenched dawn – sun playing hide 'n' seek in and out of clouds now casting dappled beams. Each phase an ongoing drama played out in nature's amphitheater – always something to see – always something to feel on sunsoaked/ rainsplattered skin. Anything but boring.

But, I'd almost prefer a little boredom to the jelly fish sting of Sailor's 'narcotics' comment.

Especially since the entire O-Blu crew is pretty much in earshot top deck, sailing past dotted islands. Once again in Bex's brown one-piece with blue wrap tied at the waist, I'm slouched on the slatted bench as Sailor takes the few steps back to the big wheel having run below and back above deck to turn up the music – which unfortunately drowns out the scenic serenity surrounding us – but doesn't drown out William. He's sitting opposite me still talking Wilhelm's ear off about whatever world/sports issue he thinks needs 'fixing' while Wilhelm continues to nod his agreeable 'ja, ja'.

Mimi the Model is standing nearby on the sail deck statuesque in a red bikini similar to the blue striped one she had on the day before. Bex is lying beside her, her bikini top straps pulled down dangerously close to Euro topless beach burlesque. T-Rick's standing on the bridge deck grinningly putting the pressure on Sailor to get us to a surfing area, which Sailor's resisting, because he has the perfect spot in mind for snorkeling and no one else surfs.

"Is that true?" I indignantly ask T-Rick – trusting him to tell it like it is, but with a degree of tact – unlike narc Sailor who's perfected both his moves undercover and that other type of 'undercover' – the 'nothing between us' special op. A 'hardly know ye' pose intent on captaining us from point A-to-B without a smidgen of 'night before' gossip. But, he's kinda overdoing it.

"Does anyone understand what she's saying?" he'd appealed to whoever was in earshot when I'd attempted some admittedly lame jokey comment. The punny kind he'd instantly get if we were back at the Karaoke joint and I was opposite City Sailor. But, I'm opposite scary Skipper Sailor and floundering on deck, back to being 'fish out of water'.

T-Rick has stepped up as the proverbial 'nice guy best friend' with a surprising ability to notice things – but articulate them diplomatically. I know this, because he attempted to teach me how to surf yesterday.

"You're doing great."

I just wiped out. While lying down on the board.

"It's a tough board," he smiles away my skepticism, infectious with can-do surfer cheeriness, as he helps me roll back onto the board – keeping himself aloft beside me with the graceful arm swish/paddle of a boy born by water.

"It's narrower than a normal board," Dolphin T-Rick explains.

"The pointy front seems to make it harder to keep it upright."

"It's more for pros – more built for speed." He grips the side – steadying the board. "See, you have to actually hold it still with your body – use your stomach muscles."

"That would actually require stomach muscles."

"Everyone has stomach muscles."

"Na-uh."

"Trust me, you have stomach muscles – you just need to learn how to use them."

Well, I'm craving cheesecake. Does that count as 'using stomach muscles'?

"Okay, let's try it again," he says like a dad teaching a kid to ride without training wheels. "I want you to try paddling now."

"I thought surfers were supposed to be laid back," I stall.

"That's a total myth."

"It is?" My mind thrills to peek into a foreign culture.

"That whole surfer 'dude' laid back thing is a complete stereotype. Real surfers are thrill seekers – always in search of a bigger wave – willing to fly to remote places they've never been to before and dive in."

"Adventurous."

"…and driven by the need for bigger and bigger thrills…"

"That Hawaii Five-O big wave…"

"And competition," T-Rick grins. "Not just to surf the biggest wave – but to do it better than anybody else." His surfer pride lights a little go-for-it Olympic flame, "Not laid back at all."

I paddled then – just a few feet before yet another waveless wipeout – but I did appreciate the mind expanding redefinition of 'surfer'.

"Do I look like I'm on narcotics?" I plead now, 24 hours later, turning hooded eyes up to T-Rick from my slouchy bench seat pose.

"No."

I mentally stick my tongue out towards Sailor in na na na na boo boo satisfaction, but then T-Rick steps past and sideswipes with…

"It's just that your eyes are so sensual. I noticed it at the Decap. They're mesmerizing. Like you're making love to a man with your eyes."

You… he… what?!

He disappears below deck.

15. THE HOTTIE LENS

Binoculars pressed to my eyes, I scan the horizon. Anxious.

"I don't see him." Worry seeps out.

"I doubt he'd go out that far if he didn't think he could handle it," Bex murmurs, hand shielding eyes like a visor as she joins me on self-appointed lookout duty.

"Yeah, but he could have misjudged the distance."

I scan again – watching the breaking waves on the distance form white caps – looking for a lone surfer who paddled out of view.

Nothing but water.

No T-Rick.

Now I know why it's such a miracle if anyone lost at sea is spotted.

I don't mean to ramp up the anxiety level, but he's been gone long enough to let my imagination run wild with everything from a shark attack to him accidentally getting hit on the head by the board and slipping under…

Or maybe, I'm just trying to return the favor.

To make sure he's seen.

Because, that's how T-Rick made me feel with that out of the blue compliment, which elicited a giggle burp of "Thanks", instead of the requisite art deco cigarette holder and smoke ring puff of, "Charmed, I'm sure". Or, if that's too retro I could have gone for a more au currant, "Killer cleavage and all you can talk about is my eyes?!"

Nope – none of that – just a gawky giggle burp worthy of a breathless entry in a teen diary.

Embarrassing how much a little compliment can ballast my tank. But, on the night I defined myself as a 'step-something to a hundred Cinderellas' – someone was looking at me with a hottie lens. It makes me wonder how many people dwell on their perceived worst – while someone else is noticing their best. T-Rick has just one upped me in the 'seeing the good in others' department.

Wait.

Damn.

This means the American has out-niced the Canadian.

Was that a rogue wave – or did the earth just tilt on its axis?

"He knows what he's doing," Sailor shrugs off my crossed arm concern when he returns from visiting Creepy Ghost Ship. It's now anchored beside us again in the 'snorkeling' zone. In the light of day it's more of a luxury vessel, owned as it turns out by a relative of Julisa's. He dished the neighborly gossip with Sailor as if this were Wisteria Lane.

Jeez, even out here you can't escape the suburbs.

And perhaps that's exactly what T-Rick was trying to do. Shrug off the same old and find a spot to test drive that sleek board of his on waves he's never laid eyes on before. Not just for the momentary 'thrill' he enthused about, but for something that lasts a lot longer and can be exported back to his own 'burbs: bragging rights.

"He's been surfing since forever – I'm sure he's fine," Sailor insists.

"Then why can't we spot him – even with binoculars?"

"Diego," Sailor calls out and Spanishes him into the row boat, guiding Diego towards the distant waves with the original GPS – a pointed finger.

Still no sign.

By the time T-Rick paddles back my false alarm was starting to look like a real one.

"You're hurt!" Bex zeroes in on T-Rick's abs.

Red scraped raw. Streaks of crimson like he's been in a fight.

"It's just the board friction. Paddling that long…"

"How long?" I grill him – half angry 'older sis' – half awed groupie.

"Forty five minutes there and back."

"Forty five minutes?! Each way?! Plus you surfed in between right?"

"Yeah," T-Rick shrugs, as if being scraped raw paddling through salt water is no more hassle than driving to the liquor store for a six pack.

And speaking of which…

"T-Rick, you've got a six pack!" Bex wide-eyes the scrapes on his abs like she's seeing him for the first time.

"Oh, I think it's more of a three pack," he flushes modest.

"No, it's at least four and a half – five even," I assure him, staring at the ripples on his now neon glowing abs.

How did I not notice how utterly hot he is? How could I have missed what is now oh-so-obvious?

I glance over at Sailor, now back at the big wheel.

That's how.

The 'scallywag' moody moon of Sailor eclipsed the good guy sun of T-Rick.

These American beach boys are gonna be the end of me.

"Lila, have you been putting on sunscreen?" T-Rick asks, a tad suspicious, like he already knows I'm guilty of epidermal neglect.

I scrape glue-stick eyes away from Sailor at the wheel (is that the sound of my retinas ripping?) and come to rest on T-Rick sitting opposite me on the bench, oblivious to his own war wounds.

"I think you need some," he insists, concerned. "You're starting to burn."

I blink at his sun, looking directly into it with invisible opera glasses that finally spot a near-extinct species I haven't seen in a very long time.

BOYFRIEND MATERIAL.

Flashforward to Midnight...

I'm lying beside him, though I swore I wouldn't.
His hand is on my shoulder...
Instinctually comforting the tear streaked girl beside him. Gentle... careful... restrained. Yet, one lit fuse away from igniting to flame.
And all it would take is my turning into his arms – face pressed into his hard chest.
Then looking up to find his eyes in the darkened cabin and murmur 'thanks', only to bring lips too close...
Would mine press to his first – or his to mine?
Don't do it – don't turn!
His hand is on my shoulder...

Back to now...

Still on the bridge deck, tilting my head slightly to the left – eyes still on the newly returned T-Rick as he leans back in the bench seat rehydrating with gulps of water – I sharpen my view. Not of the ethereal vista surrounding the O-Blu with turquoise glasswater lapping out from our anchor point to waterwind its way around idyllic micro gold strip shorelines of Island after Island before escaping the San Blas 'hood and flowing to a deeper, bluing sea. Not of the expansive sky that suspensefully flits between brilliant cornflower blue and grayish overcast. But, rather, of something near extinct I confirm upon closer examination.

Yep, affirmative...

BOYFRIEND MATERIAL.

The hot AND sweet allure of the outwardly sexy and inherently kind. It's not that I'm picking out china patterns, but I can look can't I?!

Of course, wherever the near extinct BOYFRIEND MATERIALREXASAURUS appears he is usually accompanied by...

"Next time ya gotta bring Alicia," Sailor calls out to T-Rick, who nods agreement. "She'll love this."

Alicia. That can only be...

"Is that your girlfriend?" The squeaky tilt of surprise in my voice raises it an octave north of Minnie Mouse.

"Oh... uh... yeah," T-Rick smiles a blank smile. He would seriously rock at strip poker.

I, on the other hand, have alert raised eyebrows wiping out any last remnant of sleep deprived 'narcotics-eyes'.

Um... you could have mentioned...

None of your business, Li.

Okay, I know it's not a prerequisite that all co-eds on a three day boat trip should tattoo their single or marital status on their foreheads – but a hint wouldn't hurt! Like I need the stab of guilt for my thoughts. If I'd known in advance I could have at least imagined him in a fat suit or something…

"How long have you guys been going out?"

"A couple of months."

Oh, so new enough for 'what am I getting myself into' doubts. Maybe that's why he didn't –

None. Of. Your. Business!

"How did you meet?"

"We kept running into each other on and off over the years – same crowd kind of thing."

Okay, Lila you can stop interrogating now…

"That's nice, but how did you actually meet?"

My tone is pleasant, curious – but it's like he's a prime suspect in a police investigation that just avoided answering a direct question and I'm wondering where I can get a lamp to shine in his face.

"Well…"

15.2

Afternoon is giving way to evening. The rockabye lap of waves and humid rain threat of San Blas lulls me into a perpetual hammock. One with a still stunning view of the closest Island with its inviting, private micro-beach from which William, Wilhelm and Mimi now watch us – having snorkeled out for the reverse view of the O-Blu framed by ocean.

I envy them land – not trusting myself to swim out that far and back – feeling weak from sleep deprivation – and not the most athletic at the best of times.

"Sometimes you joost have to jump in," Wilhelm had thrown my way as he and Mimi treaded water waiting for me to pluck up the courage to leap off the stern in flippers.

I stood frozen for some inexplicable reason – inwardly eye rolling at the irony of neutral 'go with the flow' Swissbaby telling the girl with a Ph.D. in 'impulsiveness' to take a flying leap.

Instead, I eased into the water for a quick dip into the warm silk – barely a Carib baptismal – before crawling back on board and drying off. Restlessly in search of comfort, I settled instead for folding the damp towel onto the bench seat and resuming my slouchy lounge pose – stomach ever so slightly lurching at yet another tilt.

Steady girl.

But, now I know what they mean by 'sealegs'. Legs that constantly adjust as if on a perpetual surfboard. The wobble, sway, wobble that is boat livin' is slowly unbalancing what little equilibrium I brought on board.

Someone jumps off the stern to snorkel.

The boat rocks.

Someone climbs back in the boat to slather on sunscreen.

The boat rocks.

And now I'm about to rock the boat too.

"I'm afraid it's gonna rain again."

"Maybe," Sailor says, eyeing dark clouds gathering from the top deck, still in his shirtless, boardshort 'uniform'.

"We're going to have a severe bed shortage if it does."

"I wouldn't worry about it."

There is a power vacuum on this glorified raft – one in which Sailor seems a bit oblivious to the logistical discomfort – a leadership step one ladder rung too high for him to step up. Clearly, his 'normal' is my 'roughing it'. And if there's one thing I tend to step into like a hapless park pedestrian stepping into unscooped doggy deposits – it's a power vacuum.

"Three people slept top deck last night. There's no way anyone will be able to tonight if—"

"We'll sort it out."

Really? How?

This morning's rain splattered the bench 'beds' on either side of the bridge deck through the open sides of the canopy. There goes my coveted Separate Bedroom. Not to mention that while the Mimi and Bex girl power duo might be willing to share a cabin all night – I fear William will get violent if Wilhelm so much as eyes his pillow. They've been sleeping in shifts with the elder 'world authority on all things' William taking the night – and babyface 'peace out' Wilhelm sleeping on the long galley table bench seat opposite Diego's bench then crawling into the 'real' bed early morning as William vacates their 'shared' cabin.

"You're not the one who's gonna have to sleep on a soggy mattress."

"You can have my cabin," Sailor white flags with a 'whiner alert' tinge.

"I don't think that's such a good idea," I knee-jerk martyr.

"Why not?"

Why not?

Because my ears are flinching from the crack…

…crackle…

…CRACK of eggshells I'm walking on.

"I just don't think it's a good idea."

"I don't see why not."

Well, 'cuz… 'last night' looms between us like a question mark. While I feel like running through a field of daisies in a flower print dress, you've been radiating 'I shouldn'ta done that' ALL DAY.

One glance in the galley and your returned smile felt like the strained effort of an American diplomat bumping into his Russian counterpart in the lobby of the U.N. during the Cold War.

One quick 'that night in Bella Vista' banter about your rum 'n' cokes vs. my half a margarita before the talk is shut down like a clandestine aborted mission when the subtext becomes too obvious to anyone on deck.

My look would say 'the night before' was transcendent – even meaningful.

Yours says 'I was drunk.'

And you're killing my buzz.

"Diego!" Sailor spots an issue, "Spanish!"

Diego sprints over to address it and Sailor joins him to 'supervise'.

Okay, Yeah, I get you're 'at work'.

"Spanish! Spanish" Sailor's gesturing while Diego checks the anchor line.

And you're not a complete Queeg. You did lend me your laptop to sign onto Facebook – sprawled on your bed in a parody of your own Facebook engrossed sprawl – to email a 'don't worry, we haven't sunk yet' message to Sib.

"I don't see why you can't just accept the offer," Sailor circles back.

Sigh.

Because, for all your half naked Captain 'uniform' you're wearing 'back off' aloofness like a stuffed shirt. And if 'visiting' your cabin results in this level of code red awkwardness the Morning After – I don't want to know what taking your cabin will do.

Fantasy Island is quickly unraveling into Gilligan's Island as I've marooned myself way outside anything resembling a comfort zone.

"Thanks, it's okay. I'll figure it out."

"Okay, but I can sleep anywhere," Sailor insists. "I'm used to it."

I fix him an 'oh really?' look.

"Well, not 'anywhere', but I don't care about a little rain."

"Just what we need; for the guy driving the boat to get no sleep, so he can be tired at the wheel the next day and hit a reef like you did when my brother was on board."

T-Rick grins, "You hit a reef?"

"It was just that one time," Sailor retorts sourly.

Visiting hours are over!

15.3

Ominous clouds move in, bathing the blue with gray...

"You can share my cabin," T-Rick says out of left field from the opposing bench after yet another of my Cassandra 'it shalt rain and we shalt perish' anxiety attacks. One that interrupted the 'why Grolsch beer is better than Heineken' boy debate raging on the bridge deck.

"You're welcome to join me," T-Rick adds genially. "There's plenty of room."

I look at him like he just copped to breeding unicorns for a living.

Mimi, William and Wilhelm swim in from their private Island postcard back to the boat...

Rock, sway, rock.

... and clamor onboard from the stern, until most of us are crammed on the bridge deck benches. The boat swells with blithely carefree touristas.

Crowded.

The swimmers dry off as Sailor goes below to fiddle with the playlist again. Mimi follows him – her only concern being DJ input.

"Sorry, what?" I make sure I heard T-Rick right.

"You can share my cabin."

Well, it's not quite 'ladies first', but it's tempting.

"Sailor! Sailor! Sailor!" Bex has taken to tripling his name every time she calls him. She claims it reminds her of a song, but I suspect she's countering his lackadaisicalness with a hyped urgency over all things large and small.

"Yah?" he calls up from below.

"You've got guests!"

They paddle in alongside the O-Blu and hover.

Swish, paddle, swish.

Two shorter 'cousins' to Termite Wedding Longboat. More like Termite Bat Mitsvah boats. Captained by smiling, welcoming Kuna women selling more Kuna Squares, though Diego's wife has the inside edge as he's displayed her handmade offerings on the galley table. They stand apart with a distinctly good design sense and I wonder what life is like for him at home with an artisan wife and baby son.

A teen Kuna girl leans up to hand Sailor her cell and he takes it below to charge.

Teenagers and cell phones are indivisible even here. Is that progress? Or a sign of the apocalypse?

What is now obviously ancient is the sealegs the Kuna are born with. These locals are far beyond the main Island we first landed on. The hard edged 'city limits' I naively imagined – turn out to be merely launch pads to a fleet of Island hopping navigators, who seem just at ease bobbing on a vast sea laced with hundreds of islands as I would be weaving in and out of Hollywood traffic on the 10. And while it was men who guarded the borderline into Kuna territory – it's women who are the ambassadors.

"Ass anyone zeen my top?!"

Mimi re-emerges on deck only to find her blue bikini bottom suspiciously solo. Drying where she left it on a railing sans the top, which appears to have gone overboard.

"Merde!"

Bex jumps to her aid, scanning the surrounding water. And while T-Rick, Wilhelm and I help search, it's no use. Mimi's bikini top is fish food.

Not quite the Bermuda triangle of disappearing ships – but there are other triangles brewing.

"No, thanks," I smile T-Rick's way, declining the close confines of his shared bed – however comfy. "I appreciate the offer, but I'll be fine."

"Honestly, I don't mind."

"That's really nice of you."

Keep your secret weapon abs behind the yellow line.

"But, I'll figure something out."

"Well, if you change your mind – the door's open."

His good guy smile chisels my ice. I try to gauge the intent in that smile. Is he rescuing a damsel from distress? Or is this a 'party for two' proposition? A last grasp at bachelorhood before he settles down with New Girlfriend? But, I pick up no subterfuge – no inappropriate agenda – just the proverbial 'nice guy' once again being... well... nice. It's something I would do – offer without thought to implications. Still, I think we may be taking this co-ed crew thing a little too far.

"Thanks, hopefully it won't come to that..."

AKA: No way in hell, Stealth Hottie!

"It's no problem if it does." He radiates 'white hat'.

15.4

"I'm beginning to feel like I'm on a floating commune," I muse aloud shortly after from my bench seat opposite T-Rick, William and Wilhelm. They're lined up like a haphazard rock band minus the guitars.

"A floating commune?" T-Rick echoes.

"Yeah, all of us living in such close quarters like this. It's very… Woodstock. I feel a sudden urge to braid the girls' hair, give free massages to the men –"

"I'll sign up for that," T-Rick starts in.

"Ja, me too."

"Crikey, if you're offering."

I'm three for three with the shirtless T-Rick, Wilhelm and William proving my point.

"Let's just be clear that when I say 'massage' I mean in the massage clinic sense – and not the massage parlor sense. Big difference."

"Yeah, of course," T-Rick does a mock serious throat clear 'ahem'. "We knew that."

As The Doors warble through the speakers, I return to my musings.

"All we need is some tambourines and we can start singing from the musical Hair." My own curls have already puffed up with the humidity in a 'curls gone wild' spiral upon spiral. "I might even go topless if this floating commune thing keeps up. It's Woodstock on water."

Light My Fire – Jim Morrison concurs from the grave.

"Well, we're not wearing shirts, so please feel free," T-Rick grins.

"Because, it's all about equality, right?" I grin back.

"Absolutely, equal opportunity nudity."

Let the sunshine in.

I take in the trio of no shirt/no shoes *caballeros* for a moment, trying to see with T-Rick's positive lens. The way he tunes into each person onboard and tries to be helpful if he senses a need – not just in my case – but for all. The way he gets along with everybody.

Well, here goes.

"William?"

"Yeah."

"Do you find in your work you're constantly having to troubleshoot and respond to problems?"

He grunts a "Duh".

"So, you're always having to fix things?"

"24/7."

Well, that explains a lot. I smile at him then with an understanding I've been withholding in favor of judgment. He's a 'fixer' and the very armchair critic thing that's been putting me off – is the very skill he needs to do what he does. Wiry, and lean, he's in remarkable shape for a guy whose hair has grown snow-cap white – his pale blues keen and watchful. They may lack warmth, but they spot the iceberg in a wider world. He wants to be useful – and there's always a need for a good lookout.

Wilhelm's peepers on the other hand are large and open. Wide-eyed where William's narrow – optimistic where William seems cynical – as though he's still a baby faced kid in a world of wonder though he's pushing thirty. His direct gaze startles me as his eyes catch the straining rays of sunlight peeking through the clouds. They match the waterline where turquoise turns to azure and then a darkened near navy blue. Easy to underestimate with his teddy bear belly amiability, he listens more than he talks.

Which means he knows more than he tells.

"Are you going to keep traveling, Wilhelm?" I later ask.

"Ja. But, I vill go home for Christmas."

"Oh, is that a special time in your family?"

"Ja. Vee all go to my parents'."

His waterline blues sparkle with anticipation.

"So, are you an uncle already, with nieces and nephews?"
"Ja. Two nieces von nephew."
"Do you want kids too?"
"Ja, von day."
"So, family is important to you."
"Ja. It is vat is most important in life, no? It's nice to travel, but nicer to go home."
"Especially at Christmas."
"Ja."

All of a sudden Wilhelm manages to be both grown up wise and plush toy kid sweet. Or is that one and the same?

In a place so beautiful, it becomes easy to see the beauty in everyone.

Especially if you're staring.

On cue, my curls toss towards Sailor, still leaning over the rail talking to the Kuna teen girl. She's paddling in place – expertly keeping her canoe-like boat alongside the mammoth in comparison O-Blu. He's animated – talking with his hands as much as his voice – making her laugh.

It hits me then that this is Sailor's 'hood 'n' home – and how hard it would be to have to open up your home to strangers to keep… well… afloat. I'm guessing he didn't factor that in when he worked for ten years to get this rig. I know he didn't factor in his wife meeting another guy across a crowded marina.

Now, the only 'ball and chain' in Sailorworld is a gorgeous on the outside 50' gas guzzler that specializes in high maintenance.

Sailor waves bye to the teen girl, who paddles away to whatever Island she calls home. He takes a seat on the slatted bench where a political debate ensues in which he reveals himself well informed and slightly more left leaning than I imagined. He then proceeds to entertain T-Rick and the boys with Tall Tales. That bar in South Africa where he ran into a posse of unfriendly locals and had to talk his way out of getting his ass kicked, that accident that landed him in a remote Panama hospital where he coulda died, but instead got patched up for $50 bucks, that time he was sailing to Mexico and ran afoul of an overzealous coast guard in the dark.

This is Sailor's 'buried treasure' – the travelogue of his life he hopes to one day put in a book. Only being here living it takes up so much time, he can never quite finish enough to get there. When Diego asks him something he scrambles off the bench – back to Captain duty.

Seemingly most comfortable when in motion.

Once done, he stops to talk to Mimi for a moment as she stands by the sails – modeling her remaining intact two piece – the red striped bikini. Mimi, who despite emerging as a more introspective, music loving shutterbug than the vapid long leggy catwalking stereotype – remains our resident starlet.

Only, at this moment I don't envy Mimi her figure. Okay, maybe just a little. But, even more, I envy the curvaceous Bex her immunity to the onboard testosterone.

I look away from Sailor, but am drawn to look back by some invisible tractor beam, only to catch his curly head turn towards mine. I look away again quickly – caught sightstalking.

So close.

In this tight space.

So… male.

In this unspoiled place.

Slightly more tough – a little more wild.

A roughness that is at once disconcerting – and tilting just enough to seductive to make me squirm.

And in this conflict between 'he fascinates me' and 'he's prickly like a porcupine' – I withdraw into myself again.

The doctrine of 'advanced civilization': be cool.

A 'don't let it show' barricading of oneself behind the façade of 'couldn't care less'.

Only 'cool' is also synonymous with 'cold'.

While here – my emotions run hot.

And what irks me most – is that it shows.

Yet, the more I bury desire – the more it intensifies.

Bubbling to the surface like lava.

Like the Arenal volcano. Rising up deceptively immobile – a black cone of ancient stillness as though God was in a darkly introspective mood the day he crafted it.

Motionless.

Profound.

The Buddha of mountains.

But, for miles around its internal explosions rumble.

"I think we'd better start dinner," Bex passes my line of sight and down the stairladder to the galley. She starts chopping vegetables for her now famous Salad Buffet only to be joined by Sailor…

"Seriously, I don't understand why we can't just toss –"

"You can help chop or you can leave this galley."

"It's my galley."

"Yes, but I've got the knife."

And they're at it again.

16. MOONLIGHTING

"You guys are like a buddy movie where the protagonists are also each other's antagonists," I typecast Sailor and Bex over dinner by moonlight. "Like Lethal Weapon."

The O-Blu crew is gathered around the fold up table on the bridge deck for our own profane 'last supper'. A meal in which the menu may be a simple seafood/salad sequel – but what's also being served up is camaraderie – increasing layers of 'getting to know you'.

"I'm curious, Bex, what is it you do?" Sailor had leaned in towards her the night before at our late lobster dinner, finally playing host and zeroing in on the most discerning client.

"I'm a translator," she had answered like she worked for the Queen, candlelight flickers making her face look even more 'don't mess with the best' VIP.

"Really? How many languages do you speak?"

"Several."

I told myself he was just being a good Captain, but the subtext was something else. Bex posed a challenge – and Sailor was warming to that challenge. Coaxing her out of her Brit accented aloof shell, though she didn't make it easy for him.

"Okay, but which ones?"

"French, German…"

"That's impressive."

"Not really, many people in Europe speak multiple languages."

I wondered how she could be so impervious to the very same attributes that render me weak. Drawing him in – by forcing him to draw her out.

"Espanõl?"

"A smattering – I'm just learning that one," she modested.

"Spanish, Spanish?" Sailor hit her with a few choice words.

"Spanish in your Spanish," Bex lobbied back.

"That's pretty impressive for someone who's just learning. But, I suppose knowing a lot of other languages helps. Like for me growing up with Italian and now Spanish…"

"Well, and English. If you learn more than one language before the age of five…"

And they're off. He's found her soft spot. Grammar. Multilingual grammar.

And…

"It's not always easy living an international life. I have to have a mobile profession," Bex admits.

"Is that why you're a translator?"

"Yes, Skype – Internet – makes it possible to live in St. Martens."

"But, where's home?"

"That's a little more complicated," she smiles. "Where's yours?"

"You're sailing on it."

I see the moment Sailor breaks the ice. The moment she warms up from 'this guy is not on my radar' to 'this guy is interesting'.

Not that 'true love' is about to ensue. But, that she's no longer a hostile.

"Lethal Weapon?" Bex brings me back to the present.

"Yes. Opposites who snipe at each other but are forced to work together for the greater good."

"Are you saying I resemble a rather tall black man?" Bex critiques my casting.

"Yah, not so sure I wanna be compared to Mel Gibson," Sailor also thumbs-down while reaching for some tomatoes for his salad.

"Not DUI raving lunatic Mel – but the character he plays in the first Lethal Weapon. The rule breaker."

"I can see that," Bex smiles wryly at Sailor and I follow her gaze to see the resemblance even more sharply.

Mimi, on the other hand, stands up for Bex's right to be the female lead, "Ow about Moonlighting, no? Rremembehrr dat show?"

"Cybill Shepherd and Bruce Willis. Yeah, that fits too," I

grudgingly agree, chafing a bit at the romantic connotation even though I brought it up. Ahem, there's a reason I said '*buddy* movie', okay?

"Remington Steele!" Someone calls out like we're in some romcom smackdown.

"Pierce Brosnan and Stephanie Zimbalist." I nod and the die is cast – Sailor and Bex are box office gold.

The onboard romance if only in the phantom movie sense.

"Boris and Natasha," T-Rick grins, unwittingly twisting the knife.

My volcano rumbles.

16.2

"I need to sleeeeep…"

Sailor baby whines up at me from his prone position flat on his back. His cabin is dark – lights out. The door's open and he's only just climbed into bed.

I'm standing beside him like a cat burglar caught mid-burgle on the way to the family jewels.

"Uh…"

Bed Girl Stalking.

"I just…"

Awwwkward.

"I just wanted to say good night." The whisper sounds more like a hiss.

"What?"

Oh for freakn' cryin'outloud!

I lean down closer, fierce whisper countering the soft words…

"Sweet dreams!" said unsweetly.

"Close the door," he growls.

I yank the door handle – only it yanks back – plunging me into an impromptu tug of war with the bungee cord that I now realize is holding it open – and the cord is winning.

How I ended up here is a casebook study in how not to play 'hard to get'. The anti-femme-fatale guide book.

I was fine.

Really.

The O-Blu crew had dispersed to their cabins or makeshift beds – with Bex taking the opposite bridge bench to my 'separate bedroom' of last night and Mimi rolling the dice on the clouds to vacate her cabin for the bow deck and sleep under the stars alongside Wilhelm, who might have scored a midnight kiss, but for Mimi's boyfriend 'back home'.

I was propped up on the half bench at the galley table. Enjoying my martyrdom.

Diego had graciously gestured to his long bench, but I shook my head, 'no thanks'.

Martyr Rule 1: refuse the first offer of help…

Rule 2: refuse the second offer of help…

Rule 3 (you get the idea).

But, I couldn't deprive the lone, hard working, real crew member his spot of comfort for the night.

And the long bench opposite him would soon be occupied by Wilhelm – whilst Mimi would seek the shelter of her cabin. Of this I was certain having found a new career as a weather vane.

So, I capped my volcano, with its alternate rumbles of desire and sliver of miffed girl-hurt, and set up camp on the short half-bench of the galley table within tickling distance of Diego's feet.

Well this is cozy.

I fluffed my pillow with a couple of good punches and leaned back to its yielding fabric.

See? Not so bad after all.

But, I could still feel the hardness of the bench – feel the wood under the royal blue padding.

I fluffed my pillow again…

Punch… shake… punch.

And leaned back one more time.

Sigh. I FLUFFED…

Thinking about seduction… watching Sailor and Bex interact – the final admittance – that I never will be that femme fatale disappearing into a wall with a dismissive 'goodbye you stupid good lookings' complete with fake Russian spy accent as the volcano island explodes.

Too incapable of withholding affection for one who affects me.

A full on love nerd.

How big a nerd?

Musicals big.

I would buy Gene Kelly's house in Beverly Hills if I could

A Hot Sailor, A Cold Margarita, and... Trouble

afford it big. I geek out on the fact that Singing in the Rain and Bandwagon were written by the same screenwriting duo, Comden and Green, which means they worked with both Kelly and Fred Astaire big. I work my ass off when in production by telling myself if Fred Astaire could rehearse like a tap junkie just to make a little dance number on screen look effortless then I sure as hell can order dinner and keep working big.

Corrupted by the musical at an early age.

And this would be the Act End Tango.

Sailor may have leaned in for that first kiss, but it only sparked the pull close – push away – dance that followed. The idea that romance draws us in – is not as powerful as how much having it withheld does.

I might have drifted off while sitting up, silently humming *On My Own*, and fantasizing about one day winning the mirror ball trophy...

But, then Sailor walked into view. Exiting his cabin to get a glass of water before bed, his back to me as he stood at the sink silhouetted in the darkness – half visible – half shadow. And once done, he moved away from the sink, saw me bundled in my little corner – then turned on his heel and walked back to his cabin with a little hand wave.

And the volcano erupted – not in passion – not even in anger – but in scandal at the breach of propriety – the fundamental unforgivable faux pas of bad manners. Rising up from the Britmonarchy protocol (we got da Queen on our ka-ching) upbringing of a Canadian immigrant. The ire of the Politeness Police spotting a major infraction.

He didn't say good night!

Weeehooo, weeehooo – the sirens flash on.

I leap off the half-bench – a civility superhero flying into the night.

An etiquette vigilante.

Only, instead of floating gracefully into a smooth landing, I debalance at a minute tilt of wave that pitches me forward and I have to grab the back of the long bench to steady myself.

Not to mention the landmine BANG as I walk into something I can't even see but sure hear.

Freeze!

I stop breathing, convinced I've just alerted William to my nocturnal creeping, since his cabin is right next to Sailor's, door open to circulate air. I take one leap-step forward to propel myself through Sailor's equally open doorway.

"I need to sleeeeep…"

Is what greets me when he glances up from the bed.

I need to sleeeeep…

Said in a tone of such whiny irksomeness it's as if my being there is the hugest inconvenience ever.

As if I'm the rude one.

My eyes turned devil red. Maple Leaf red. If I'd had a hockey stick handy this might have been a prison diary. Okay, so I don't know a slap shot from a slashing, but I believe in higher education.

"Close the door…" he had growled from his pillow….

Which is how I ended up in the bungee cord tug of war.

Yank!

Sproing!

I yank harder.

Sproing!!!

Rustle, yank, sproing, rustle, SPROING!

Sailor leaps out of bed, pulls the bungee cord out of my fumbling hands with a sharp tug and releases the door, closing us in.

He turns and we are face to face in the dark.

Okay, buddy. We can do this the easy way or the Canadian way.

Never underestimate nice people – they will smile and smile while you hang yourself. Do NOT push them over the edge.

Only, before I can say, "I get you're at work 'n' all, but auditions for 'Insensitive Smartass 1' are over—"

His lips crush mine in a killer kiss that knocks the breath out of my startled lungs.

16.3

WHAT?!

Uh-uh – no way! You presumptuous self-entitled – Libertarian my ass!

He yanks me even closer into him, arms encircling me into a steel cage hard embrace.

Fuck you! You're high if you think I'm gonna—

But, his next kiss is even more ardent.

Fuck You!

Not just passionate…

FUCK YOU!

… but devouring.

Ohhh, God, yessss – Fuck me!

He's gone from 'go away' to 'come here' in .07 seconds – accelerated ardency like a Bugatti Veyron Super Sport jumping the curb – pimped out black and red with a vintage American Muscle Car style spoiler.

An intensity of desire that shreds the lie of indifference.

And one-ups even my desire for him.

We wrestle onto the bed in a flurry of hardcore kisses, bodies crushed together, clothes rocketing off as his hands feel everywhere at once – over every inch—

Oh yesssssss that feels soooo…

His hand shoots to the flashflood of desire between my…

Oh my God!

Fuck me!

No wait, fuck you!

But my legs wrap around him, inviting, urging as my hands return the favor – stroking every available surface of him as he hovers above me lingering with a sudden holdback to careful – like a gentle knock on a door or swiping an access card. I could deny entry — but instead I reach up for the next hard kiss — security clearance flashing green — and he barges in.

Inside me in a blaze of passion.

Ohhhhh… God… YES… FUCK ME!

Volcano exploding — molten lava rivering around us — carrying us away on a glowing flash. Incinerating all sense, but pure — raw… wild ferality.

Primal.

Origin of the species primal.

A crazy, intense coupling as he pleasures me whilst pleasuring himself — bypassing the constructs of conflict and convention to an eroticism that strips me to carnal core.

Fuck dinner and a movie.

Passion dizzily increasing in speed and frenzy — contrasting quiet but for the rustling of sheets — senses alive in a sex-meth blend of bodies — scaring me with its intensity — shattering everything I thought I knew about sex and love by shooting me up to a height of the one — without the other.

But, before I can go 'all the way'…

"I'm cuming," he rasp whispers.

Figures.

16.4

Panting from a blend of exertion and whipped up lust, I lie beside a satisfied Sailor.

The silence, but for breathing, is deafening.

Great, I've just had Angry Sex and I'm not even married.

In a microcosm of how a relationship goes from the first blush of recognition – to 'how did we turn into strangers' – miles apart even while lying next to each other – I am in one of the most stunning regions in the world feeling not just isolated, but trapped.

Staring at the ceiling.

Angry at myself.

Staring at the ceiling realizing…

He left the hatch open.

Sailor stands up on the bed, having spotted the skyview and pokes his head up through the hatch with an…

Ohh shit!

Look on his face as he ducks back down – realizing – there be people up there!

Mimi and Wilhelm to be precise – likely prone and also staring upwards for a star view. An open sky ceiling. Holding out in the hope of a dry night.

And no doubt privy to some extracurricular sounds that just emanated from the cabin below – the barbarians among the civilized.

Sailor's 'ooops' face – though understandable – only infuriates.

I yank on wrinkled clothes and bolt from the bed.

Violently opening the door, I grab the stupid bungee cord to secure it.

Fumble, fumble…

Sailor's hand shoots to mine to relieve me of this tiresome task.

It's like being reverse Tasered – instead of volts of pain – it's a deep bolt of tender beauty. Where the searing heat of lava morphs into the warmth of heartlight.

And, there it is again. The tenderness underlayer. A brief, moving moment of blissful connection. A match struck in a darkened room.

And I flee from that room – running more from that with this particular man – than from anything else.

Only problem is… I have nowhere to go.

17. THRESHOLD

I'm standing in front of T-Rick's cabin door – hand poised to knock.

Damn.

I lower my hand.

Hesitating.

How did I get here?

I slink back to the half bench and corner into it.

Stabbing pain from a back protesting the coziness betrayal. A bench that looked promising. Looked comfortable with a little pillow/blanket padding. Luring me in…

Sleep with me.

But, in fact is a torture device of…

Smack!

Ache…

Proportions.

Like attempting to sleep on a paddle.

I close my eyes…

I am in a soft easy chair… in a five star spa…

Tabacon Hot Springs. Yeah, that's it.

Back spasm.

The bench snickers.

Shivering slightly from the cold shower I took a half hour ago, letting the water sting my skin, before mercifully raising the temperature to a warm cascade. No longer caring who did or didn't wake up, until both guilt and the outhouse smell drove me out. Emerging clean and clothed in my bedtime gear, crawling back into my corner. Determined to be comfortable.

And failing.

On all counts.

Laughing at the absurdity of it all, until I noticed the slight force to that laugh.

Ha ha.

Sob.

A woman in sex is like a flower opening. If she blooms into a cold room – if there is not a ray of sunshine – or a drop of water – the petals shrivel. Contracting into themselves – curling in at the edges.

I feel like a blowup doll minus the easy-clean plastic.

Well, isn't he your blowup doll too? I mean, isn't this what you want? No personal entanglements?

Yes, and if we could just remain within the borders of a bed where the erotic connection sears through every cell… but, the moment we step out of it…

The Iceberg.

And, this moment is proof positive that I am not now nor have ever been a man.

Since the 'free love' seventies someone's been trying to convince women that true liberation is equivalent to the Hustler "relax, it's just sex" motto. The phrase played out over the loudspeaker at the flagship store on Sunset Boulevard in L.A. like some Communist Party slogan played out in Red Square.

But it's a *male* fantasy.

And, if this were 'just sex' then…

'Who do I have to sleep with on this low rent Love Boat to get an orgasm?!'

I mean, I've heard of Tantric Sex, but I think even Sting would be cranky by this point.

Um… Li? Could you induce a climax in a woman?

Shut up Fairness!

Pop Quiz: where is the labia?

Uh… is this multiple choice?

Pop Quiz: what is the geographical distance between the clitoris and the G-spot?

Uhhh… um…

This is harder than I thought.

And what would I say to a female lover, "Hold on while I figure this out?" or, "Just a sec, I think I've almost got it?"

"Ow," would be her likely response. Or worse, the glazed look of ennui and a deadpan, "Try a little to the left."

The female Hoo Hoo = my Waterloo.

Well, at least I brought ice cream to the post coital party that one time I had a woman in my bed…

Vancouver's East Side circa 1993

Two nude redhead femmes, one flushed with afterglow, sit up in bed sharing ice cream. Chocolate Swirl. Her favorite.

"Assume the position," She had commanded early into the night, slapping the long thin switch against her hand for emphasis.

"Excuse me?" I turned away from the stove and met her stern gaze across the kitchen island.

"You heard me." Switch slap on hand.

"You're kidding, right?

"Now!"

Jeez, good thing I studied improv. And what's the first rule of improv? Never block a creative offer – just go with it. So, I turned my back to her and bent over my kitchen counter.

"Do you know why you're being disciplined?"

Giggle.

"Was that a giggle I heard?!"

"Um…"

Giggle.

Whack!

"We agreed to 7 p.m. and you're still cooking."

"Well, at least it will be hot."

"Your insolence will only make it worse for you."

Whack!

Giggle.

"Was that another giggle I heard?!" She was trying to sound

severe, but I thought I heard the hiccup of a stifled laugh. "Well? Was it?!"

"Um… no?"

Whack!

"No, what?"

"No, um… Mistress?"

"That's better. But, it still won't spare you."

Whack! Whack! Whack!

I was trying so hard to hold back the laughter I had tears in my eyes.

Dressed in a pure white babydoll mini dress atop plaid patterned stockings imported from England, I was a variation of the 'naughty schoolgirl' and she was the tweed clad Headmistress. Though, if she was going to spank me, it should probably have been for my lack of cooking skills, not the lateness of the meal. Not to mention that when I finally got up the guts to reach for her you-know-what – she pinned my hand to the bed with surprising strength and refused entry with probably the sexiest words I've ever heard. A breathlessly hissed, "You're going to make me disobey my Master!"

Figures. The one woman I've ever really been attracted to – already in a femme triangle. And while we had 'permission' from all parties with the caveat I could only touch so far – that made me the square.

But her imagination was playful – her long red hair silky – the curve of her waist a Montmartre paintbrush's wet dream – the full, firm breasts. The softness of pretty lips. The revelation of what I'd always suspected – that a naked woman is nature's masterpiece – mysterious even when in full reveal. The reflection an unexpected wisp of reassurance to a fragile ego that had endured one too many blows.

Not to mention that to stay my hand – she focused her girl on girl powers solely on my pleasure.

And, it's not just about the… whoa… O… she so artfully induced two hours later – a confident career lesbian Mistress to my awestruck newbie Submissive – it's not just that she understood:

good sex has a build up beginning, Mardi Gras middle and acute pleasure release end – it's that we both understood the need for a sweet aftertaste.

Chocolate Swirl, the afterglow of champions.

And while my head and Hoo Hoo may agree to disagree – it's sobering to realize just how much my Hoo Hoo is in cahoots with my heart. That who we love romantically defines our sexuality far more than sex actually does. If only I could have stayed a lesbian instead of the bi-curious girl who discovered she was more Hetero on the Kinsey scale than she'd hoped. I mean, we could have shared clothes. Plus, women are so much more cuddly, y'know?

It ain't about the 'ultimate embrace' – but the missing one.

Back to now...

I de-contort myself from the spank bench and stand once again at T-Rick's door.

Hovering at the threshold.

How did I get here?

Toronto 2002 – Ghost of Threshold Past

He swaggers down the aisle between tables, largesse dwarfing the multi-ethnic blend of locals, tourists and the lone redhead-with-notebook packing that breakfast joint in The Beaches. The one with two restaurants: a narrow one in front and an expansive back patio with its own doorway in back.

Clink of metal cutlery on porcelain plates, a kid bangin' his spoon like a drum solo, and it all fades in his wake.

A Hercules body-double passing my sightline. Vintage tattoos. Pre-Ed Hardy designs of a youth gone wild. A slight self conscious flash in the eyes – a half smile on a complicated face. A sensitive bull in a china shop.

I follow him, as if pulled out of my chair by an invisible force, until I reach the doorway to the back patio. And am stopped by an equally invisible force field.

What I saw walk by me was a single man. On the prowl. A hunter.

The image that greets me as I hover on the threshold is the polar opposite.

"What did you see when you saw us sitting there?" Trouble will ask months later at our first long call – me pacing the kitchen – him on cell from the car.

"A happy family."

"Just goes to show, looks can be deceiving." He sounded bemused – and bitter.

Well, looks can be deceiving, I analyzed – staring from the doorway at a man I'll later call Trouble, his wife and kids having brunch.

If this were my family that would be 'the uncle'. Or, that time Sibling's errant dad moved back in for a few months 'cause he was recovering from surgery when Sib was too young to remember. If this were my high school best friend's family, the 'parents' would be legally separated, but living together because the company they both worked for went under and the house didn't sell.

Vaguely, underneath, is a sadness to realize – I no longer know what 'family' means unless it's fractured.

Hovering at the threshold.

I glance back to my table. If the overtaxed staff has already set it, cutlery wrapped in a paper napkin, a mug awaiting the obligatory pour of coffee – I'll go back, sit down, open my notebook, and burrow again into my own little world.

But, it's not set.

Hamlet Hesitation.

Hovering…

Oh, for crying out loud! I propel myself through the doorway.

I just want to meet him – it's not like I want to marry him!

So, the first lie was mine.

"What makes a person cross the line like that," I asked an undercover Mountie friend after a drug money bust caught dirty cops in its net. "A person who never set out to hurt anyone?"

"Because you cross it one line at a time," Mountie said from the vantage point of a real life Bruce Willis complete with eerie resemblance. "One line at a time until you look back and realize you've moved the line of right and wrong so far back that you're on the other side wondering, 'how the hell did I get here?'"

Back to now…

Knock knock knock.
T-Rick's muffled 'come in' has me turning the handle.
Damn you, Trouble.
I wouldn't be here if you hadn't caught me when I chased you.
For in the inquisitive eyes looking up to decipher his – he saw something. Something that reminded him of himself.
Unusual cells.
The harder truth is that I wouldn't be here if I hadn't been overconfident in my ability to resist the very temptation that had propelled me out of my chair in the first place. So sure it would be just a second look – or at most a quick 'hello' to a stranger I'd never see again.
Mistaking love at first sight for idle curiosity.
Stepping into his orbit. Too close…
I step into T-Rick's cabin.
He's reading in bed. A paperback from the collection left in the room, Michael Connelly being the pinnacle pick of today's boy talk. Back of his head towards the door, T-Rick cranes his neck up and smiles friendly when he sees who it is.
"Hi, I hope you don't mind…"
"No, of course not. Come in."
"It's just that, the bench thing isn't working and…"
"Please, make yourself at home," he puts down the paperback.
"Oh don't get up. I'll just…"
Awkward.
He scooches over to the right, giving me the left side of the bed.
Awkward[10]
I close the door behind me.
"Thanks," I mumble and maneuver feet first, sliding in careful to avoid the overhanging indentation from the deck above.
Careful to stay on 'my side'.
"This is…" I'm about to say 'cozy', but it's way beyond. "It's

A Hot Sailor, A Cold Margarita, and... Trouble   225

like sleeping in an MRI. Not that I've had one, but wow."

"Are you okay?"

"Yeah, I just didn't plan on being in a coffin until death."

"Do you want to switch sides?"

There's more ceiling space above him.

"No, it's fine, I'll adjust."

Martyr rule 4...

"The bed's nice," I smile, realizing how ungrateful I've been sounding.

"Yeah, it's pretty good for a sailboat."

There's nothing to do in this room but lay beside each other. And notice...

He's lean with a lovely energy in repose. Beside me in a bed flush to three sides of the room. T-shirt tight to his body. I'm all too aware what's underneath it. All too curious what's underneath the boardshorts.

Breath shorting out.

Big inhale.

Think of Gandhi.

Not the peace Gandhi – but the ascetic yogi sleeping with virgins to prove his detachment from all desire Gandhi.

Big exhale.

"Are you all right?"

Gandhi.

"I just get claustrophobic easy, that's all."

He turns to me on his side, lean muscles flexing under the shirt.

Silent Gandhi sneeze!

"Um... thanks for sharing –" I cover smile.

"It's my pleasure."

Om Namah Gandhi...

The overhang presses down on me – shrinking the space – sucking the air out of the room...

"Are you sure you're okay?!"

Clawing breath... zero oxygen.

"Uhhh... would it be all right if we opened the door?"

T-Rick scrambles up and opens the door, and as the available air space expands...

Deep breath in.

Exhale.

"Thanks, that helps."

"Are you tired, do you want the light off?"

"It's up to you, I can sleep with it on if you want to read some more. Do your thing, dude."

T-Rick scrambles back into bed beside me, sliding in feet first. Two pairs of feet point towards the far wall. He reads and I adjust to the confines, relaxing into the blessed feel of a bed under my back.

Stab.

Oh man – what now?!

Stab, stab, stab.

I force myself still and drift in and out until T-Rick gets up to turn off the light, plunging us in the dark, which only serves to make the distance between us contract.

Stab.

As he lies back down beside me, I confess...

"Um... brace yourself... I have to remove a piece of underwear."

"Panties?" he says hopefully.

"Not actually wearing those. You don't need to with yoga pants."

"So, you're like commando?"

"Dude, I'm completely covered up here. I'm wearing longer pants than you are."

"Yeah, I noticed. Aren't you warm?"

"I was born in Haifa. I can handle heat – it's cold I can't."

"But, you live in Canada." He sounds amused.

"Yeah, feel sorry for me, beach boy."

A quiet chuckle from 'his side' of the bed.

I scooch over even further and reach behind to unhook my

pushup black bra that's digging into my back like a Borgia dagger. I tug at the clasp… and pull… despite years of practice, my bra unhooking dexterity is no match for Sailor's one-handed maneuver.

Tug, pull… snap…

"Need some help?" It's rhetorical. And amused.

"No thanks, I got this."

I fiddle with the eyehooks until – sproing! Finally, it springs free. I pull a strap down my arm and out from under my T – then the other one – until finally I wriggle free.

Ahhhhh… that's better. Legs stretch out – toes wiggle in comfort.

I bury the bra in the sheet to my left, out of his sight lest in the cold light of morning I'm outed for plain, oversized practical, when a girl with allegedly 'sensuous eyes' should be packin' lace.

"What about the shirt?" T-Rick asks, still amused.

"That stays on."

"I seem to recall you promising to go topless…"

"Threatening more like it. And I was just kidding."

"Oh." He mocks disappointment.

"Yeah, I'm really all talk. When it comes right down to it – I prefer to save my sluttiness for behind closed doors."

Beat of silence.

"I think we better close that door," T-Rick says soberly.

This makes me laugh out loud.

"Good one."

A laugh that lets me breathe.

"Great delivery."

I thumbs up in the dark as humor dials down the tension – cleansing the room like sage.

Easing the chit chat until I realize what this is… pillow talk. Chaste pillow talk. But, pillow talk nevertheless.

T-Rick also clues in that by offering to share his cabin, he's put himself in awkwardville.

"Lying beside an attractive woman," he admits, "it's hhhard."

The way that word comes out on a rough breath – no double

entendre – just real – lets me know.

I'm safe.

"You think you've got problems? You're not the one lying beside a hottie with a six pack."

"I think you're doing pretty good just as you are."

Deep breath.

Gandhi, Gandhi, Gandhi.

We shift – flat on our backs – staring at the ceiling.

"So, two months, huh?" I make room for New Girlfriend. Vaguely aware from my on-deck interrogation of earlier that elicited his confession, "she's the nicest person I've ever met" and, "she's smarter than me" that this is not just a passing fling. He's found 'The One'.

"Yeah, two months," says the unsuspecting future groom.

"And before that you were single, right?"

"For quite a while."

"But we meet now," I say. "Not three months ago – not even nine weeks ago – but now."

"Yeah, the timing sucks."

"It blows," I agree. "And not in a good way."

It's his turn to laugh.

And mine to be honest – even though it's a misguided loyalty to someone who hasn't asked for it.

"Well, it's also that I met Sailor first."

"You have a thing for him?!"

Cute. 'A thing'. That's adorable.

But, his shocked tone stings.

"Yeah. A thing."

Seriously, Sailor – what's with taking 'don't kiss and tell' to this OCD level? I thought the point of having a 'best friend' was to tell each other everything? Proof positive Sailor is not now nor has ever been a woman. Proof too that in his little black book, I don't even rate a sticky note.

'I'd have shared the flat sheet' my ass!

Hey.

Hey.
Take your 'hey' and stick it up your…
Light flashes – blinding in through a small, round portal.
"Was that lightning?!"

17.2

CRACK! Lightning. CRACK. Thunder.

The sky has finally unleashed its heavy rainfall burden. And I scramble out of bed, concerned for Bex above.

"Are you okay?!" I speak directly to her feet, having found her with legs bent at the knees, dangling over the top of the stairladder – the rest of her flat on her back still on the bridge deck. She bears a striking resemblance to a murder mystery victim except she's still breathing.

"Yeah, it's the one dry spot."

The now soaked bridge deck has yielded a narrow strip of dry floor under the canvas – but not enough to fully stretch out.

"Bex! Come below!" I urgent-whisper from my position at the bottom of the stairladder, looking up at her thinking that can't be even remotely comfortable. I'm simultaneously trying not to wake the O-Blu snoozers, who're sleeping through the downpour. You'd think everyone would be wide awake, running around screaming, "Bail you varmints, baaaailll!"

CRAACKK! A million little splashes hitting the boat – hitting the water!

Greeted by…

Snore… snarfle… rhythmic breathing.

"RUMBLE!!!" sulks the sky at the lack of audience for its killer drum solo.

The stargazers have been driven below, with Mimi now stretched out in the Bex/Mimi cabin and Wilhelm confined to the long bench opposite Diego.

"There's still um… a half bench…" I worrybead, "Or maybe, if you don't want to wake Mimi, we can figure something out to take turns in T-Rick's –"

"Can't," Bex sighs. "Too claustrophobic."

A Hot Sailor, A Cold Margarita, and... Trouble

I thought mine was bad.

"I won't be able to sleep a wink below."

"Oh, sorry, honey. Is there anything I can get you?"

"No, I'll be fine. I'm so knackered at this point I'll probably nod off, no problem."

Wow, Bex can out Martyr me at fifty paces!

"Okay, then, if you're sure..." I say uncertainly.

"I'm sure, honey."

"All right, well, nighty night then. See you in the morning." I turn back towards T-Rick's cabin.

"Sweet dreams," Bex says from the flat of her back, legs still dangling over the edge. Classy and courteous even when contorted. I gape up at her with Brit upper crust envy – then carry on.

Preoccupied, I reenter T-Rick's darkened cabin.

"Everything okay?" he says from the bed.

"Yeah, sort of."

I'm answering while still in motion – too fast for such poor visibility – scrambling onto 'my side' of the bed—

CRAAACK!!!

Just as loud – but not thunder.

My forehead has hit the overhang at full velocity.

Now I know 'seeing stars' is not just a metaphor.

The dark room is blackened further as a pitch void fills my eyes in from the corners.

Stars swirl in that blackness then flame in and out like fireflies. And then... pain.

17.3

T-Rick's hand is on my shoulder…

Instinctually comforting the girl beside him, who answered his, "Are you all right?!" by bursting into tears.

Hot, stinging, tears.

As much from embarrassment as from a stubborn head hitting a harder, unyielding wall.

Dislodging my composure.

Projectile tears involuntarily shooting out as I lay face to pillow. The CRACK in the dam, spidering out a thousand mini-cracks through which tears escape into a total loss of structural integrity, bursting emotion wide open.

Pain tears masking grief-wracked sobs.

Grief – the control bandito who gangs up on you, sneaking past loss into present circumstance – until you're confronted with not just one blow – but all the past blows this one reminds you of. Surrounding you like an outlaw gang on a deserted road. As if it happened only yesterday. And that's what takes you down.

His hand is on my shoulder.

Neither judging nor superior in this moment of weakness he's witnessing up close.

Simply kind.

This only makes me cry harder.

Unraveling me by being a safe harbor.

This is the real Lethal Weapon. A hot man with protective instincts.

Not control instincts – *protective* instincts.

The man who's secure enough in himself to be strong for you when the feminine burden – sensitive to nuance – to the world's wider pain – to your own inadequacies – devastates.

Even if he thinks your tears are just a headbang owie – like a kid who just scraped her knee.

Comforting – without presuming you need 'fixing'.

T-Rick's hand on my shoulder is a simple, 'decent thing to do'. But, it incites a war in the girl laid out beside him. She's fighting with all she's got. Not just to hold back insurgent tears – but to hold back from turning into his arms.

Toronto 2003

I TURN

Into the crook of his arm.

The strength of his contracting muscles, lending me a wisp of valor – breathing in a little courage.

Side by side.

His other arm reaching around for me – hand stroking my back, as tremulous eyes find his in what little light seeps in – lips so near.

Hovering.

He closes the remaining tiny gap and finally… the gentle, but insistent feel of rediscovery. Of his lips parting mine, like the first, best taste of a forbidden fruit – like the first time a human tongue touched whipped cream or the first, crisp bubble of champagne.

Fluidly, I lengthen along him, vaporizing any remaining distance between us – fully cuddled into him now, awakening to his masculine certainty – making me feel soulfully feminine – pretty in all the places I feel compromised – his hand now tracing lines on my skin as if he can't ever touch me enough.

"Why…?"

I struggle to find the words.

"Why what?"

"Why does this – this which should feel… wrong – this situation… WHY when I'm this close to you – I only feel an overwhelming sense of…"

"Yes…?"

"Innocence."

Pure and faultless. Only…

Rightness.

"Don't you know who you are to me, yet?" he asks.

Shake of head, 'no'.

"You're the love of my life."

Trouble says the words like an indelible song – a moving melody you can't get out of your mind. And my one tear turns into a torrent as his massive arms pull me into his naked perfection as he murmurs...

"I've been waiting for you all my life."

I cried deeper then. Because I knew it was true for me too. The hardest truth. That each moment was like the first – out of time – out of place – like none before or since.

Eden in a snow storm.

And mingled with the quiet joy-relief of recognition was the inconsolable, because I knew...

This is gonna hurt.

A lot.

Love in conflict with principle steals the joy it arrives with.

Back to now...

I blame the Caribbean. How it drew me to this place like a siren call – as if it knew my real name. A girl born on the Mediterranean who just had to see that other celebrated body of water. Who had to see for herself how the Sapphire compared to the Turquoise. But, the picture that drew her in didn't prepare that girl for the real thing – for how the Caribbean colludes with sensuality – the air heavy with downfall – monsoon giving way to trickling rain drops as I lie beside T-Rick, face still down in the pillow – tearathon subsiding – but mind galloping fast forward like a dimly lit blue foreign film.

Flashing contraband images in front of my closed eyes – fantasy-shifting me into T-Rick's embrace. A back-of-mind sub-surface dive into the wrap-around-me comfort mingled with the rush of how his lean-muscle hardness would feel along the length of my curves.

Would he push me away in alarm? Or, join me in the rapids?

A riskable outcome. He pushing me away would sting but not destroy – and the pleasure of feeling his arms wrap around me – biceps flexing strength – pulling me closer in – looking up at him in the dark – the quick to smile surfing prof's lips finding mine – deepening from soothing to ardent in the 2 seconds it would take for him to register I'm reaching for him – would be worth the risk.

He's the kind that telegraphs he'd care to please – the kind that sparks my desire to give in turn – to trace my mouth along his lean, hard chest – to lift the shirt and find the healing scrapes and kiss them better – until I make a left turn at his abs...

The quiet ahhh... moaning out on his gasp...

...what he sounds like when taken to that height.

Lying back receiving...

Until...

He'd tussle me onto my back – cradling – dropping kisses – tasting the residue tears he's simultaneously stemmed. The tide turning from pain to pleasure. Sparking a little rivalry of who gets to give more.

There's nothing like a man who inspires your sensuous generosity.

Would he lift the shirt off my body or wait until I lifted his? First-touch hand caressing skin... discovery of the 'topless' raising the stakes as we would cross the divide from dreamy to hardcore... he sliding off my pants to touch the rumored 'commando' underneath, me undoing his boardshorts in one motion... discovering his secret places in the dark.

Hardening him further with my caress.

His kiss blocking out the view of the room we're in – seeing only him above me.

Would he rush to enter – clamor over the last barrier between us?

Or, slow to savor – pulling it back.

Languid. Not just touching – but exploring.

Like a mist mid-storm. Slow motion hand traces holding back time – elongating it as if we have some say in eternity – as if we can freeze frame this second by sheer will.

As if we can sidestep tomorrow.

But, tomorrow will come. Blue Foreign Film scenes shift from cinematic to natural stark-light – shift to the look on his face I might see as midnight bled into morning.

That Look.

The 'what did I do' wince – hidden quickly by a reassuring smile – sparing my feelings – because he seems like that kind of guy. But, I know all too well how one moment can domino into a lifetime of emotion.

This will hurt you more than it will heal me.

It glimmers then – that this is the Genesis of every affair – the moment you turn to person B for tears over person A. Or because of boredom. Or fear... that it will never get better.

One isn't the loneliest number. It's being one-half of two when it's not working – a .5.

I have turned – and been turned to. And the irony of The Other Woman is that the mistress often isn't the cause of a man leaving his marriage – she's the solace or spark 'on the side' that allows him to stay.

And, this is not my dream. I didn't grow up playing with 'Mistress Barbie' while the girl next door got the dream house.

"I just need a moment to be a baby, if that's okay," is my sniffly signal. Tears finally dry – face still in the pillow – clothes still on.

T-Rick takes his hand off my shoulder then. Moves ever so slightly further into 'his side' and lets me find my own way to composure.

Until we settle back into calm waters.

There's a scientific rumor that we think tens of thousands of thoughts a day. I think a woman has the same number of thoughts as a man – plus an additional 10K about the man in her orbit. Complete with future projections, pie charts and a PowerPoint presentation entitled "Cost/Benefit Analysis".

All unsaid. Instantaneous.

The intricate lattice-work of the female mind.

"Sorry 'bout that."

I shift a little – as does he on 'his side' of the bed.

"No need to be."

Platonic pillow talk resumes, pleasant like a hammock…

18. DAY THREE: EVE'S REBELLION

Eyes flutter from a sleep robbing nightmare. Open to my nemesis – the smug overhang. Head still smarting. Glaring at it – naming it – and the first near imperceptible lurch of what will be endless hours of takedown seasickness for what it is.

Slut Tax.

Wincing in 'oh-oh what did I do?' life hangover.

Nothing wrong… a little voice whispers. You got naked with the single guy and not with the unsingle guy. In modern terms that's practically Victorian.

But… head hurts… nausea lurches… like retribution…

And foreboding. The portend of a 'last day at sea' that will leave me plastered to the top deck lying on damp Alligator Mattress praying I don't embarrass myself further by throwing up. Seasick beyond what I thought was even possible – willing myself to hold it together until we reach land.

Getting a little help in the humiliation department from Sailor.

"Oh, that's a bad bargain," will be the rough equivalent of his rolled eyed comment when I ask to borrow $2 towards Termite Wedding Longboat's return.

Not daring to risk even a grain of white rice at the Chinese restaurant that suddenly appears atop an isolated hill as we cross the divide from San Blas back towards Panama – fearing I'll have to insist we pull over on the highway and slow down our return.

Relieved feet alighting out of the packed SUV at Sibling's gate – with a side of reluctance at the goodbyes. Smiling at T-Rick's new-to-Facebook invite and Bex's 'let's meet for coffee soon'.

We'd traveled from strangers to crew to friends.

Culminating in Mimi's lost at sea bikini top being waved like a flag – ahoyed by the garlic 'n onion neighbors who'd fished it out of the water and caught up with us miles later. When we realized what they were waving, we erupted in wild cheers at this 'nautical miracle'.

"Yay! Woohooooo!!!"

Mimi clutched her top in happy surprise as a grinning Wilhelm pronounced, "Zat vas zeh best moment of zeh whole trip!"

A collective memory. A temporary tribe.

I will never forget…

"Ahem…"

I will turn back to Sailor still in the packed SUV at the gate to Sib's condo complex, window rolled down. Wondering if he wants a hug bye – some friendly gesture I've missed – but his 'ahem' clarified by a tilted head towards the driver.

Flushing red, rushing back to hand Ronaldo the last $25 I had saved for his services home.

"Oh, sorry," I blush. "I'll probably open my bag to discover I've forgotten something on the boat too." Embarrassment covered with the sheepish smile of self ribbing.

"I don't think that would surprise any of us," will be Sailor's cold quip from the coveted front passenger seat.

The rumored 'poison dart' delivered courtesy of the 'cool guy' disavowing the quirky girl in front of the 'popular kids'.

I will turn away then – walk up the path to the door, bedraggled and starving – the SUV trundling away behind me.

'Well, at least now I know what it's like to be voted off Survivor,' I'll shrug.

Shrugging off shame. As if Sailor's ill-timed dig was somehow just punishment for the crime of passion – as though in giving into our Close Encounters of the Naked Kind – I've given up all right to kindness. When in fact I was reaching for it in his touch all along.

It's not that I wasn't prepared for his daylight distance – it's that I kept hoping to see the better side of him – the one I could feel under the surface of my skin wherever his caress left a trace. Only, the stubborn optimism that serves me well in a tough profession was a liability here.

Though I'm not sure which I prefer – Sailor's blunt honest running commentary that always lets me know what he's thinking – or Trouble's sweet words that blind me to what's really going on.

Either way, neither will likely ever have to confront the key contradiction of sexual politics: that men are still 'heroes' for 'scoring' but women whores for the same ardency. Derided when arms are welcome. As if mutually consensual sex were a conquest and we the vanquished village. When in fact receptivity – that willingness to let the man in – is a gift. A portal to paradise – a union of masculine and feminine that can transcend earth bound constraints – and soar us to how the divine must have felt in Creation.

At least it can be.

When it's magical.

And yet, that deepest form of intimacy – still used to whip women. Both figuratively and in some unforgivably 'dark age' corners of the world – literally.

Until we learn to whip ourselves.

Until we hand over the keys to our own jailor.

Until I come to a life changing conclusion.

I don't have to collude in my own oppression.

"Will you marry me?" I turned to Sailor at the passport checkpoint, when mid-highway we had to clamor out of the SUV and show our visas to a Panamanian official, so we could continue on towards the city.

Sailor's wide eyed startled expression was priceless – and predictable.

"If I brought a groom, I mean." I smiled, cheekily clarifying as the euphoria at being back on land made me reckless. "I've always thought it would be cool to be married at sea. As Captain – could you officiate?"

"Technically, I suppose yah – I think you can get certified on the internet or something. But, why would I perform a ceremony that I think will ruin people's lives? If people want to get married, fine, whatever. But, not on my boat." And with that he huffed into the checkpoint building, while I stood outside with T-Rick and grinned...

"You know what I wish for Sailor?"

T-Rick raised a 'what?' eyebrow.

"I wish a woman would come into his life that knocks that chip right off his shoulder. A woman that makes him fall so far in love that she hands him back his heart on a silver platter."

Because one of the greatest gifts of love is how it can knock us off our high horse and remind us just how human we really are. And it would be a shame to miss that. Though, admittedly, I wasn't sure if I was blessing Sailor.

Or cursing him.

And while the dish served up to me on a silver platter that last morning on the boat was Low Self Esteem Soufflé chanting, "Eat me! Eat me!" – lying there in T-Rick's cabin, stomach pitching to the boat's unsteady wobble, I decide not to partake of that salty dish.

Nor its side dishes. Neither the bitter You Whore Hummus (not to be confused with the delicious, moderately spiced Live and Let Live Hummus I've enjoyed at fine establishments on three continents) – nor the bland Just Sex Desserts.

But rather, to find meaning.

Whether it's in the quiet stirring of morning after the rain – or an inexplicable visceral connection.

Because, what is freedom if not the ability to discover for ourselves? To make our own mistakes and suffer the twist to the heart until we learn? To venture too far out to sea – and then have to find our way to shore. And most of all, to define what is – and isn't – meaningful for ourselves.

Lying beside T-Rick, staring at that overhang in the moment before that Last Day at Sea, a song softly strains in from the galley. A song that will stay with me throughout what's about to follow.

Johnny Cash and Joe Strummer. Singing Bob Marley's 'Redemption Song.'

Soothing my rough edges. Reminding me of that distant first love… stringing words like pearls…

"We are going to emancipate ourselves from mental slavery…" the original line from a Marcus Garvey speech that inspired the lyrics, "… none but ourselves can free the mind…"

There has to be a place for poets and dreamers.

Or what's an Island Eden for?

I turn for a better vista then – shifting face to face with T-Rick – still fast asleep on his side towards me, arms across his chest – the soft lines of sleep smoothing out years until I'm looking at the boy next door Towhead Surfer of another era.

Gentle yes, but I stir to a streak of determination in him. Intel – subliminal signals – his Mr. Congeniality a mask for a strong will. I'm surprised to pick up this radar – that if it were a choice between meeting Sailor, who can come across the impulsive hothead, or the more benign T-Rick in a dark alley – I think I'd rather clash with Sailor. If he's Butch Cassidy – T-Rick is the deceptively calm, squint into the sun sniper, Sundance.

Best friends. Reverse mirror images.

T-Rick the blonder beach boy – the more thoughtful 'tuned into people's feelings' likable guy. But, with an unspoken line you don't cross lest you see the blade flash. Lying beside him I sense it like a double edged sword. The hard under the sweet.

I breathe relief to have made it through the night – in the clear. But, morning also brings the clear light of him.

Whispering…

"… It's been less than 60 seconds – you still have time. A last stealable moment… a slip of the hand… straying accidentally on purpose to the front of his board shorts… waking him to a brush of palm against his…"

He stirs, sleepy eyes slowly opening. My hand remains at my side…

"Good morning," I smile as relief slams into regret.

A line uncrossed. The moment lost.

The playlist cues the next song.

19. RELATIVE STRANGERS

November…

The blessed feel of cracked concrete under shoes. Diesel lungs. Noise. Ahhh… downtown Panama City in all its sun glinting off urban grime glory.

Mark waves to a lanky Caribbean-Panamanian walking in the opposite direction in a white collared shirt and black slacks typical of a guy on his way to the office. He grins back from the sidewalk across the street with a wave of his own.

But, there's a cheeky irony to the nod…

"How do you know him, Mark?"

"He's my brother."

"Oh! Well, do you want to stop and talk to him – I'll wait if you want."

"No, I don't know him. It's not like you and your brother."

"Oh, you mean you didn't grow up together?"

He shakes his head, 'no'.

"Well, I have a brother I've never met in Bucharest. From my father's first marriage."

"I have many brothers and sisters from my father… he…" Mark chuckles and shakes his head.

"How many?"

"If you put us all in one room? You'd need a whole restaurant – like a banquet."

"That's one big family reunion."

"I don't even know how many."

"Are you telling me your father spread his seed all over Panama – populating it with his offspring?"

The laugh is 'yep' – the shrug 'that's life'. But, Mark's a diplomat – a former soccer player who knows how to smile for the cameras after a loss. This among the things I know of him having pelted him with questions from the passenger seat. But, no matter how he much he tells me about himself, 'two kids, one a lawyer, sure I'm proud of them, still married to their mother…'

Only time is the tell…

And under the 'tranquilla' bodyguard he insulates me with as he leads us to the immigration office, through the tangle-lines to a fast track he's arranged to stamp me 'approved' for an extra week lest I be barred from leaving the country for overstaying my visa – or worse – have to call my brother collect from jail – coils the spring of frustration.

One that will explode in "I will kill you" with a hand gun threat when a year later he tangles with Sib over money – leading to a lawyered cold conclusion to their association. Signed agreements and a terse adios un-amigo.

People reveal themselves.

Some, like Bex, delight. The haughty vibe a veil for a nurturing nature.

"You made us all omelets and you don't even eat eggs?!" Sailor had sounded so surprised that last morning in the galley as she whisked and flipped. "Bex, I misjudged you," he'd added, as if the girl most likely to mutiny just snagged 'crew of the month' award.

She meets me on rainy afternoons – Monsoon Mall Girls matching stride for fast stride across the expanse of Multi-Plaza. Tangling with her smartyboots brain, debating everything from Internet dating to whether 'the universe' contains a force-of-good 'creator' or is just a lot of gas floating around a bunch of spheres with the occasional black hole. Cerebral one minute – 'ooohing' like prom girls over her new black dress the next.

"But, I really think you do have to love yourself before you can be loved," she pronounces over cappuccinos with little hearts drawn into the foam.

"Bex, if I waited to love myself before I found love I'd be 98 years old on my deathbed and then maybe some cute doctor will walk in – and I'll be like 'oh Doc I finally love myself – what are you doing Friday night?' And BAM – white light!" I close my eyes, dropping head to shoulder in a 'death' pose.

"Oh, Girlfriend you're too funny – but do you honestly believe you can love another without accepting who you are first?"

"Guys do it all the time! Do you think some guy who just got dumped is sitting around reading self help books thinking 'oh Jeez, I guess I better love myself before I get banged' – no way! He's down at the bar flirting above his Cuteness Factor!"

"Yes, and he's going to veer from one bad relationship to another."

"Or be loved by a warm, kind, pretty woman – because he believes in miracles – and got out there to find one."

"Or, he could be like my ex and tell me I'm *too* loving."

"He didn't!"

"He did," and her eyes well up.

"So, he takes the one thing that is great about you – the one thing you know makes you worthy of love in the first place – that you have this magnanimous, caring nature – and trashes it."

"Well," she sniffs, "maybe he's right."

"Or maybe he grew up in a home where affection was frowned upon – and the need for love seen as a great weakness – but instead of just admitting he's uncomfortable with receiving love – he blames you – as though your capacity for love is some fatal flaw."

"Oh, I see you've dated him too," she laughs and wipes away a stray tear. "The wanker."

"You, on the other hand, are 'Mr. Congeniality,'" I had cast T-Rick in the SUV on the way back from San Blas. Having dubbed William 'Coach' because he wanted to fix the world, I had turned my attention to T-Rick re-canned into the third tier backseat wedged by the window. He grinned that quick-draw generous smile – the one that made it easy to miss the Wild West under the Beach Boy. The guy who just hunted down his own stolen truck when the police failed to find it.

Incongruity.

It can draw you in like a maze – fascinated at unexpected

corners even as you're anxiously in search of the exit.

"I have a five year plan," Trouble tells me seven years too late. The King of Contradiction – he's a capable, hard working, fiercely loyal-to-his-kids responsible businessman who does what he sets out to do.

Except in matters of the heart.

There, he seeks his emotional and physical happiness 'outside' of a vow he claims is a prison sentence. One he won't escape from even as the cage door swings open.

I don't think he ever means to lie to me – he holds on to the belief – so sincere – so convinced – it feels heartless to tell him, "You're living a lie – and it's killing you."

But, I am an easy mark – moved more by words than actions – so caught up in staring into someone's eyes – I miss what their hands might be doing.

And some don a disguise to prey on you from the moment they spot a score. Watching from the shadows…

20. THE POLITENESS THIEF

We race through the night – Sailor in the lead – me trying to keep pace in high heels. A wannabe Charlie's Angel.

Sailor looks back and grabs my hand – ostensibly to steady me across the broken pavement – but it's a yank forward and I pray I don't stumble as he pulls me along.

"You had to wear those shoes," he throws a quick-pique glance towards the black formals with their rhinestone straps across peekaboo pink toes.

"Didn't expect a high speed chase," I mutter in my best Jacklyn Smith purr offset by a Drew Barrymore badass squint.

"C'mon…" he tugs.

Ow. Pinch the heels.

Fuck Charlie. Blaspheme squished toes.

We round a corner towards the Marriott. Glittery Night Life Bella Vista now feels ominous – a thief's den – twisting corners in an underworld – as though we'd stepped through a rift in reality to a dark matter dimension.

"Stay here, it's safer." Sailor parks me in an alcove across the street from the Beirut patio and turns away to chase down the bad guy. Around the corner.

Out of sight.

Too late for me to point out – he's taller than you – and what if has friends – the kind with matching tear tattoos under the eye? Part admiration for Sailor's courage – part fear he'll hothead himself into a worse situation while I stand here. Alone. With a drop-kick feeling.

"Well, you see…" my mind jitters into what I'm gonna tell Sibling. "We were just sitting there minding our own business… and I had your cell phone on the table… yeah… the expensive one you lent me… the one you put my SIM chip into and asked me not to lose…"

When the shark disguised as a dolphin caught our scent – my scent to be exact.

How long he stood outside watching through the window on the darkened street, I'll never know. Was it a split second? Or did he take in our exchange with amused surveillance? The curly haired duo at the corner table. Back to the 'scene of the crime'…

Sushi Express.

Same brightly lit interior, same colorful menu.

Me once again trying to channel Gandhi – not the ascetic 'sleep with virgins' to prove his impulse control Gandhi – but the peacenik 'non-violent' Gandhi who would frown on me acting on my own current impulse: to punch Sailor in the face.

"You came to dinner," he says, irritated, "and you already ate? Who does that?" Sailor shakes his head and stares back at the menu, going to plan B, since I've just nixed his 'let's have what we had the first time' plan A. Making me out to be the one lacking in social grace – by himself being spectacularly rude. It's a brilliant sleight of hand.

Who does that?

The woman who only has $10 in her purse (three of which is for the cab ride home) and while that's embarrassing – it's also helping me hold onto November. Huddling over my laptop hour after hour coaxing out a page count. Hence I can't 'split the bill' like we did last time. Double Hence: the socially awkward hunger strike.

"It's nine o'clock at night and this was fairly last minute," I remind him non-violently, whilst my left hand casually clenches into a fist under the table.

Why am I even here?!

"Oh, no doubt there's a crazy, intense connection," Sailor had said over the phone earlier that evening – part of the olive branch that got me out tonight. But, this 'crazy intense connection' doesn't give us a manual on how to talk to each other.

"Okay, well… if you're not gonna eat anything…" Sailor

orders a mix of sushi and sashimi from the black clad waiter.

C'mon, Gandhi, just one punch – open hand if you prefer – just one teeny smack.

Gandhi shakes his head while adjusting his dhoti, "*Om Shanti*, little hellion. Om Shanti."

Did the Watcher notice me overcompensating?

"I'll pay you for the 'food and gas' as soon as I can."

"No problem. Whenever you get the chance."

"I'll add extra for the $2."

"Sounds good," he completely misses my sarcasm.

"And extra for the wait."

"Okay, thanks."

"It just might take me a little while to get it to you."

"Don't worry about it. I know where your brother lives - haha."

Grrrrr... Gandhi!!!

* * *

"He charged you?!" was Sib's aghast reaction to an offhand comment. He stood in the living room with his painting behind him. I stopped in my tracks on the way to the kitchen – turning back towards him – startled at his tone.

"I offered," I explained, stripping smooth the residue hurt bubbles, refusing to admit them. "I think he's struggling and too proud to admit it."

"Well, so are you!" Sib glanced up to the ceiling with a little head shake as if supplicating some divine being for patience. "You don't..." brotherly shudder as Sib grasped for the sanitized version... "You don't *kiss* a woman and then expect her to pay to go on your boat. It's just not the gentlemanly thing to do."

"Well, at least you know your sister's not a gold digger."

Sibling fixed me with a look, "In your case you might want to take a workshop."

"What? Gold Digging for Amateurs?"

"Something like that. Then at least maybe you wouldn't offer what you can't really afford."

"I think if he didn't need it, he wouldn't accept it – just like if I could offer more I would. You never know what someone's going through beneath the surface. Most people don't mean to be mean."

Sibling looked at me as though I just said the sky is made of blueberry icing and clouds are candy floss.

"It's not like I've never done him any favors," he countered. "I ask for one thing and he—"

He cut himself off while I stared at him – mind flashing to Sailor's first 'friend of your brother's in town' text.

Oh man.

Did Sibling ask Sailor to 'look in on my sister while I'm away?'

Is that what started this whole chain of events?

Do I really want to ask him that question?!

About as much as I'd like to hike through North Korea in a T-shirt that says: CIA agents do it undercover. But, if he did – then that does give me a greater insight into Sib's point of view.

"Look, I don't want to be the cause of a friendship ending."

"You're not. He's just not the friend I thought he was."

"But—"

"Sis, do me a favor?" Sib interrupted.

"Uh... okay."

"Step away from the buttheads."

I laughed, "Step away from the buttheads?"

"Just step away." He stood in front of his painting like a sentinel of the heart and made a shield gesture with his hand. Protecting his sister's honor. "Just... step away."

Back to now...

"What did you tell your brother?" Sailor asks, chopsticking a tuna roll into his mouth.

"No details, if that's what you mean," I murmur, weary of the topic.

"He's changed." Sailor is countering with clues, like a trial lawyer cross-examining a witness he suspects of perjury. "He's not joking around on Facebook like he used to – just a one line reply every once in a while. And, he never comes out anymore."

Jeez, how many breakups can one non-relationship have?!

"You and my brother are completely polarized. He thinks you should have talked to him if you wanted to... uh... kiss his sister – and you're strictly 'don't ask/don't tell'. You think it's not something that should ever be discussed."

"Damn right, it's sick!"

"I'm not talking details," I repeat for the endless time. "But, in his mind there is a guy code." And it has been irreparably broken.

Sigh.

I was better off sticking to the polite, cheerful 'thanks for the great trip' email...

* * *

"You sent him a thank you note?!" was Lewaa's aghast reaction.

"I'm Canadian, aren't I?! Besides, he's given me the fulfillment of a seven year dream, there's no point being churlish."

"Why are you defending him?"

"I'm not!" I snapped defensively.

"Then why even go out tonight?"

"I'm trying to avoid Ryder's mistake."

"Ryder's Mistake?" Lewaa looked dubious, "Who the hell wrote that?"

"No! Ryder – Prague. Remember? It's not a book – I told you about him! He missed the last night we could have spent together. And when I called him seven years later – he admitted how much he still thinks about that – how much he wishes he'd made it back in time and—"

I caught Lewaa's smirk.

"Damn it, Buddy!"

He grinned wide, onyx eyes shooting haha sparks.

"Well, anyway," I huffed – half fuming – half laughing, "You only get one chance at a last night."

* * *

But, I was beginning to wish I'd avoided this one. Better to have left it with a 'thank you' note – to stick to the truths that don't offend – avoiding the difficult... 'I was... lonely...' tracks that only slam down steel doors like a lockdown.

"So, you were lonely on the boat..." Sailor repeats, wary, taking a pull on his beer.

"Yes, it was... challenging."

"But, you know I couldn't... I mean..." he bristles. "It's my place of business—"

"I get that. But, at a certain point if you don't... acknowledge someone... it's like you're ashamed of being seen with them."

"Don't... don't go there. That's not how it was..." Sailor shakes his head, sounding offended I'd even suggest that. "And I did not just wave my hand – I did no such thing."

"Well, it was dark," I shrug. "And I was busy being bench slapped."

"I told you three times you could have my cabin!"

This non-relationship is sounding an awful lot like a bad relationship. Jack Nicholson yelling, 'you want the truth – you can't handle the truth' looping in my brain.

You will only look at me and cite 'unfair expectations'. I will only look at you and say it's unfair not to expect expectations.

So, instead I simply ask...

"You never did find my yoga pants, did you?"

"No. Sorry."

Lost at sea.

Lost in silence.

So much for a graceful exit.

Sailor sits opposite me chopsticking his last salmon sashimi – not one bit less sexy than the first time I saw him – and completely defensive at every word I utter especially if it starts with "I felt". I'm confused as to how Sailor, who can debate politics with a depth of knowledge and social conscience, can't hear what I'm feeling with a fraction of the empathy he'd show a cause. I'm beginning to wonder if this is some Pavlovian reaction – like if Sailor hears anything close to…

"I felt…"

… He panics as if he knew all along….

'Didn't I call it?! She wants a relationship!'

"I feel…"

'Told ya! She wants a relationship!'

"And then I felt…"

'Sonofabitch! I knew it!!! She wants a…'

You get the picture.

I'm beginning to think if I so much as eye twitch towards a man, he'll think I want to drag him to the nearest altar and make him my Mister.

Assume the position, buddy!

But, while I may not be the poster child for coupledom, I will posit the theory that it takes three things to make any union work:

Mutual attraction.

A deepening to love.

Shared relational values.

The latter being the least factored, yet most important, because it speaks to how two people will treat each other on a day to day basis. Will they build up – or tear down? And while most people may settle for two out of three – or in the Lila/Sailor axis a damn extreme one out of three – I can't amputate my own relational values just because the guy doesn't share them.

He was the siren call I tried and tried to ignore but couldn't until I was naked and then naked again – but no matter how incredibly we do horizontally – the ship is going down fast on whatever remnants of a friendship we might have been able to salvage. And, now *both* of us are sitting here thinking…

Extract! Extract!!!

At least I know I am.

I was sad it was going to end this way when the front door of Sushi Express opened.

The tall, too slender man stood there looking in – bedraggled, tired eyes... hungry.

Our eyes met and I feel for him... for his sorry state.

But, my hand automatically reached for my purse sitting on the chair to my left, intent on placing it below my own chair – out of reach.

I stopped myself. Stopped myself, because I feared how that would make him feel.

Suspected.

Thinking how people will see a potential thief trolling for cash – but maybe he's just a homeless man in search of a good meal. And it would be hard going through life having people recoil every time they see you walk in the door.

I allowed the tall man with the gaunt, haunted look in then – mistaking a shark for a wounded dolphin as he cut through the restaurant towards our table.

Unconscious of whom he reminded me of – flashing my mind elsewhere...

Bucharest – November – 1994

He is so thin. His suit looks twenty years old – his eyes haunted and hungry despite the smile of recognition when he sees his little girl has not lost her curls. His curls.

"Hello, Dad." I say it in English as I hug him, shocked that he feels so tiny to me when the last time I saw him he was a tower I had to look so far up to.

I have such pitiful resources – how am I to help him when I've come to find my father only to find him in distress? The fall of a dictator – the devalued lire – the steep price of a hard won freedom from a cruel system that demanded cult like allegiance to 'the party' – neighbors informing on neighbors.

A child censored in what she could write to her ill father – lest she get him in trouble with the authorities. A father who went 'back home' for a lifelong pension now evaporated.

A child who missed him seems meaninglessly selfish next to this…

Back to now...

"SPANISH LOUD SPANISH," the tall, gaunt stranger is in Sailor's face. Standing over him. Irate. As if he suspects Sailor cheated him at cards — dwarfing our table at the back of Sushi Express with his aggression.

"LOUD SPANISH" Sailor quick-reflexes back still sitting in his chair, looking up.

I eye my purse still on the chair beside me. Vaguely aware this feels like a thief's diversion — so the sleight of hand can pickpocket the distracted tourist. I know. I was robbed in Bucharest and this is how it was done...

But, my purse remains unaccosted.

Chiding myself for the mistrust clanging like a peeling bell.

"SPANISH!"

Eyes turn. The entire restaurant is now riveted on the altercation — until finally...

"GET YOUR SPANISH OUT OF MY SPANISH," Sailor volleys, and the tall man slinks back through the restaurant and out the door.

Eyes turn back to their own business.

"Did he take anything?" Sailor leans in towards me.

I shake my head. "I don't think so."

My own eyes completely missing the obvious until ten minutes later... I reach into my purse and... a sickening lurch.

"The cell phone. It's gone."

Sailor catches the stricken look on my face. Concern flashing across his — then immediate action. Not to dial 911 and wait for the inevitable 'not much we can do' shrug from cops arriving too late on the scene — but to instantly go after the offender — a warrior of one.

Leaving me standing 'safe' in the alcove, still trying to figure out how to explain to Sibling, "I forgot the cell was on the table — and I never saw his hand move." It's not so much the phone — but the photos and contacts — that Sibling's private world is even now possibly being scrolled through.

The fact that Sibling will shake his head at my distress and say, "It's just a cell phone – you're more important – as long as you're okay," is a day away.

The fact that Sailor will email him attempting to take the blame – a noble gesture – is also a day away. Right now there is only guilt:

Kill Sibling's plant – check.

Sleep with Sibling's friend – check.

Lose Sibling's expensive cell phone – checkaroo.

If there's a Sister from Hell Award – I'm the frontrunner.

I shift weight to my left foot, giving my right foot a break as Sailor rounds the corner back into view – passing me with a determined look on his face as he keeps searching down another side street – another dark corner out of sight. Resolved to help me without factoring in the risk to himself.

A knight in tarnished armor.

I glance over to the few stragglers in the Beirut patio across the street tossing me odd looks. A Suit opens a fire door into the alcove and glares at me for a moment as the casino sounds bing and ting behind him. He then closes the door again with a slam.

What?

Wait.

Do they think I charge by the hour?!

Don't they see my hair tied up in an 'I'm NOT trying to seduce you' bun?!

I'll show you Librarian!

Well, except for a few protest curls sticking out.

And the last-minute switch from flip flops to the whimsical heels I'm sorely regretting.

Ho heels – librarian lid.

Great. I'm a Hobrarian. Let me Dewey Decimal you, big boy. What am I gonna do for the john – read to him?! Is there even a going rate for that? Do I charge by the hour or by the page?!

"C'mon," Sailor doubles back – grabs my hand. "I think I've seen that guy before around the Veneto. Let's go."

And we're off across Balboa for The Thief's Tour. I steel myself to run in heels as Sailor yanks me towards El Cangrejo.

20.2

Sailor is four sips into his post-chase beer when he mutters, "Where's T-Rick when I need him to run interference… keep me out of trouble."

I look up in surprise from my half beer, having poured the other half into Sailor's glass.

He seems to wrestle with himself for a beat, then leans over the rickety wooden table in the hole-in-the-wall tropical bar and kisses me.

Soft.

Sexy.

Sweet.

He sits back in his chair and raises the glass to his lips while mine tingle.

Sip.

He reaches for my hand – not to yank – but to hold. Fingers caressing electric currents.

It suddenly dawns on me that Sailor feels safer chasing a nefarious thief down dark alleys than being alone with the woman at the table.

Caress…

Kiss.

"I see you put your hair up," he observes, though it's been up all night.

"Uh-huh."

"It's nice. It's nice down too." I sense a preference for the latter, but the fact that Sailor would have any opinion about my hair seems far-fetched. And yet…

I get up – go to the ladies room – only to find the smallest mirror known to humankind. What is it about Panama? Stunningly beautiful women – tiny reflections.

I reach for the tight scrunchie holding up my hair.

This is it.

The fabled moment where the Librarian unties her bun and lets down her gorgeous, glossy mane – letting it cascade past her shoulders while she sexily shakes it out.

Only, as I pull out the scrunchie with a flourish…

Nothing happens.

The curls refuse to budge. They stay sproinged up – stubborn. Defiant.

I shake my head.

Nothing.

They remain as if sculpted. Exactly in the same updo bun as before.

I shake my head again – hard.

The curls ignore like feuding schoolgirls.

I run my fingers through tangled locks – tugging downward.

Now my hair is sticking straight out sideways.

I desperately run the tap and wet my fingers, running them through tyrannical locks, tugging down the protest curls, until finally I emerge with a somewhat frizzled, but 'down' hairstyle – slipping back into the chair beside Sailor adopting a nonchalance despite my head having just grown to three times its normal size.

"Better," Sailor mutters between sips – our hands clasped.

20.3

He caresses the length of me as we lie on a hard mattress for transient expats. The stare-smile is one I only see when he's hovering above me – shy and jokey-smoldering at the same time – like he's about to give me a good time and he knows it, but doesn't want to appear too arrogant about it.

He reaches down for another slow, long kiss.

Then pulls back to meet my eyes again as his smile deepens into the view I came here to see for the last time. Not just his hard, hotboy nudity – but the undefended lover-look he gives me when he knows no one is watching and he's safe to be that side of himself – to go to *that* place. All tough-guy pretense dropped to the floor along with his clothes.

Drop and give me twenty, hotness.

"How is it I'm once again naked and you're not?"

"I don't have a problem with that," I shrug.

"Uh huh. I bet."

He reaches for my top, again demonstrating his one-handed bra unhooking maneuver. Caressing, kissing my naked breasts.

"Satisfied?"

"Hardly." He slips a hardening nipple into his mouth, swirling it into aching desire.

Mmmmm…

My fingers twirl into his curls, still silky and sensuous.

He reaches back for another kiss and holds my gaze with that one-of-a-kind soulful smile.

I thought Sailor was akin to a sailboat on tropical waters – but he's more like that hike I once did that had so many tripwire brambly twists and turns I swore I'd never hike again – until I got to the peak and saw natural beauty so startling it nearly scarred my irises.

Only, what was wild in the wild has become gentler, even familiar – his practiced hands now easily finding the 'soft part underneath'... his kisses slow... tracing... already nostalgic.

"Why do you wear such complicated clothing?" he shakes his head when again confronted with the dreaded tights – tugging – even as I restrain the laugh and tiny flash of annoyance – reaching to help while wondering if in Sailor's perfect world I'd be sporting Velcro tear-away panties.

But, his hands are appreciative – caressing – once skin meets skin. Tenderness now fluidly under – and over – layered.

In his embrace.

In his eyes.

Fusing into one.

Congruent.

I smile back up at him, feeling the sweetness envelope us as he pushes into me one last time. The rhythm building slowly – the one time we actually have no time left. Wrapping arms around arms, kisses upon kisses, as he drives deeper into the tight yielding – alternately receiving and thrusting up to meet him.

"Mmmm... that feels good," I murmur, touching him everywhere I can reach, trailing my lips along his neck as he thrusts deeper and deeper into my lust.

"Ooohhhh...." I murmur his name.

He rhythms us higher – increasing the ache of pleasure now radiating outward from every point of contact.

Where we touch.

Where we lock.

Where we...

"Ooooohhhh... Yes." It's a whisper.

He closes his eyes, thrusts faster, intensifying.

His breath ragged, he slams even harder into me as he reaches that climactic sequence – the sudden escalation – the waterfall torrent currenting through me as my legs wrap around him tighter – taking him as deep into me as I possibly can – until the final plunge of his sexual force driving into me one last time – and now

it's his turn to gasp-moan – as he arches back and empties.
    Soft caresses.
    Kisses trailing along my neck.

20.4

We lay side by side, just looking at each other. Face to face after our last Close Encounter of the Naked Kind – still in fact... naked.

I study him, already sentimental, oblivious to the expression on my face until Sailor says...

"You look at me the way Homer Simpson sees the world when he's drunk on Duff Beer."

"Excuse me?" I'm confused, half twitch of a smile, half 'huh'?

"When Homer's drunk on Duff beer he sees the world not as it is – but as this magical place. Everything's beautiful, better, brighter. Like a trip on really good mushrooms or something."

Uh-oh.

Busted.

"And your problem with that is?"

"It's not real."

"I don't know about that—"

"I read what you wrote about me," Sailor counters, "I don't recognize myself. That guy you see – that's not me."

I flash to the excerpt I posted from our first night – and smile.

"See? THAT look," Sailor says in 'I rest my case' finality.

"Well, it's probably a good thing you don't see yourself the way I do."

"You're romantic," he tries a 'not that there's anything wrong with that' tone, but coming from him it sounds like a near fatal disease.

"And you're not?" I sound skeptical.

"I'm about the least romantic as they come," says the guy who sees palm trees every day.

I raise an eyebrow. But, I'm also aware of the threadbare room. The ancient, scarred dresser, the lack of any paintings or architectural beauty. The constant scrambling to get clients for the next tour – the long hours – the frequent repairs. The price of a life outside the 'work downtown/sleep in bedroom community' norm.

"I mean, look at me – I'm just a guy with bad tan lines," Sailor argues for his own downgrade. "I barely have time to write – the one thing I most want to do – and I haven't hit the gym in weeks! I'm even getting love handles! Look!" he attempts to demonstrate by pinching at his imaginary 'love handles' whilst I continue to lay beside him in all my curvylicious glory, bemused and entertained.

Wondering if Sailor's American practical/sensible side is a teeny bit in conflict with his more impulsive 'that's amore' Italia side.

Huh.

You never really know a person – not 'all the way' – not all the layers. Even if you spend a lifetime with them – they can still surprise you. Let alone a brief peek.

"I'm just a guy in need of a new boat battery. And you're a romantic," he says again, as if he's throwing his hands up in the air in a 'don't look at me – it ain't my fault' gesture.

As if that explains everything.

"You're Homer," he concludes. "And, I'm the donut."

I adopt the glazed, gluttonous expression Homer Simpson usually gets when faced with his favorite confection – only I'm looking at Sailor as if he's the confection, "Mmmmmm… donut."

"Uh huh" Sailor adds. "You want some ice cream with that?"

How did you know?

I grin and his face breaks out into a reflective smile.

Laughing.

And talking – about romance vs. realism – about future plans in different cities – about one sentence leading to the next…

"That was one strange trip," he shakes his head. "I'm not usually like that."

Yeah, well, get in line. This isn't my 'normal' either…

"Again with the compliments," he says a little while later when I try to explain his lovehandles are nonexistent and he should really see someone about that body dysmorphia.

"You know, the response to a compliment can be, 'thank you',"

I say, wondering what the hell they taught Sailor in kindergarten. "You can even say something nice about the other person in turn."

"I told you," he drops a light kiss on my lips, "I like that you're passionate."

"Oh, I didn't realize that was a compliment," I grin. "I thought when you said that it was more like 'oh goody, I'm about to have a good time'."

"I like passionate people," he shrugs and reaches for me, wrapping his arms around only to notice a little tear escaping.

"What?!" he sounds alarmed. "Is it the cell phone? It's just a phone, your brother will understand."

I shake my head, 'no'.

"What then?"

"I hate goodbyes."

His embrace tightens, encasing me in strong arms, my face buried in his chest.

"This doesn't have to be goodbye," Sailor soothes.

Nice try.

I know an ending when I'm in one. My fingers may dial/he may friend me on Facebook, but this is it. Though, if I'm going to tear up every time I'm in bed with someone, I should maybe invest in a publicly traded tissue company. Or, get a monogrammed white vintage hankie. Linen with pink embroidery for the initials – oooh and scalloped lace around the edges and—

Focus, Lila!

"It's a small world," Sailor caresses my hair. "You'd be amazed how small. And we'll see each other again."

"It won't be the same." I'll be shoveling snow.

"Yah, that's true – you'll totally pass by me like 'whatever'."

"What?" I crane to meet his face and see he's serious.

"I'm telling you – if you ran into me in New York or L.A. you'd think 'that guy? No way'!"

"That's not true."

"Yah, it is. You'd fit into that urban setting – you'd be doing your thing – and I'd be the fish out of water."

I want to shake my head 'no', but it glimmers he's onto something.

I imagine running into him in L.A., try to picture him in a suit at the Beverly Wilshire, meeting me for lunch at The Blvd., at that table where I used to have breakfast and write when I was a little flush with cash. Seeing him pull back the chair opposite me and adjust his tie – elbow to elbow with studio heads, black suit/white shirt D-Girls – a goateed screenwriter with a serious A-list look on his face meeting his high-powered agent who's still sporting peach fuzz. And, even Lewaa, that time we shared a hamburger due to being broke, but I dragged us there anyway, because an über-stylist had done my hair for free and for once I looked like a photo-op.

But, I can't do it. Sailor is MIA in a scene that for me is The Mother Ship.

I flash imagine him into his standard shorts and T walking towards me with that 'que pasa' easy grin and... there.

That's better.

Remembering him always in motion on the boat – at the big wheel – diving in to rescue Bex – tanned and grinning into the wind – slightly inebriated yet still able to sauté the best damn lobster I've ever tasted. Pulling me towards him in a hardcore 'don't fuck with me' kiss one minute – inverse Tasering me with his tender touch the next.

Come visit me.

The great thing about him is the very thing that from day one would have ensured this would only ever be what it is.

Sailor is always Sailor.

"But, don't you think – it's Panama?" he says as we shift – again face to face – still au naturel.

"Panama?" I repeat, unsure of where he's going with this.

"It's hot here."

"So?"

"It heightens things. Everything is more intense here. Everything is more... extreme."

I stare at him, and the fever breaks.

20.5

The second last image Sailor has of me – before seeing me into the cab – last glance – last kiss – is of a tumble on a darkened street in El Cangrejo.

I was feeling very proud of myself for having made it through the night without an ankle twist – proud of my mastery of Charlie's Angels heels – when I hit a miniscule crack in the asphalt and – splat!

Down on one knee in an accidental proposal.

Sailor turned back at the…

Gasp!

… only to find me looking up at him kid-height short – feeling last week in town (should know better by now) tourista stupid. He rushed to help me up from the pavement.

Months late he'd type, "I'm just the guy you seduced with your quirky/sexy moves…"

Still, even then, I could never bring myself to confess. I was going to – but at the last second I pulled back – recognizing I was too raw – too vulnerable. And that maybe some things are best saved for when it feels right. I had tried with a gesture – reaching for him – whilst still in bed. But, he'd playfully swatted my hand away.

And the question died on my lips. He was right – it was late. And I won't blame him for denying me what I never asked for. Surprised to find I had my own way of withholding. My own little emotional safety net courtesy of self denial.

He would remain that echo ache of blinding desire.

Un-satiated.

A provocative postcard from The Fever Coast.

And, I would wait until I was with ONE. The one man I could say everything to…

21. COMPLETION

December…

"Dear Jesus…"

I am standing mid-aisle, dwarfed by a Golden Altar and vaulted ceiling in a famed church in 'the old city' – Casco Viejo.

"… I know this is a rather unusual request. And, let's face it – I was born Jewish. But, then again, so were you. So, I'm hoping you'll give a sistah some divine intervention. If you need references, I watch White Christmas religiously every year around this time, not to mention that ill-fated attempt at caroling during a blizzard. And while Christmas and Chanukah may have different origins – in a way both celebrate light at the darkest time. So, if you could just see your way to granting me this one additional wish…"

I had already prayed for loved ones and world peace – feeling its possibility in the still peace of this house of worship. The soundwaves of hymns and prayers having left an invisible trail of hope.

As mesmerizing as the Golden Altar was, it didn't feel like the source of the beauty of the room. It was the heart of everyday people who'd gathered to worship something greater – to give praise to something sacred. They had raised the roof on spirit and I could feel its presence – its stillness.

And so, I'd joined my prayers to theirs.

Outside, ruin argued with renewal as the buildings of Casco vacillated between past and present – some hollow – burned out and broken – vying for real estate with gentrified shops and eateries, a first ever taste of lavender ice cream on the last day.

Sibling had remained on his cell in the plaza by the statue of Simón Bolívar, while I prayed for him and read about the Golden Altar – how it had once been painted black to save it from the plunder of pirates.

I thought: this is how I see people – as the Gold. I could choose to only see the painted over view – the camouflage of all that glitters – but then my life would be poorer for it.

"I'm sorry," Trouble said the words I never expected to hear the other night. Through tears I never expected to see. "I'm sorry I wasn't strong enough to do what had to be done to bring us together."

He broke down then – crashed down to rock bottom so hard he left skid marks.

And while I wanted to shout out, "No! Don't say it!" because that would mean he'd given up on Us Possible – I knew from having stepped into the screensaver that Paradise had come and gone – and it had been a solo journey in the ways that matter. I touched the screen, wishing I could gather his tears into some Holy Grail chalice and offer it to an altar of redemption. But, instead I was destined to say the wrong thing, too overcome by my own culpability in his pain and the pressure he'd felt. Witness to his relapse – knowing Trouble is troubled.

Large of stature – a small, fearful boy peeking out from wounded eyes. Lonely, but for a crushed pill.

"You are more than this…" I will try to tell him in different words.

The love will bubble up as it always has – the fingers dial – but this is the Genesis of 'goodbye' – the moment I truly realized my love for him is as much a burden as the beacon he's described. He will suffer harsh withdrawal – clawing his foot out of the addict's bear trap. But I'll be in a different city by then. As ever, impressed with his immense ability to do what he sets out to do – but aware the same woman always stands by him while I fly.

And it's too late to heal my father… will be the thought that humbles me.

One year will turn into the next when the Kuna will rename themselves the 'Guna' to better reflect their original language and San Blas will become Guna Yala. A self-definition akin to an artist naming a masterpiece.

By this time Lewaa will have completed The Star Kingdom – an adventurous, fantastical, funny, moving story – only to hear the same "I love it, but…" that we predicted. He'll keep writing anyway – words racing on the page in defiance of speedbumps – GPS set to a dot on the horizon only he can see – pedal to the metal.

A breathtaking vision.

In turn, Sibling will finish his chipless, beautiful painting – the blossom now preceded by a bud. Bud promise – blossom joy. And without any awareness of the irony parallel in my life he will entitle it: Our Love and Our Future.

He and Gisele having transitioned to friends, single Sibling will call me one day.

"Can you keep a secret?"

As long as it's not about a relationship. Is what I don't say.

"I'm seeing someone new."

Sigh.

But, there will be a look in his eyes, one I haven't seen in a very long time – and my mind will flash to…

She's about as perfect a woman as you're ever gonna meet…

Oh no. Sib, don't tell me!

Julisa.

"We ran into each other – I hadn't seen her in a long time – and it was this instant attraction."

And with Sib's friendship with Sailor reduced to the surface polite 'hey, how ya doin' at accidental Expat run-ins – I guess he figured the 'guy code' no longer applied.

"She just needs a chance to tell her ex – you know – Sailor – they're still friends, and he should really hear it from her."

And when I finally meet *her* face to face on Skype and see them together – I understand. "Beautiful" doesn't come close. Even as I will grin like a fool at the awkward coincidence – I will not be able to help but notice her dazzle factor.

I will watch Sibling fall hard – complete with 'meet the parents', and talk of popping the question.

Until...

She stilettos his heart with her own ex-haunting. Yet another past entanglement intruding on the present like an epidemic.

And I will marvel at how incredibly – optimistically – Sibling bounces back. That, for all of his challenges he always finds a way to rise up on steady legs, tall and sure. "Another day in Paradise" being his fave response to "how are you".

After fall – get back up.

And something Sailor said on that last night will come back to me, "You know, sometimes you get into a relationship and it detours you from the course you're on – a course which might have worked out better for you down the road if you'd stayed with it."

If Trouble taught me love's eternal flame – Sailor taught me I don't have to throw myself on the pyre.

And my hopeless hope chest – the love that had always outrun me no matter what city I had landed in – will lock away in the dusty attic of what might have been like a vintage trunk in storage. I will break the lock occasionally, peek in and wonder – picking up the tiny antique bejeweled wish-pin before it stings me again and I slam the lid shut.

Still, it's a compelling idea – even for someone who reaches for it just as much as she slaps it away – the one with whom love can blossom – the one with whom great dreams can come true. It beckons just beyond a hazy horizon.

The Love Possible.

"And so, Jesus, in conclusion..." I complete my prayer as I step out of the church – from the sacred back out to the profane, "please send the man who can give me a Happy Ending."

Epilogue

Calgary – November 2010

"OH MY GOD!"
He is a classic column of tall, dark and handsome. 6'3, "and a quarter," he'd joked when I'd asked him how tall – but I wasn't prepared for his skillz.
"What are you doing?!"
Quick with a joke and deadly attractive – he was standing by the café counter in black slacks, collared gray shirt and black leather jacket while I ordered from the pretty, Irish owner whose own curls brushed away from a friendly face in cheery whorls. He was frowning at his phone, no doubt work emails already clogging his inbox at 7:30 a.m. He looked up, caught my notice of him and smiled a smile that reached all the way to his eyes.
What is a guy like you doing in a town like this? Was my thought at first sight. And I wanted him. And only him.
Prince Disarming.
That was six months ago.
"How are you doing that?!"
His chocolate brown bedroom eyes flicker amusement. Smug.
But he never breaks contact – never stops touching – intent only on the pleasure he's inducing. In control.
The short red skirt I'd worn over yet another pair of black tights – the plunging top – are now on the floor at the foot of my bed.
The pre-bed negotiations were worthy of a U.N. Summit. Six months of friendship – the mutual spark leading only to hand holding, a kiss, glances. He took me to the river the day before surgery – a gloriously blue sky sunny day so common in Panama – but rarely that warm in this 'Iceburg' where summer is but a

fleeting butterfly and winter a cruel daemon with every icy shard against skin.

"Whatever you're doing – please don't stop!" I gasp, arching back.

Heat radiates off his body – a furnace on a bitter night. He makes the fireplace at the restaurant seem like a mere flicker. I had waited for him, draped on a vintage velvet couch of rich ochre. I had waited for him, from the first second I saw him. When he arrived to sit beside me, his legs stretched out in the jeans he'd gone home to change into after work – the ones with a fray here and there in all the right places. He lifted the edge of my short, red skirt when the waiter wasn't looking and I slapped his hand away.

"Do you think I'd expose you?" he ran his hand up my thigh, "Trust me, he's not looking." His fingers came dangerously close to the V-Zone. "You're warm... oh and..." quiet chuckle... "Wet."

"Shhhh...!" I flare, "people can hear you! Besides, you can't really tell that through the layers!"

"No, they can't – they're busy with their own conversations," but he removes his hand as the waiter turns. Only to place his hand on my chin and lift my lips to his with a whisper pre-kiss, "And yes, I can tell through the layers."

I lean back and take a long pull on my wine glass.

"You're blushing," he says, amused.

"Yeah? Well, I'm looking in a mirror then." But, it's hard to see a blush through his darkly handsome olive skin and he knows it.

"And, you're overthinking again," he grins.

"I'm a writer." I blush deeper. "I overthink for a living."

"Then think about this," and his hand brushes over my black top caressing breasts 'through the layers' just as the waiter turns to keypad in an order.

"I dare you," I had said a few weeks ago, arms crossed.

"I Double Dare you," he'd countered with a knowing smile, then got serious. "It's just the right thing to do – you never sleep with a woman and not make sure she's taken care of."

"But, if she doesn't ask –"

"She shouldn't have to." He won the staredown.

"How the fuck?! Ohhh mmyyy Goddd!!!"

For a woman who hates having to ask – a man generous enough to absolve her of the burden is the ultimate aphrodisiac. Prince Disarming didn't just make me feel safe in the most embarrassing of topics – he's applying the same idea of mutual pleasure without prejudice – in other words – every woman deserves exactly what he gets – not just the one he's in love with. There is a genuineness to that – a sense of fair play.

New motto: No pets, no plants, no holding back.

"Oooohhhh YESSSS!!!"

My eyes squeeze shut, but they're imprinted with his 'hottest guy in a hundred mile radius' vista. I open them again and his chocolate browns hold mine, his kiss possessive. His touch urging me to give it all.

His fingers finding pleasure centers beyond imagining – pulsating euphoria throughout awakened nerve endings like a joyride under the skin. Revving ardor higher, harder, faster to a sex-sense peak that flings me over the edge out to the blue.

"OHHHHH MYYYY GOD!!! YOU ARE AMAZING!!!" My alto voice reaches the dizzy height of a coloratura soprano as I cry out his name and my body arcs in skyrocket ecstasy.

"Oh yeah, baby," he kisses my temple as I shudder to stillness.

I collapse into his arms. "That. Was. Brilliant."

And, way too intimate. I mean, WOW. Sex is one thing – but this is too personal to share with anyone, except someone I deeply trust. Worth the wait.

He holds me close, caressing, coaxing final little blissquakes.

Even though Prince Disarming is wasting his skillz being a serial monogamist – even though his talents would be a public service to women the world over – I feel like hoarding him like Frodo with that ring – forcibly restraining the urge to rub his chest and mutter, "My precious."

"What?"

"Oh, nothing," I smile and snuggle in closer, knowing deep

down I'm the wing-fluttering bird to this tree who's deeply rooted in his hometown.

He strokes my arm. "You have soft skin."

You have a Genius Lover IQ.

He holds me closer – I hold my freezing feet against his long, hot legs.

"Remind me to call you next time I need an ice pack," he murmurs sarcastically.

"Mmmmm... cozy," I sigh, content. "You're better than an electric blanket."

"It's what I do," he jokes – then reaches down, face nuzzling into a deep post-bliss kiss.

Must not fall...

    Must not fall...

        Must not... I catch myself.

Some prayers do come true. And, it had occurred to me, as I'd walked out of that church in Casco, that while it's easy for me to spot the gold in others – I often view myself as the 'painted over'.

"You don't see yourself as you really are," Sibling had said. His parting words spoken on the dusty high noon road to Toucemon airport – him at the wheel – me the cranky passenger hating to leave Panama. Wishing I could will the car to turn around. Sibling's generosity having reached the limits of his savings and my own bank account planted at zero with no new contract in sight.

"Sib, I'm a fortysomething woman with a negative net worth – you said so yourself."

"Your bank account shouldn't be the basis of your value."

"May I remind you – you're in finance!"

"Then I of all people should know. You're more than your wallet. You think you have to do something to be 'successful' – but you were successful the day you were born." Sib booted it up the Tocumen airport turnoff.

"I'm basing my life on a feeling," I murmured – riddled with self doubt – but no longer able to deny the peace that defies logic when I sit down to the blank page – even as it terrifies. A sense of being compelled – even as I struggle to make it through the day in exhaustion and pain as the bad days get worse – even as I have no clue how I'll survive. "It's a very insecure way to live."

"Look, you're rolling the dice on yourself. That's more than some people do in a lifetime. See it as brave – see it as your next great adventure. Now's the time to stop running. Now's the time to heal – and finish a book. And maybe then you'll realize – you're more than you think you are."

Sibling popped the trunk, hauled out my suitcase and turned to me with that brilliant smile that flashed me back to Baby Sib and our shared childhood.

"Pura Vida," I reached up for a hug, so touched that the phrase he taught me escaped on a tear in that last moment under the Panama sun.

"I wish you could borrow my eyes." His blues met mine, "Because if you could see yourself through my eyes you'd never have another bad day."

The best people in our lives remind us of the best in ourselves. Of truths we know and have forgotten – and in turn grace us with the privilege of seeing the greatness in them. Pointing us towards our own soul when we think we've lost the way...

Destiny is the insistent inner voice that urges you to fly
even as you crawl along the sidewalk
face down to see the cracks
thinking that's the way to avoid them.
What would happen if you looked up
and caught a glimpse of sky?

xo Lila

CELEBRATING

Thanks again to David Richer for too much to mention including the wickedly awesome cover art for Sex, Love, and Paradise!

Lewaa Nasserdeen kept his promise and was my sounding board, story editor, and superstar hero from idea to final word (literally down to the wire)!

Maureen O'Brien let me into her café at 6:30 a.m. (even though it didn't open until 7) and caffeinated me with the best espresso north of Panama. Cheery, super energized and just all round beautiful – her Gardens' Grace Boutique and Coffee Bar closed after 9 years and 90,000 muffins (before this book could be released), but she made cold, dark Calgary mornings worth getting up for, and is now a friend for life. The 'GG Crew' included: Barry Lindgren – fastest wit in the west. Dianne Davis – a 'tiny dancer' with a mighty heart. Jane (The Janester) Vander Meulen, Lanette Heintz – a true craftsperson. Lauren the Crazy Cupcake rock star (and the O'Brien/Symon/Davis clan for inviting me to their Christmas festivities), The Teachers, Tina Wilding, Susie De Giusti, David Finch (Historian/Author), Shane Butler, the lovely GG baristas I drove crazy with my 'special orders' (Chelsea, Kyra, Clare, Shannon, Meghan, Roisin, et al), the extended GG 'family' of customers who every day would ask 'how's the book coming along' and the person who said, "It's a memoir – you already know what happens – why is it taking so long?!" It's done, okay?! Sheesh!

Sara Klinghoffer and Little E for the shared family moments. Cuzzie, keep singing and songwriting – I'll be in a club one day soon dancing to your song!

Carmen Olsen – the Eagle Eye editor who can spot a typo at 100 paces – and marketing smartyboots.

Harry Dino Sideris for being a supremely nice guy. Bettina Hari for being a supremely nice woman.

Carver Irish for listening to early chapters with equal parts intelligence and enthusiasm.

Brendan Richardson for those hyper-smart writer-to-writer comments.

Amy Knippshild for the constant reassurance that 'everything will work out fine'.

Andrew Forbes for the cover art and interior design – thanks for your amazing dedication and knowledge.

Patrick Russo for helping me to better understand the language of images and for being so great even when it's last minute.

Carolyn Hay for sooo much plus the .5 joke (can't wait to see Yorkville, The Musical)!

The McArters, The Tarofs, the Klinghoffers, Shimon Sarelle, the Spinu family – forever love. A special mention for Kaeli McArter and her debut EP – LEAP – which features our song Get Lost (www.kaelimcarter.com).

Elaine Allenger, Madeleine Wakefield, Megan Johnston and my friends at BVC. Phay Wills. Sean Wintraub for Super-D's moniker and the Vice Girls: Alicia, Amy, Jolene, Megan, and Harriet. Also a shoutout to Linda (Alyx) Roche, Paula MacPherson, Harry Tucker, Al Watts, Elizabeth Johnson, and B.C. artist Ann-Marie Brown. The Roomies who were awesome to share a domicile with: Ashley

Mitty & Nic Sharkey, Yolande Mitty, Michael Malone (thanks for Dewey Decimal Joke), Yvonne D, and the ever popular Jessica Kill.

Toshi at Carino, Najam at Prime Tandoori House and Misato & Mitsuru at Cerezo.

Thank you also to the Alberta Foundation for the Arts for providing me with a grant to adapt this book into a screenplay.

Double Yay to Tim Baloi and the staff at the Indigospirit bookstore in downtown Calgary for my first book signing event.

To the people that appear in these pages – however disguised – thank you for being fascinating. Sorry for staring (no, I'm not).

If this was an award show and I won some dubious honor like the 'Most Mixed Metaphors Award' – the music would have cued by now and I'd be hustled off the stage.

xo

The End

Lila Z Rose

A writer currently living in Canada, Lila Z Rose set out to write her first novel – and got completely sidetracked by life. A Hot Sailor, A Cold Margarita, and... Trouble is the result of her many distractions.

Twitter: @lilazroselove
www.lilazrose.com

To view David Richer's paintings: www.davidricher.com

To find out more about Lewaa:
Twitter: @LewaaNass

Made in the USA
Charleston, SC
28 January 2014